British Women Mystery Writers

British Women Mystery Writers

Authors of Detective Fiction with Female Sleuths

by Mary Hadley

McFarland & Company, Inc., Publishers
Jefferson, North Carolina, and London

An earlier version of Chapter Two was published as "Jennie Melville: The Forgotten Case of the Police Procedural" in *Clues: A Journal of Detection* 21:2 (Fall/Winter 2000).

Library of Congress Cataloguing-in-Publication Data

Hadley, Mary, 1949–
   British women mystery writers : authors of detective fiction with
female sleuths / by Mary Hadley.
       p.   cm.
   Includes bibliographical references and index.
   ISBN 0-7864-1242-9 (softcover : 50# alkaline paper) ∞
   1. Detective and mystery stories, English—History and criticism.
2. Women and literature—Great Britain—History—20th century.
3. English fiction—Women authors—History and criticism.   4. English
fiction—20th century—History and criticism.   5. Women detectives in
literature.   I. Title.
   PR888.D4   H33   2002
   823'.087209352042—dc21   2002002059

British Library cataloguing data are available

On the cover: From left to right: Judith Cutler, P.D. James,
Jennie Melville, Susan Moody, Joan Smith and Michelle Spring

Manufactured in the United States of America

*McFarland & Company, Inc., Publishers
   Box 611, Jefferson, North Carolina 28640
   www.mcfarlandpub.com*

To my beloved husband, Charles,
and my children,
Katherine and Christopher

Acknowledgments

My book would not have been written without the help of many people.

First to be named is my dissertation director at Reading University, Dr. Tom Woodman, without whose encouragement and advice I would never have continued writing past the first chapter.

In addition, I would like to mention several of my colleagues at Georgia Southern University, especially JoAnn Steffen for her help with editing; Michael Mills, who also enjoys detective fiction and read several of my chapters; and Dr. Larry Burton and Dr. Eleanor Agnew, who gave me so much support.

Also Suzanne Metcalf at the Henderson Library's Interlibrary Loan office and Jim Rickerson at Statesboro's Regional Library are to be thanked for all the help they gave me tracking down sources of criticism and works which were out of print.

And finally my gratitude goes to all the authors whose works I examine. I was amazed how much time they took from their busy lives to answer my questions either in person or by e-mail. I certainly could not have accomplished the writing of this book without them.

Contents

Introduction

"To take on the genre; to rethink it, reformulate it, re-vision it: this is the challenge to contemporary authors" (Klein, *The Woman Detective*, 227).

British female authors have written about female detectives, police women and amateur sleuths since the 1800s, and although many changes have occurred since then in the ways they are depicted, critics such as Kathleen Gregory Klein and Anne Cranny-Francis, among others, felt by the 1980s that it was time the genre was reimagined. Klein states in *The Woman Detective*:

> To re-imagine the genre an author will want to consider both content and structure.... A feminocentric novel does not necessarily need a feminist detective but it cannot evade questions of gender... [The text should be one] which urges readers to solve not only the problem of the crime but also the problems of the social system [227].

Although a great deal of critical attention has been paid to P.D. James, far less has been paid to Jennie Melville and the other authors included in this book. I aim to redress that lack by showing how the authorial intentions of British female detective writers have been affected by both feminism and societal changes so that they are putting women's issues at the forefront of the narrative. When I use the term authorial intention, I am referring to my personal interviews or e-mail interviews with several of the authors discussed, or to my use of interviews given by the authors to others in which they explain their attitudes and motives in their writing. In this book I will also demonstrate that they evince basic similarities to American female detective authors but are also, in some

1

respects, distinctively different and have created new types of female protagonists. I first describe how 1960s authors P.D. James and Jennie Melville moved their female detectives away from those earlier conventions which depicted female sleuths as sidekicks to the all powerful male protagonist and as sexually unappealing, dependent or eccentric spinsters, to the 1980s assertive controller of dangerous situations. Next I analyze four other 1980s and 1990s authors, showing the innovations in their works and how feminism, with its emphasis on social consciousness raising, changed both the subject matter of their novels and the protagonists themselves. Finally I examine the latest voices coming out of Britain in the late 1990s and project where I believe the female detective novel is going.

Although the female sleuth has existed for over one hundred years, her early form, according to Patricia Craig and Mary Cadogan, was "rudimentary" (11). These critics provide a detailed survey of this early material in their work. In particular they demonstrate that: "The apparent feminism of many of the early stories featuring women sleuths is at odds with the sentimental endings which popular authors often felt obliged to append to their works" (12). Many of the writers of female detectives were male, and we see that:

> The early female criminal investigators prided themselves on their ability to tackle situations with panache; but actually they trailed a genteel aura of discreet scent, elegant gowns and earnest tea-cup tête-à-têtes. Their exploits are rarely spiced with authentic danger, and the stories rely heavily on coincidence [Craig and Cadogan 16].

Baroness Orczy's books, for example, featuring the female detective Lady Molly who first appeared in 1910, have a "curiously archaic" tone. "The Lady Molly stories flirt with feminism, although this is of the wooly, romanticized variety and bears no relation to any of the organized suffragist movements of the time" (Craig and Cadogan 30).

During the period between the two world wars, sometimes known as the Golden Age, British writers produced a detective genre which "developed out of a desire to modernise the crime fiction of the past" (Light 66). As Alison Light also describes, this whodunit genre had certain distinguishing characteristics, including an emphasis on a convoluted puzzle, suspenseful plotting and the idea that criminals were aberrant personalities even if they could be found in small villages. Some of these authors, such as Agatha Christie and Dorothy Sayers, created female detectives who were brave, clever and successful, and, even if they did not make social commentary in the same way as the authors of today, the conventions they followed did allow them creativity. Julian Symons describes in his seminal survey of detective fiction, *Bloody Murder*:

> The period in which [the Golden Age detective stories] were written was one in which the number of unemployed in Britain rose to three million and remained near that mark for a decade, in which boom in America was succeeded by slump and slump by depression, in which dictatorships rose to power. These things were ignored in almost all the detective stories of the Golden Age. In the British stories the General Strike of 1926 never took place, trade unions did not exist, and when sympathy was expressed for the poor it was not for the unemployed but for those struggling along on a fixed inherited income [96].

However, Dorothy Sayers evinces major concern in *Gaudy Night* for the problems of the career woman, stating several times that she may have to choose either marriage and children or a career, thus denying herself either intellectual or biological fulfillment. Many of Harriet Vane's thoughts about Oxford women are also Dorothy's as she says in a letter to Muriel St. Clare Byrne, "*Gaudy Night* is not really a detective story at all, but a novel with a mild detective interest of an almost psychological kind.... [T]he plot, so far as it goes, is part of the theme" (Reynolds 354).

Written to support their female authors financially, but with the abovementioned view to entertain with the convoluted plot or puzzle formula, these early detective novels had a more limited function than the detective fiction of today. As Ernest Mandel states, what characterizes them is "the extremely conventionalized and formalized character of their plots" (25). When we read the books, it is not simply the authors' worlds which may appear dated, but the very fabric of the detection. Although, according to Anne Cranny-Francis, Agatha Christie's Hercule Poirot was modern to his audience, a "neat travesty of conventional British masculinity" ("Feminist Fiction" 73), and he often analyzes the motives of the criminal, he only rarely questions his own behavior and seldom criticizes himself or his actions. This is very different from P.D. James's Adam Dalgliesh, for example, who states in *Death of an Expert Witness*, "It was possible to do police work honestly; there was, indeed, no other safe way to do it. But it wasn't possible to do it with-out giving pain" (340). Gwendoline Butler, aka Jennie Melville, writing her John Coffin series has Coffin almost hit the woman he loves in *Cracking Open a Coffin:* "A strong, hot anger swept over him. Without conscious thought, his right arm raised itself. He saw Stella's eyes widen, the pupils black. He knew fear when he saw it" (141). Although there existed unheroic detectives in earlier fiction, they only rarely evinced any soul-searching or criticism of their own actions.

So why did the Golden Age writers want a puzzle formula and very little social criticism? Alison Light in *Forever England* indicates that the reason Christie and other female detective fiction writers between the wars had a special need to write in a soothingly entertaining fashion was as a reaction to the traumas of World War I.

> The whodunit between the wars came rapidly to be as insensible to violence as it could be. As a literature of convalescence it developed a strongly meditative framework, relying upon a kind of inturned and internal ratiocination rather than on what would stir or shake the reader... Fleshiness, [of characters] either figuratively or literally, was perhaps in gross bad taste after the butchery many had witnessed. Vio-lence is literally bad form [70].

Thus, the focus of these earlier writers is on deliberately avoiding social consciousness because their readers wanted to be healed and comforted through entertainment. In addition, Christie basically appealed to a conservative audience who wished to have its position within the patri-archal society ratified, as they solved convoluted mysteries which made them feel in control of their world.

In contrast, when the first female hard-boiled detectives appeared in the United States, they were seen, in the words of Maureen T. Reddy, as "less part of an existing tradition than a distinct counter-tradition" ("The Feminist Counter Tradition" 174). This countertradition moved the female hard-boiled genre not only away from the more traditional post–Golden Age British detective fiction but also from the American male hard-boiled tradition. These male hard-boiled works, first intro-duced in the pulp magazines of the 1920s and 1930s, had come out of the action adventure story and were themselves a deliberate break from the perceived gentility of the Golden Age. The hero was physically tough, a loner, proficient with a gun, preferring his own brand of justice to that of society's which is indeed often shown as corrupt. Since his quest is more important than love, and since woman is often shown as evil, he is forced to eschew a loving relationship.

The early 1980s female hard-boiled novelists, beginning with Marcia Muller, who debuted in 1977, and continuing with Sue Grafton (1982) and Sara Paretsky (1982), had enjoyed reading the earlier male writers but were faced with the major dilemma of reconciling traditional femininity with the conventional private detective. They solved it by altering their narratives to include subject matters which concern everyday life and, most especially, relationships. Susan Wittig Albert says those authors' protagonists "display a deep fascination with human motivation, with the searing emotional drama of splintered relationships, with the corrosive friction between the individual and society" (100). And Ian Ousby expands this view:

> Female private eyes ... are implicated much more deeply in their stories.... In the female private-eye novels personal involvement is not just a convenience to get the story going but a signal that its theme will be the detective's own self-discovery and self-definition. She is not just there to solve a mystery but to learn about herself by understanding women from her family past better, or to see herself more clearly by comparing her life with the fate of women friends [186–187].

As I mention later on in this book, even though these 1980s authors move several traditions of the earlier detective genre from the center stage, they sometimes keep a fantasy element, a larger-than-life not totally socially realistic element in their depiction of their protagonists. According to Kimberley Dilley, "The mystery novel is one form of mass-produced fiction in which women have been able to push the accepted and create new possible narratives. They have used the mystery as a forum for experimentation, discussion, fantasy, debate, foolishness, and practice" (136). Because the mystery novel attracts such a wide-ranging readership, it is eminently suitable as a medium for discussion of serious themes, both feminist themes in particular and wider themes of social justice to which a feminist slant contributes.

As Maureen Reddy explains, these feminist writers suggest above all that "there is no single, universal truth ... rather truth is always relative, dependent on the perspective and on circumstances" ("The Feminist Counter Tradition" 176). Kathleen Klein claims that Sue Grafton's Kinsey Millhone adopts "individual solutions for societal problems" (*The Woman Detective* 206). In the view of Anne Cranny-Francis, "tracing the social and institutional consequences of injustice—institutionalised corruption, personal trauma—is as crucial to the development of the narrative as is the identification of the criminal" (170).

In both the U.S. and Britain, the sheer numbers of women writers have been amazing. As Kathleen Klein says in her preface to *Great Women Mystery Writers*, "between 1980 and 1993, sixty-eight women private eyes appeared in print, sixty-four of which were created by women" (7). In addition there has been a huge burgeoning of the field of mysteries. Willetta Heising in her compendium of mystery series facts and figures, *Detecting Women*, catalogs about 130 writers in the 1960s, 186 in the 1970s, 630 in the 1980s and 992 from 1990 to the end of 1995. Along with numbers comes power, and the detectives of the 1980s clearly reflect women's growing power as they question societal expectations, reject the attitudes of the earlier male detective model and develop new codes of behavior. We will see how the female characters today are portrayed less as innocent, stereotypical victims and more as capable, complex role models dealing with violence, crime and justice in a fictional world which closely parallels the day's society.

In the 1960s, both in the U.S. and in Britain, the role of women was clearly defined and usually narrow. There were very few women in positions of authority in the workplace, and the general social expectation was that they would marry and stay at home. Kenneth Morgan states in his analysis of the 1960s:

> The 1961 population census showed that women numbered 32.4 per cent of the employed work force, including 65.9 per cent of the clerical grades, notably secretaries and other office employees. But the wider presence of women in public life, in politics, the law, the universities, or the civil service was a limited one. Only 9.7 per cent of "higher professionals" in 1961 were women. A dominant administrative figure like Evelyn Sharp in the Housing department was a relative rarity [206–207].

Also, although there existed rampant sexism in many areas, very few women questioned their treatment but rather accepted inequities as the status quo which could not be changed. Although huge strides were made in the next 20 years, the problems of discrimination were still very significant even in the late 1980s. Indeed in 1988 author Caroline Heilbrun wrote, "I think that this openness about the prison of gender is one of the detective novel's great claims to fame" (7).

It is not surprising, therefore, that until the 1980s much detective fiction was dominated by male protagonists. In the early 1920s and 1930s the hard-boiled school coming out of the United States only had male protagonists, while even the great female writers, who had some amateur female sleuths, used male detectives or private investigators. However, the new professional female private investigators of the 1980s reflected the growing numbers of women in the work force, women who chose to be single, who were extremely efficient at their jobs, who could defend themselves physically and who constantly questioned the patriarchal society in which they functioned.

As we move into the 1990s, we see a new range of lesbian, black and ethnic female fictional detectives. While these types of detectives proliferate in the United States and have attracted the attention of many critics such as Anne Cranny-Francis, Maureen Reddy, Kimberley Dilley, and, of course, Kathleen Klein, there are fewer in Britain and, with the exception of Sally Munt's work, few in-depth studies of them.

This book focuses on six main British authors, all of whom have created these new types of private detectives, police women or amateur sleuths that have changed the genre. P.D. James created a different type of professional female private investigator from those of the 1920s; Jennie Melville, a more modern police woman; and Liza Cody, a hard-boiled type of serial private investigator. Val McDermid has created an overtly lesbian amateur detective; Joan Smith, an overtly feminist, professor amateur detective; and Susan Moody, a black amateur sleuth. Although this analysis will concentrate on these innovations, it will also examine other aspects of these authors' writings as they impact on the genre. All of these writers have chosen a serial detective, which has allowed them to make their characters dynamic. Readers react to the characters and their worlds as well-known friends and feel involved in the dilemmas they face in a way they don't with a single novel. As Priscilla L. Walton and Manina Jones say, "Because of the [series structure], authors can explore the varieties and nuances of the genre and its themes in an extended way and from a single point of view to which readers develop both a personal attachment and a political engagement" (54–55). However, as we shall see with several of the authors, there are problems with creating a series if either the author or the readers grow tired of the detective.

P.D. James has long been hailed as the new Agatha Christie, an accolade she did not particularly like since she preferred Dorothy Sayers as a writer. Although her first book, written in 1962, had Adam Dal-gliesh as the detective in charge, she later introduced Cordelia Gray in 1972, who was a new type of professional private eye, albeit very different from later American female private investigators. James is very much a product of the old school, a Tory member of the House of Lords, a believer in the system, justice, rules and regulations. Her character, Dal-gliesh, lives by these rules, but James is also a feminist. When the second Cordelia novel *The Skull Beneath the Skin* was not the success hoped for, James created Kate Miskin, a police woman, who shares many of Cordelia's characteristics and blends feminist concerns with modern police procedures.

Jennie Melville (pseudonym of Gwendoline Butler), whose first book also appeared in 1962, is just as interesting as James since she is the creator of a very realistic British police procedural with a female protagonist. Her main character, Charmian Daniels, who begins as a humble police detective but ends as a chief superintendent, gives us real insight into the problems of being female in the British police force. Another fascination with Melville is that much of her writing is far in advance of its time and reflects views and ideas which made her unusual in the 1960s and 1970s.

Liza Cody, the first author to have a hard-boiled type of private investigator, wrote her first novel two years before Grafton and Paretsky. Anna Lee is important because she is, in fact, very different from the American P.I.s, retaining some of the characteristics of the earlier more traditional Cordelia Gray. In addition, Cody's second series introduces Eva Wylie, a very different, almost antihero amateur investigator.

Val McDermid is a remarkable writer who has moved the detective genre in several new directions. Lindsay Gordon is an overtly lesbian amateur detective. Kate Brannigan is a hard-boiled detective who has a committed relationship and functions in a northern city, Manchester, and Tony Hill is an innovative serial killer profiler who shows how the detective novel-cum-police procedural is moving towards the horror novel.

Joan Smith—like McDermid, a former journalist—created a feminist amateur sleuth, English professor Loretta Lawson. Although the novels contain clear feminist messages, they do not slide into didactic tracts which fail to entertain. Smith manages to blend the best of the cozy traditions with a modern consciousness raising.

Susan Moody has two series, both featuring amateur detectives:

Penny Wanawake, a black world-famous photographer, and the bridge teacher Cassandra Swann. The first black protagonist, Penny, though wealthy and beautiful, is highly unusual, and so too is her message criticizing British upper-class traditions. Cassie Swann brings a fresh new look to the mystery novel since she is very far from the typical cozy or hard-boiled sleuth. Young, dynamic and critical of social ills, she is a far cry from Miss Marple. However, in her overweight, unathletic ways, she is also nothing akin to Kinsey Millhone or V.I. Warshawski. Like Smith, Moody manages to blend the best of British and American traditions in yet another new and exciting fashion.

In the last chapter, I examine some of the newest voices in detective fiction coming out of Britain. I have picked authors who have begun to write novels in a series or who have written three or four such, featuring either an amateur sleuth, private investigator or police woman. I have also chosen novelists, some of whom have won prizes, whose works are easily obtainable in the United States. In their fiction we see how many trends mentioned in this introduction are evolving and how the genre is moving in multiple directions.

As society has changed since the 1960s, we see parallel changes in the female detectives portrayed in novels. These changes include such things as looks, sexuality, attitude toward marriage, family and friends, as well as violence, patriarchal institutions and justice. An interesting study by Kathlyn Ann Fritz and Natalie Hevener Kaufman entitled "An Unsuitable Job for a Woman: Female Protagonists in the Detective Novel," analyzes 52 female detectives from the 1920s to the 1970s and shows how the changes in the types of detectives from unattractive, elderly or single women to attractive career women reflect the social change in the image and status of women in the United States. Their findings are reflected in Britain where the fictional detectives move from stereotypes of women to ones who "mirror the dramatic, political, legal, economic, and social changes of recent years" (106). The authors also describe the interesting shortage of married female detectives, which they feel leads to a lack of realism in the detective genre. The fact that, to this day, fictional female detectives are nearly always unmarried continues the traditional detective fiction's view that one cannot be married and have a career, especially one that is dangerous. Since this is patently not the case in real life today, one wonders why this aspect of the sixties and earlier societal beliefs has continued in detective fiction. When Val McDermid interviewed real-life private investigators and reported her findings in *A Suitable Job for a Woman*, she found that many were married and most of them had children. Fritz and Kaufman point out in their article that "by the 1960s most male detectives are married. This is apparently part of a trend toward greater realism in detective novels" (112). The male's marriage serves to make him seem "more like a real man, with personal problems and concerns" (112). So why does the female have to have a family of friends but no husband and often no parents? Why doesn't the fact that she is married make her seem "more like a real woman?" Fritz and Kaufman explain the discrepancy between the males and females:

> In detective fiction the detective must occasionally neglect his/her family for work. Apparently the idea that a married woman, with responsibilities toward her husband and her home, would neglect them to pursue a murder hunt is not consonant with the audience's beliefs about the proper role of women [113].

Thus, the fact that Melville depicts Daniels as married and later, after her husband dies, getting remarried and solving the problems of juggling a personal life with her career, is particularly relevant and is just one of the areas in which she is ahead of her era. Whereas in the past "[t]he over-thirty career women in detective fiction were depicted as 'characters' whose peculiarities cost them their femininity" (Fritz & Hevener 115), today's private investigators are personable, attractive and in no way outlandish. In the past, the career detective often couldn't get a husband because she wasn't attractive enough; whereas, today's private investigator doesn't want a husband because he would cramp her freedom. Today's authors have protagonists who lead lives similar to their readers' in many respects so that they are easily able to empathize with the characters, rather than seeing them as alien creatures. For example, Daniels takes a long time to decide whether or not to get remarried because she feels that her new husband may dominate her, and she enjoys her liberty. In addition, although Val McDermid's Kate Brannigan has rather unusual living arrangements because she doesn't like to live with her boyfriend all the time, many women might view those arrangements as the ideal alternative to getting married.

The changes in attitude towards the sexuality of the female detective is also of particular interest in post 1960s detective fiction. In novels of the '40s and '50s, the sexual life of the female detectives, whether young career woman or older spinster, was never discussed. In the '70s and '80s, detectives like Cordelia Grey, Kinsey Millhone, V.I. Warshawski and Anna Lee have liaisons but do not want someone permanent in their lives because they see this type of commitment as detrimental to their work, especially when the man tries to change them in some fundamental way. On the other hand, in the '90s, detectives have male friends and lovers who have no desire to change them and really do enjoy egalitarian relationships, even if Kate Brannigan's boyfriend always insists that they eat Chinese food when they go out to restaurants. The detectives' sexual encounters fall into two categories: they often enjoy a totally committed or fairly committed relationship to one male whom they are choosing not to marry at the moment, although it is implied that this situation may change at some point. In addition, they think nothing of having several short-term sexual relationships with whichever good-looking male they happen to be working with. These relationships are usually entered into with eagerness on the part of both parties and finish without any apparent sense of guilt, regret or hurt on the part of our female detective. In these relationships the female detective is acting like the "love 'em and leave 'em" males who exist in all societies, thus blurring stereotypical differences in gender.

The problems of gender discrimination are the basic feminist issues which all of the writers in this study examine, to a greater or lesser extent. One of the writers, Liza Cody, focuses on it often. Cody's protagonist, Anna Lee, works for the Brierly Security Agency as an investigator but is regularly disparaged by her male boss and is even nearly fired in *Dupe*. B.J. Rahn discusses in *Great Women Mystery Writers* how Cody has said that she wants to change the system which puts women in a second-class situation and aims to do so by showing the gross inequities which exist in white collar business (72). The investigator as victim is also analyzed by P.D. James in *An Unsuitable Job for a Woman* where Cordelia is always on the defensive to prove that she is able to do her job successfully. On the other hand, although both Charmian Daniels and Kate Miskin have some difficulties with their male colleagues, we really do not get a sense of their being unfairly treated or condescended to by their male superiors. Finally, Kate Brannigan, with her kick boxing and strong self esteem, is definitely very far removed from the victimized Anna Lee. Thus, as women gained greater recognition in the workplace in the '90s, and much of the work of the feminist movement became institutionalized in law, so, too, do the protagonists of the latest detective fiction reflect this newfound power.

Not only do many detective novels criticize male behavior toward females in the workplace, they also contain other criticisms of social inequities and act as social commentaries. Sara Paretsky says that "the quickest way to kill your fiction is to be writing sermons with it" (qtd. in Trembley 267). Despite this, many post–1980s authors do use the medium of the mystery to pinpoint areas which need change. Paretsky herself clearly indicts patriarchal society by making traditional male-centered institutions the focus of V.I. Warshawski's investigations, and all the authors in this survey criticize different aspects of the society of the time. James also touches on the idea of the victimization of women, a theme which is more central in Cody's work. While Melville is concerned with many issues arising from violent crimes towards women, McDermid unveils the difficulties of being lesbian and the prejudices of our culture. Smith, among other issues, depicts the problems of women in academe, and Moody discusses such contemporary issues as world poverty, child abuse, the efficacy of the penal system, classism and agism. Even though there continue to be numerous female detective writers whose only concern is to present a gripping plot, I feel that the authors analyzed in this book, because they include social criticism, add a dimension to the genre which may make it of greater appeal to many readers.

In all these writers too there is a more general reconfiguration of the idea of criminality and justice in the genre. In the 1960s, although there was some interest in the psychology of detectives and criminals, profiling of killers was still to come, and there was still a belief that someone like a serial killer was a totally aberrant personality. Thus, if such a person were convicted and removed, society would be able to return to being a fundamentally just place.

However, as feminist writer and critic Anne Cranny-Francis points out, the 1960s and 1970s justice system had major flaws, and it is writers with a feminist perspective who are likely to see the limitations of a patriarchal justice system. One of the roles of the 1980s feminist hard-boiled novels is to trace "the social and institutional consequences of injustice—institutional corruption, personal trauma—[which] is as crucial to the development of the narrative as is the identification of the criminal" (Cranny-Francis 170). When we read Christie or Sayers today, their books may appear unrealistic simply because the detection work is shown as unnaturally easy and successful, and they do not dwell on the judicial process. As Alison Light states:

Christie's conservatism is not one which likes to dwell upon the processes of the law; she is much more likely to play down both retribution and punishment; the majority of her murderers commit suicide or remove themselves conveniently and she evinces little interest in the judiciary [101].

In earlier detective fiction when criminals were protected, perhaps because their motives were good, they still usually died at the end of the book. On the other hand, Anne Cranny-Francis points out:

[Today] in some of the more radical texts, however, the criminal gets away with murder. This conclusion is disturbing for readers, and only acceptable if they accept the social criticism of the writer; that is if they accept that the social order with which they are familiar is not as just and harmonious as they have been taught to believe [173].

Several of the authors in my book explore the question of who is the final victim and, in the manner of the 1930s male hard-boiled writers, describe the realistic, dirty side of crime. They show that powerful figures whether in industry, government or even in the home often misuse their power and even go beyond the laws.

It is clear then that since the 1960s, detective fiction with female protagonists has changed a great deal, and especially in the 1990s we saw a very different private investigator and police woman and very different ideological assumptions. However, Britain appears to be lagging behind the United States at least in one respect and that is in the representation of ethnic minority female protagonists, which reflects its generally more conservative society. Although both countries have burgeoning numbers of lesbian writers with lesbian protagonists, in the United States there are about ten black female writers with black female detectives or private investigators. In Britain there is only one so far. In the U.S. there are several ethnically diverse female writers—Chicano, American Indian, Hispanic—while Britain does not have any to date. This last difference is particularly interesting.

If we consider detective fiction as reflecting society, and if we look at the 1970s' immigration wave of people of Indian or Pakistani origin, some of whom came from Uganda, the numbers would suggest that 20 or 30 years later one could expect to see these minorities reflected as characters in detective fiction and possibly becoming writers themselves. However, although some of the television police dramas have a token

Indian or Pakistani, the books I have examined have very few minority secondary characters and only one primary one. Why are minorities not as visible in British writing? Jennie Melville has one theory which will be addressed later, but even Val McDermid, although she does have some ethnic minorities as characters in her books, does not examine crime from the point of view of the large Indian and Pakistani population of Manchester.

One major change in the 1990s British detective fiction was a significant shift of location, however. Whereas pre–1960s detective fiction had two main settings, London and its surroundings or the country village, today's novels are set in numerous cities both real and imaginary. What is interesting is that an industrial city, like Manchester, has, in McDermid's books, finally found itself in the limelight. With the focus on this cosmopolitan city, the types of crimes described have also changed. McDermid examines white-collar crime such as fraud, as well as crimes related to drug trafficking. The small country village of many of Agatha Christie's books lent itself to the description of "cozy" crimes. Manchester, meanwhile, with its easy access to other cities by means of its airport and numerous motorways, is the center for any types of ugly crime; therefore, McDermid can extend the "modern seediness" element found in James's earlier works (Porter 13).

Many of the works in this book fall into the category of female hard-boiled detective, yet Joan Smith and Susan Moody's detectives are all amateurs, and Loretta and Cassie have many similarities to characters in the cozy genre. This term has been used by publishers and booksellers to denote more traditional mysteries, either in the genre of the Golden Age puzzle or pertaining to more rural settings, or as described by author Carolyn Hart, who has written numerous novels in this genre, as being like a "parable." It doesn't have so much to do with crime as with relationships, with the writer exploring what led to the problems between the victim and another person or people (71). In addition, the cozy is popular because it offers "humour, entertainment and satire" (72). Hence the cozy, far from being insulated and an inferior subgenre to the hard-boiled detective fiction, has a great deal to offer. Hart claims that one of the strengths of the genre is that cozies "excel in voice" and that voice is the author's world-view where the writer puts their own "spin on everything from politics to love to morality" (73).

Although there continue to be new writers of the cozy genre and numerous new amateur sleuths of all ages and occupations, perhaps the

Golden Age puzzle genre of detective novels will gradually disappear unless the novel has a protagonist who is herself fascinating and also analyzes social issues. Puzzles and convoluted plots alone are not going to sustain us because we need more than an intellectual tease when we read. As society changes, so too may those "raw nerves" and the issues which we consider important. Today we know that justice is not always achievable, nor is crime in reality something which will never touch our lives.

The authors analyzed in this work have proven themselves in their series to be innovative and appealing to contemporary audiences. Those who began in the 1960s are still widely read today. Those who began in the 1980s and 1990s will assuredly continue to be popular in 20 years. By examining where our current female writers are taking the detective genre, we witness the new roles of women in society and can empathize, as Kathleen Klein states, with "real women portraying authentic lived experience" (*The Woman Detective* 228).

Where will British detective fiction go in the future? As previously mentioned, there will probably be greater numbers of ethnically diverse authors entering the market and, before that, many more immigrant characters appearing in texts. In addition, the advent of victim support groups, which are the norm in even small towns in the U.S., implies that we may witness an even greater focus on the psychology of the victim than we have at present, and more novels may combine social documentary with mystery. Along with this, there will probably be greater violence and overt sexuality in novels by female authors as the differentiation between what is acceptable in books by male authors and female authors becomes blurred. As our medical knowledge grows and the forensic scientists become increasingly expert, we may see a return to the puzzle element, this time with the pathologist acting as detective rather than the police, as is the case with Patricia Cornwell's Kay Scarpetta. As women gain more positions of influence in the police force, we may see more series with characters such as Charmian Daniels who have several male subordinates working for her. These women may even be shown not only married but with children, since McDermid discovered when she interviewed real female private investigators for her nonfiction work *A Suitable Job for a Woman*, that most were in relationships and were mothers. As crimes and criminals cross borders and oceans, some of our detectives may start an investigation in one country and finish it in another, and as our authors gain knowledge of computers and international law, so too will the detectives. Although it is difficult to pinpoint exactly the new directions of the mystery novel, one thing is certain: whatever the detective fiction of the future, British writers will continue to excel in the genre.

Chapter One

P.D. James

Women detective fiction writers have come a very long way since the Golden Age of Agatha Christie and Dorothy Sayers. P.D. James, who began writing in 1962 and also earned the title of "queen of crime," acts as a bridge between the traditions of the earlier genre and the greater feminist thrust of the detective fiction of the post–1980s. James is a paradox since she is a Tory and a High Anglican. She uses the closed-room puzzle formula of the traditional detective novel; yet she has many feminist features, and her books are contemporary and insightful. In James we still have the male detective as hero in a style sometimes reminiscent of the earlier writers, but she also created the female private investigator and uses the new type of female detective. Because she thus straddles two eras by means of her protagonists, she is particularly suitable to begin an analysis of changes in the genre. As she says in her latest autobiographical work, "Because the detective story is usually set unambiguously in its own time and place, it often gives a clearer idea of contemporary life than does more prestigious literature" (*Time to be in Earnest* 59). James is concerned with psychological analysis, both of the victim and the murderer. In addition, her detectives—whether the male, Adam Dalgliesh, or the females, Cordelia Gray and Kate Miskin—are far more reflective than those of the earlier genre, although they are different from the later feminist detective heroes in certain respects. James's use of introspective detectives and concern with justice and punishment, as well as her feminist issues, all make her a far more profound and serious writer than Christie and a clear originator

P.D. James

of the new type of detective fiction which reflects social and political changes and issues.

Although her characterization is modern, James's descriptions of her settings often remind the reader of the traditional detective story. In her 1977 novel *Death of an Expert Witness*, the setting is the Hoggatt's laboratory housed in a "late seventeenth century ... three story brick mansion with a hipped roof and four dormer windows, the centre three-bay projection surmounted by a pediment with a richly carved cornice and medallions" (106–7). This use of a mansion, reminiscent of many of Christie's stately home settings, is at once a reminder of the earlier detective genre and a modern twist since the functions of the laboratory make this mansion anything but stately, and we are told more than once that the founder has no respect for architectural splendor. "The ceiling carvings had been removed, perhaps because Colonel Hoggatt had thought them inappropriate to a working laboratory, but the scars of the desecration remained" (108). In *Original Sin*, Innocent House is the setting for the murder of a publisher. The magnificent entrance hall of the house is modeled after a Venetian palace:

> The intricate segments of the marble floor, the six mottled marble pillars with their elegantly carved capitals, the richness of the painted ceiling, a gleaming panorama of eighteenth-century London, bridges, spires, towers, houses, masted ships, the whole unified by the blue reaches of the river, the elegant double staircase, the balustrade curving down to end in bronzes of laughing boys riding dolphins and holding aloft the great globed lamps [129].

James's masterful use of descriptions, however, is not limited to houses. In *Death of an Expert Witness*, with a fine eye for detail, she describes at the beginning of the book the fens around Cambridge, where the laboratory is situated and where a body is first discovered:

> The place was an arid scrubland between the two ends of the town, litter strewn and edged with sparse trees above a ditch.... The ditch [was] dank with nettles and sour with rotting rubbish, the trees wounded by vandals, the trunks carved with initials the low branches hanging torn from the boughs. Here was an urban no-man's-land [and] fit territory for murder [23].

James's use of the word "urban" cannot fail to remind the reader of the early hard-boiled fiction of Dashiell Hammett and Raymond Chandler with their emphasis on the ugliness of cities in the settings for crime. Later in the same novel, James has the mother of one of the clerical assistants who works at the lab compare the safety of the fen village to the dangers of London: "Liverpool Street Station was the cavernous entry to an urban jungle, where predators armed with bombs and syringes lurked in every Underground station and seducers laid their snares for innocent provincials in every office" (*Death of an Expert Witness* 40). This mention of "bombs and syringes" reminds us of the horrors of IRA bombings and the advent of drug-related crimes which have so transformed London from the city it was between the wars.

Thus, James's descriptions are reminiscent of earlier detective fiction but do, however, differ in one major regard. According to Dennis Porter, "the relationship implied between the crimes committed and the environment breaks down with James" (13). Porter goes on to say that "the typical ambiance of a Sayers or Christie novel implied the surprise of crime under circumstances of order and relative beauty" (13). While the hard-boiled tradition "posited not an antithetical, but a sympathetic relationship between crime and environment in the urban spaces of rapidly developing, unregulated American cities" (13), James shows us a "modern seediness which easily explains both the unpleasant circumstances of characters' lives and the crimes which sometimes spring from such lives" (13). In *Death of an Expert Witness*:

> Violent death might lurk eastward in the dark fenlands, but surely not under these neat domestic roofs. Hoggatt's Laboratory was hidden by its belt of trees, but the new building was immediately identifiable,

its concrete stumps, ditches, and half-built walls looking like the orderly excavation of some long-buried city [171].

James may appear to be surprised that murder can happen "under neat domestic roofs," but she has proved to us that those same roofs are not covering a world of order and tranquility. The people who work at Hoggatt's Laboratory neither labor congenially together, nor live untroubled lives outside the laboratory. The extent of the seediness of their lives is divulged layer by layer as the book unfolds and by James's descriptions of settings.

James's claim to fame as the "queen of crime" (she was recognized early by the press as a worthy successor to Christie), is mainly due to her masterly ability to get under the skin not only of the criminal and the victim, but also the detective. Although it is her creation of the first female P.I. which makes her particularly significant for this analysis, it is important to recognize the changes she brought to her male detective and his relationship with his female subordinate, Kate Miskin. James's Adam Dalgliesh is a new type of male detective who still has an air of superiority like earlier detectives but does differ from the heroes of both the British traditional murder mysteries of the 1960s and the hard-boiled American works. Superficially, Dalgliesh is different because he writes poetry and is obviously sensitive; more importantly, he is unique because he constantly analyzes his own motives and weaknesses. In *Death of an Expert Witness*, we are given one of many descriptions of Dalgliesh:

> His only son had died, with his mother, just twenty-four hours after birth.... His son would now be older than this child, would be entering the traumatic years of adolescence. He had convinced himself long ago that he was glad to have been spared them. But now it suddenly occurred to him that there was a whole territory of human experience on which, once repulsed, he had turned his back, and that this rejection somehow diminished him as a man [249].

James, herself, claimed in an interview with Diana Cooper-Clark which was published in 1983 that she "'gave Adam Dalgliesh many of the qualities that [she herself] admire[d] in men'" (28). Further she made him very professional, but not so snobbish; hence he is the son of a parson, and the poetry is "'a device ... to emphasize his sensitivity and to mark him from the ordinary, non-corrupt British detective'" (29). In my own interview with her, James also stressed that Dalgliesh is similar to her in his total professionalism and concern with ethical behavior.

However, Dalgliesh does resemble the more traditional detectives in his Godlike ways and airs of superiority, especially towards women. James has him sweeping in from London, sometimes even arriving by helicopter, to solve the crime of the moment, which he always does despite all odds. In addition, unlike detectives of the 1990s, he has no committed relationship, appearing cold and paternalistic towards women. At the end of *Unnatural Causes*, Dalgliesh decides finally to send a poem to the woman he has been dating, implying that he will propose marriage to her on his return to London. However, he never mails the letter, and she sends him a note saying that she feels she cannot spend the rest of her days loitering "on the periphery of his life waiting for him to make up his mind" (256). His response to this destruction of their love affair is simply to burn both her letter and his own and bemoan the fact that, because he has hurt his hands, he cannot wield a poker to beat both burning letters to a fine dust (256).

Unlike the feminist detectives of authors such as Sue Grafton and Sara Paretsky, who may have failed marriages or relationships behind them but have a close knit circle of good friends and pets on which they lavish a great deal of affection, Dalgliesh often seems utterly isolated in his detachment. James maintains that this lack of involvement, caused by the tragedies in his own life, is "'quite logical for the detective because his job is to observe and deduce'" (Cooper-Clark 21). In *A Taste for Death*, after a meeting with the Special Branch during which he almost loses his temper with one of the officers, Dalgliesh actually thinks, "what depressed him most and left him with a sour taste of self disgust was how close he had come to losing his control. He realized how important his reputation for coolness, detachment, uninvolvement, had become to him" (341). This ability to keep such a tight rein on all his emotions reminds us of earlier Golden Age detectives and makes it hard for us to empathize with Dalgliesh. Interestingly in her very latest book, as yet unpublished, James is making Dalgliesh less cold. She told reporter Elisabeth Grice, "'I think he may be a little less lonely in the new book.... I think it is time he got himself ... yes, I think we could have Dalgliesh in love for a change'" (25).

Another aspect of Dalgliesh's character, which makes him much more reminiscent of Sherlock Holmes than later feminist detectives, is his chauvinism. Although for many readers his attitudes might be considered quaintly chivalrous, for modern female readers his actions are more likely to be construed as insulting. At the beginning of *A Taste for Death* when the bodies of the victims who have had their necks cut with an old-fashioned razor are being taken to the mortuary, Dalgliesh muses that although he realizes that many of the forensic scientists are women, he is always glad when the more horrific bodies have been removed before they come to take photographs of the scene of the crime, since he doesn't want to upset them (44). This attitude seems a far cry from those of Val McDermid's and Minette Walters's protagonists.

One aspect of Dalgliesh's character which does, however, show a real development from the earliest novels to the later ones and makes him appealing is his questioning of the validity of his work and his own usefulness. After he has interviewed the grandparents of one of the victims in *A Taste for Death*, Dalgliesh thinks to himself, "There's too much pain in this job. To think I used to congratulate myself, to think it useful, God help me, that people found it easy to confide in me.... And if I tell myself that enough is enough, twenty years of careful non-involvement, if I resign, what then?"(324). In my interview with James, she said, "I certainly say time and time again about Dalgliesh that he's coming to realize the harm that the job he does can do to the innocent as well as the guilty. There are moral implications to this job, and he does cause pain" (personal interview July 26, 1998).

If James is interesting because her male protagonist moves away to some degree from the traditional norms, it is as the creator of the British female private investigator in 1972 that she altered the detective genre for ever. Although there were female private investigators in the 1930s and 1940s, these were very different from Cordelia Gray, who is a fascinating character for many reasons. When *An Unsuitable Job for a Woman* was published in 1972, critics hailed Cordelia as the first feminist private investigator and felt that by creating her, James had moved down a very different path. However, James modeled the character in part on her daughter, Jane, and this caused problems in the growth of Cordelia. In my interview James said that Cordelia was similar to Jane in her "straightforwardness, honesty and intelligence." She also told me what her aims were in creating such a character:

> Well, I really wanted to create the type of woman that she turned
> out to be, that is one who'd had a very lonely and unhappy early life

with no real parenting but had the sort of guts and intelligence to make a life for herself, rather fell into this job, but was determined that she would make a success of it. What I did like about her was that she was a woman with a strong moral sense, an ethical sense entering into a world where she's going to encounter people who will have a very different view of life and morals, and how can she do her job well and successfully and retain her integrity. I think she's always very much her own person, and because she's not a policewoman, she doesn't have to act according to rules and regulations and she can take a line which a policewoman wouldn't be able to take. I think that really was the basic idea. I wanted to set a book in Cambridge, one of Europe's loveliest cities. She seemed to be the right detective. Dalgliesh wouldn't have been able to operate in Cambridge because he's a London policeman and he wouldn't have jurisdiction out of the metropolitan police area, and the suspects were going to be young, the victim was young, and it really is a very young book in a sense. It was very agreeable to write about a young woman [Personal interview July 26, 1998].

Jane Bakerman compares the novel to the Bildungsroman, saying that James has altered the outcome "in a striking manner" (103). Cordelia does not compromise in the novel—"she defeats the system; she overcomes it" (104). Having served justice, she triumphs at the end, and we feel she will triumph again in the future (109). However, the triumphant, fully mature Cordelia was not to be, as we see later in the second novel, *The Skull Beneath the Skin.*

In the first novel, we learn about Cordelia's past history. She had a father who was a Marxist revolutionary who left her with foster parents and did not want her company during the school holidays. Finally, he removed her from school at age 16 so that she could be his "cook, nurse, messenger and general camp follower," until his unexpected death from a heart attack (*An Unsuitable Job for a Woman* 127). Thus, as Maureen Reddy demonstrates, a character like Cordelia, in her loneliness and lack of family situation, "resemble[s] the male hard-boiled detectives, but the resemblance is a superficial one that makes deeper differences all the more striking" (*Sisters in Crime* 105).

One of the major differences between early female detectives and those born after 1970, according to Reddy, lies in their attitude towards sexual relationships. Although these new detectives want relationships, they do not want one in which they feel oppressed (*Sisters in Crime* 105). In *An Unsuitable Job for a Woman*, Cordelia wants reassurance from her sexual liaisons and might possibly even welcome a man who wants to protect her. She describes two of her lovers and their effects on her:

> Before Georges and Carl she had been lonely and inexperienced. Afterwards she had been lonely and a little less inexperienced. Neither affair had given her the longed-for assurance in dealing with Daddy or the landladies, neither had inconveniently touched her heart.... [L]ovemaking ... was overrated, not painful but surprising. The alienation between thought and action was so complete [164–5].

Therefore, for Cordelia, sex should be the answer to her problems, a way to bolster up her own ego so that she can deal better with "Daddy" and the "landladies," both of whom make her feel young and inadequate. However, rather than making her feel strong and resolute, the sexual encounters reinforce her sense of inadequacy, but conveniently do not "touch her heart."

Cordelia also feels inadequate to some extent in her work. Although she tackles her investigative work eagerly, she is very unsure of herself at the beginning of *An Unsuitable Job for a Woman*, even with her facial expressions. When she is investigating the suicide of Mark Callender and meets the Marklands, his landlords, we are told: "She composed her face into the appropriate expression—seriousness combined with efficiency and a touch of propriatory humility seemed about right but she wasn't sure that she managed to bring it off " (80). When she visits the police station in Cambridge to gain information, she admits, "Sometimes it helped to play the part of a vulnerable and naive young girl eager for information ... but she sensed that Sergeant Maskell would respond better to an unflirtatious competence" (128–9). The inexperienced Cordelia is also horrified when Sergeant Maskell shows her a lurid photograph of Mark's body and explains the way he used a belt to strangle himself:

> Why, she wondered, had he shown her the photograph? It wasn't necessary to prove his argument. Had he hoped to shock her into a realization of what she was meddling in; to punish her for trespassing on his patch; to contrast the brutal reality of his professionalism with her amateurish meddling? [135].

Kathleen Klein in *The Woman Detective* describes Cordelia as "[lacking] the cynicism or experience which seems necessary to understand crime and evil.... [Cordelia] is reminded that hers is an unsuitable job for a woman frequently enough for her to assume that all clients believe this" (155). I do not totally agree with Klein since not all the people Cordelia interviews do believe that a woman is unsuitable as a detective, and as she discovers the truth about Mark Callender's death, Cordelia grows in confidence and even physical toughness. She is even comfortable threatening her would-be murderer with a gun, although later she does admit she could never kill someone. Maureen Reddy finds this use of a gun by the new style women detectives interesting. James, as other writers I will examine later, "[moves] the gun from the realm of the symbolic, where it signifies male power and control, to the actual.... The gun ceases to be an exclusively phallic symbol, becoming something that can be wielded by either women or men, that can be used responsibly or irresponsibly" (*Sisters in Crime* 99).

Thus, when we leave Cordelia at the end of *An Unsuitable Job for a Woman*, she appears stronger, more confident and even capable of not being intimidated by Dalgliesh. She is a powerful role model for would-be feminists of the early 1970s. In the ten years which passed until she appeared again, James's fans became ever more excited at the thought of another Cordelia novel. According to Nicola Nixon, Cordelia "achieved near cult status," and she was "a touchstone of early seventies feminism" (29–30). However, when we meet her again ten years later in *The Skull Beneath the Skin*, she does not appear to have grown either emotionally or financially. Pryde's Agency is still struggling on a shoestring and has been reduced to finding lost pets for its major source of income. The office itself is shabby, and the stains caused by Bernie's cutting his wrists as he sat at his desk still remain on the desk and carpet as permanent reminders. Cordelia is still defensively justifying her job even when the client is not criticizing: "'Don't people ever tell you ...' She finished the sentence for him: 'That it's an unsuitable job for a woman? They do and it isn't.' He said mildly, "I was going to say, "Don't they ever tell you that your office is difficult to find?"'(9). As Nixon puts it, "From the deploying of direct borrowings and allusions to the echoing of plot sequences and rhetorical figures ... James constantly directs our attention back to *An Unsuitable Job for a Woman*" (37). And in this redirecting, we realize that Cordelia is not a hard-boiled feminist role model, but still an insecure, childlike character. For example, in *The Skull Beneath the Skin*, Cordelia twice utters misgivings about her task of protecting Clarissa. Before she ever arrives on the island she says, "the envelope in her pocket confirmed that the job was real, that she would pit her brain and her wits against a human adversary at last. Why, then, should she have to struggle against a sudden and overwhelming conviction that her task was doomed to disaster?" (90). And later when Clarissa's husband, George, arrives on the island, and Cordelia is thinking that she should be pleased that he is there since he will help her, she says: "Why should she feel for the first time she was caught in a charade in which she stumbled blindfold, while unseen hands spun her around, pushed and pulled at her, in which an unknown intelligence watched, waited, and directed the play?" (158). This picture of Cordelia in a type of childish blindman's bluff game, unseeing, at the mercy of someone cleverer than she, is one which stays with us, and is reinforced by James even in the fact that after Clarissa is murdered, James entitles the chapter heralding the appearance of the police as "The Professionals." Cordelia is obviously "the amateur."

Nicola Nixon in her article claims that *The Skull Beneath the Skin* is an allegory of the political events of Margaret Thatcher's Britain of the '80s. Far from finding the changes in Cordelia surprising, Nixon sees that she is typical of the '80s female who was also being enjoined by Thatcher to uphold the family values and keep the home fires burning: "Cordelia is, both chronologically and politically—at least insofar as she adheres to ascendant Tory propaganda, at any rate—a veritable icon of post-war progress, an ideological domestic cornerstone of British (neo–Victorian) greatness" (43).

Cordelia's transformation from potential feminist role model to finder of lost pets, albeit a good one, may be explained by James's own Conservative political stance or her lack of comfort with the whole women's liberation movement, either or both of which made her unable to develop Cordelia convincingly as a strong feminist. James stated, when I asked her about feminism at my interview with her:

> I think it's a difficult label, feminist, isn't it? Because am I a femi-
> nist? It depends on your definition. I am a feminist if by being a femi-
> nist you mean someone who very much likes her own sex, admires her
> own sex, and feels that women are entitled to have equal opportunity,
> equal right to live their lives in ways that are most satisfying to them.
> But if by feminist you mean someone who is antimale, then I'm not,
> because I feel that it's like all organizations—you can get on the fringe
> people who really feel half the human race are all potential rapists,
> and they are not. And I also feel, I've always felt, that sexual equality

is strongly economic. Middle class feminists are complaining about all sorts of things in their jobs, and most of the women of the world haven't got equal economic rights; they're overworking for pittances. The greatest freedom for women has come from the right to earn their own money and the right to control their fertility. Those have been the things that have given us our greatest advantages. My mother couldn't have earned a living, and people were tied into their marriages. They had no options. But I think that a lot of the things the extreme feminists have fought for have rather backfired on women and have not made women any happier [personal interview July 28, 1998].

By the early '80s, feminists had achieved a great deal in terms of law, the Equal Pay Act of 1970 and the Sex Discrimination Act of 1975, for example (qtd. in Nixon 32). By then Marcia Muller had also created the first hard-boiled female investigator, a woman who was notably tougher than the genteel Cordelia. If, even though she herself had worked in a man's world and had been the major breadwinner for her own family, James was not fully convinced that what the feminists were doing was achieving happiness for women, it is understandable that she altered Cordelia to make her more sweetly feminine, than feminist. Support for this idea can also be found in the character of Roma Lisle in *The Skull Beneath the Skin*. Roma, a failed schoolteacher who is running an unsuccessful bookstore with a married man, is shown as an unattractively belligerent, stereotypical feminist. When she first arrives on the island, she verbally attacks her host, Ambrose: "'But you can't opt out of all responsibility for what's happening in your own country! You can't just say that you're not concerned, not even interested!'" (126). To which he replies, "'But I can'"(126). Later when Chief Inspector Grogan is listing the suspects of the murder, he describes Roma as: "a respectable bookseller, ex-schoolteacher, who's probably a member of the civil rights and women's lib lobbies and who will protest to her M.P. about police harassment if I raise my voice to her" (237). As Dr. Bonnie Plummer stated, "In the case of Roma, James not only creates a negative female character, but makes part of the negativity her association with women's rights" (PCAS conference). This description, coupled with James's admiration for tradition, possibly explains why she chose not to write another Cordelia novel. Instead she modified her heroine, made her a policewoman, and thereby created a protagonist who could resemble her daughter but be constrained by the rules and regulations of the job and would, therefore, be successful in appealing to her readers.

Four years after *The Skull Beneath the Skin*, James created this professional female detective who has numerous similarities to Cordelia and yet also with the feminist detectives of authors such as Sue Grafton and Sara Paretsky. In my interview with her, James commented on the links between Cordelia and Kate:

> I'm very interested in Kate because Kate and Cordelia have some things in common. They've both got this very bad background, poor background, both of them are very brave, both of them are quite ambitious. But, of course, throughout, Kate is a professional police-woman before she's anything else, so you'd never have Kate acting in the way Cordelia did—covering up a crime [personal interview July 26, 1998].

We first meet Inspector Kate Miskin in *A Taste for Death* (1986) where she is part of the new criminal investigation team set up by Dalgliesh "to investigate serious crimes which were thought to be politically or socially sensitive" (164). To some extent Kate is the token female in what is still very much considered to be a male domain, but she is a far cry from Jane Marple and easier to empathize with than Cordelia. Like Kinsey Millhone, V.I. Warshawski and other hard-boiled detectives, Kate is working class, single and poor. We are told a great deal about her past, her illegitimacy, the grandmother who brought her up and her socially disadvantaged background, all of which make her desperately cling to her pristine flat and newfound independence. When she hears that her grandmother has been burgled and is really desirous of moving in with her, her chief emotion is one of utter horror:

> She was seized with a spurt of envy and resentment against Massingham. Even if he had a dozen difficult and demanding relatives, no one would expect him to have to cope. And if she did have to take time off from the job, he would be the first to point out that, when the going got really tough, you couldn't rely on a woman [175].

This *cri de coeur* from an obviously frustrated feminist is one which women of all ages who have any family obligations can identify with. What is ironic in the novel, however, is that a little later on, we are told about Massingham's situation with his aged father, who is newly a widower and is clinging to his son for companionship in a way which fills Massingham with a similar guilt and horror experienced by Kate. After berating himself that he could have spared his father ten minutes of his time when he came home and before he retired to his apartment at the top of his father's house, Massingham

> thought of Kate Miskin, less than a couple of miles to the west, relaxing in her flat, pouring herself a drink, free of responsibility, free of guilt, and felt a surge of envy and irrational resentment so strong that he could almost persuade himself that it was all her fault [184].

Through Kate's relationships with her male colleagues, we see the dilemmas the modern policewoman faces and have examples of how James's novels reflect social changes and issues. Massingham's relationship with Kate is interestingly developed in *A Taste for Death* because, although he is also her superior officer, she is not as much in awe of him as she is of Dalgliesh, and they do communicate more frankly. At one point Kate complains about the victim's relationship with his mistress, saying that he tucked her away in "the equivalent of a Victorian love-nest" (292). Massingham chastises her, asking if she had to choose between the man in her life or her job, would she always necessarily choose her man? Since Kate feels very guilty because she has just broken a date with her lover, Alan, to work on the murder case, this immediately strikes a chord. This is the classic dilemma of so many modern female readers who try furiously, often unsuccessfully, to balance the demands of a career and a love life.

Kate is also a modern detective similar to the hard-boiled detectives of Grafton and Paretsky in her attitude to her cases. Unlike Miss Marple who was just an amateur who often stumbled into cases, Kate's whole focus is her work and her ambition. After interviewing a key witness with Dalgliesh, Kate thinks about the outcome of the murder:

> If this goes all right, if we get him, whoever he is, and we will, then I'm on my way. I'm really on my way. But the elation went deeper than mere ambition or the satisfaction of a test passed, a job well done. She had enjoyed herself. Every minute of her brief confrontation with that self-satisfied poseur had been deeply pleasurable [205].

She compares her current job to her past jobs with the CID, asking questions door-to-door of pathetic victims and villains, and thinks, "How much more satisfying was this sophisticated manhunt: the knowledge that they were up against a killer with the intelligence to think and plan, who wasn't an ignorant, feckless victim of circumstance or passion" (205). Thus, because Kate sees herself as intelligent and determined, she loves this new job which pits her against her equal, although that person may be a murderer.

Although many feminists might put their career above personal relationships, Kate follows Reddy's description by having "feminist values [which show] subjectivity superior to pretenses of objectivity, involvement more valuable than distance, and compassion more important than justice" (*Sisters in Crime* 14). In *A Taste for Death*, Kate interviews the mistress of the murdered government minister, Berowne, and thinks, "There isn't a man, any man in the world who is worth this agony. She felt a mixture of sympathy, helplessness and irritation which she recognized was tinged with slight contempt. But the pity won" (354). At this time, Kate also recognizes that her instincts are telling her to take this witness to her own apartment close by to offer her a cup of coffee and sympathy. She also realizes that by doing this she might be jeopardizing her professional position because

> suppose Carole were required to give evidence in court, then any suggestion of friendship, of an understanding between them, could be prejudicial to the prosecution. And more than to the prosecution; it could be prejudicial to her own career. It was the kind of sentimental error of judgement which wouldn't exactly displease Massingham if he came to hear of it [355].

The fact that she compares her own actions to Massingham's clearly shows that Kate is fully aware of the consequences of inviting Carole to her flat, but she still does it. She obviously values demonstrating sympathy above being cautious and sensible, and thus acts as a sharp contrast to Dalgliesh.

Kate Miskin is similar to many of the detectives of the 1990s in her courage, toughness, and ability to cope in difficult situations. At the end of *A Taste for Death*, Kate and her grandmother are taken hostage by the murderer who ties up the grandmother and forces Kate to make dinner for them all. Kate manages to distract the man and flings herself on top of him, grappling with him for the gun. The gun goes off and we learn that the murderer has deliberately shot the grandmother. When he is overwhelmed by Dalgliesh and Massingham, who burst into the apartment, the murderer says to Kate, "'Well, you're free of her now. Aren't you going to thank me?'"(487). This amazing twist forces Kate once again to examine her feelings for her grandmother, who would definitely have proved to be a burden to her and prevented her from advancing in her career. When I asked P.D. James why she had had Swayne kill the grandmother, and whether it was just so that Kate would be unencumbered by personal ties, she replied "'No, no. Well, that's just the way the book went. I mean, I'd never think, well, it would be nice for Kate not to be encumbered with the grandmother. In many ways having the grandmother and the personal ties would have made it more complex. It's just how it worked out'" (personal interview July 26, 1998). Later when Kate asks Dalgliesh if she is right to feel guilty and states that maybe it is really her fault that her grandmother died, he replies that it's natural to feel some guilt, but she was in no way responsible (494). Although Kate thinks that maybe Dalgliesh is just trying to pacify her, she feels that she is "tough, she would cope.... She would learn to accept and carry her personal load of guilt" (495). Hence, Kate is far removed from the type of 1950s woman police detective described by George Dove: "as every man's little sister, the squad pet who is protected by the older brothers, but ... at the same time resented and scorned because, as everybody knows, police work is a man's business" (*The Police Procedural* 151).

Kate is the hard-boiled type of feminist in that she views a sexual relationship as a threat to her independence and an interference with her career, while such an encounter is seen by the man as a way of demonstrating his ability to protect her (Reddy *Sisters in Crime* 105). When we meet Kate in *Original Sin*, published in 1994, she has been asked by her lover Alan Scully to make a commitment, either to marry him or to live with him and have his baby. If she refuses, he is going to take up a post at Princeton University in New Jersey. Like the woman in Dalgliesh's life in *Unnatural Causes*, Alan is also tired of being on the "periphery" of Kate's life (117). Kate realizes that she is not suited to marriage and certainly not to motherhood, claiming, "'I wouldn't be any good at it. I've never had any training'" (118). When Alan replies that it doesn't need training, she says that motherhood does need "'loving commitment. That's one thing I can't give. You can't give what you haven't had'" (118). Later when she is called to go to the murder scene and realizes that she probably won't see Alan again, she assesses the situation:

> She would look back on those few hours they had spent together in the flat with pleasure, even sadness. But what she was feeling now was something more intoxicating, and she felt it whenever she was called to a new case. This was her job, one she had been trained for, one she did well, one she enjoyed. Already knowing that this might be the last time she saw him for years, she was moving in thought away from him, mentally bracing herself for the task ahead [119].

Kate is clearly a woman of the '90s, more committed to her job than to her lover, although ideally of course she would like to have both. If she appears uncaring, it is because she is doing what men have done for years before her. If as women we criticize her, perhaps it is only because we know how work so often falsely appears to be the answer to all our problems.

Another way in which Kate acts more like a stereotypical man than a stereotypical woman is that she divorces sex from love. In *Original Sin* her new partner, Daniel, who is equal in rank to her but less experienced, asks her to go to bed with him. When she rejects him, saying that it would cause complications in their ability to work together, he mocks her, asking whether if Dalgliesh had made the same request, she would have replied yes or no. When she answers that she would have gone home with Dalgliesh, she justifies her answer by saying that it wouldn't have been either love or sex but "curiosity" (284). Her obvious lack of commitment to and love for Dalgliesh, yet her recognition of him as a sexually attractive man whom she could desire, makes her very different from the shrinking violets of earlier mystery stories, more manlike and far more sexually liberated.

James, like Jennie Melville, makes her protagonist a successful policewoman who can act as a role model for modern women. When Kate appears in James's latest book, *A Certain Justice*, she is practicing at the shooting range, and we are told she's very skilful. She tells her new partner, Piers, "'I wish I knew why I always look forward to a shoot. I can't imagine wanting to kill an animal, let alone a man, but I like guns. I like using them'" (109). When Piers says she likes them because she's good at shooting, she replies, "'It can't only be that. It's not the only thing I'm good at. I'm beginning to think that shooting is addictive'" (109). Piers replies that the real reason she likes it is that it gives her a sense of power (109). This more powerful Kate is one we see throughout the book. She has learned to overcome her early, poor beginnings, copes well as a single woman in what is still essentially a man's world and, above all, she is not taken advantage of by her superiors, that is, not until the very end of the book.

In the finale of the novel, Piers and Kate face the murderer, Ashe, who is holding a knife to the throat of the 18-year-old, Octavia Aldridge. After Piers shoots and fatally wounds Ashe, Kate turns to Dalgliesh and in a harsh voice asks:

> 'Why did you tell Piers to shoot?'
> 'Instead of you?' He looked at her with dark unsmiling eyes. 'Come Kate, are you really telling me that you wanted to kill a man?'
> 'Not that. But I thought I could have stopped him without killing him, sir.'
> 'Not from where you were placed, not with that line of fire. It was difficult enough for Piers. It was a remarkable shot' [353].

Kate doesn't answer. Why not? We know that she is a better shot than Piers; even if she had shot and killed Ashe, she wouldn't have done any worse than Piers. Why does Dalgliesh insist on giving the "masculine" job to the male? James is clearly letting us know that however much policewomen think they are fully equal, and however much they may want that equality, there will always, at least in the older policemen, exist a paternalism which they will have to accept in order to be promoted. When I asked her why Kate had not been given the opportunity to shoot, she replied:

> It goes on to say he [Piers] had the better line of fire.... I think that at that moment it would have been difficult not to kill him [Ashe]. He knew he was going to be captured and killed and he was going to take the girl with him, so it had to be quick. It would have been very difficult to wound him and at the same time not to hit the girl. So what was important was the one who had the best line of fire [personal interview July 26, 1998].

It's interesting to note that James talks as though she is witnessing the shooting and not creating it herself. She could just as easily have put Kate in the better position to shoot successfully or even to fail. However, like Dalgliesh, she appears to feel protective towards Kate and doesn't want her to have to face the horror of using a gun, even if she is a good shot.

The male hard-boiled fiction of the 1940s and 1950s often pitted the detective against the police and showed that he despised the shoddy work of the judicial system. This criticism of justice is one area of the female detective novels of the 1980s which is also seen in James's later works from this period. As Maureen Reddy describes, this questioning of the detective's motives in relation to justice is also a strong feminist concern:

> The detective's motives are always more centrally at issue in feminist crime novels than they are in conventional mysteries. Whereas non-feminist writers usually assign their detectives some version of the common motive of commitment to order, justice, and truth, feminist crime writers generally problematize both the universality and the desirability of these abstractions. There is no single, universal truth, these writers suggest; rather truth is always relative, dependent on perspective and on circumstances ["Feminist" 176].

We can see in James's books this "problematizing" of justice, and it is yet another aspect of her work which makes it fascinating and far more thought provoking than mysteries of the Golden Age. In her interview with Diana Cooper-Clark, James said that she saw detective fiction as a "'genre in which the problem is solved and solved by human beings; order and justice and morality are then restored'" (19). However, in *Death of an Expert Witness* when the murderer is caught, we realize that justice really isn't always going to be achieved because what the murderer wanted to avoid by killing is exactly what is going to happen now that he has been caught. Dr. Kerrison killed in order for his ex-wife not to learn of his affair because that would enable her to gain custody of their two children, and he knew that she did not really love them. The irony is, of course, that now that he has been found guilty of murder, he will go to jail, and she will gain custody, and we are led to believe that the lives of the two children will be ruined. As James says, "'The problem may be solved but other problems are left unsolved because these are problems of the human heart and problems about which perhaps nothing effective can be done'" (qtd. in Cooper-Clark 19). James continues to say that the more people write detective fiction which is realistic, the less they will be able to reassure the reader that by solving a puzzle, the detective is also able to make all right with the world (qtd. in Cooper-Clark 19).

According to Tony Hilfer in *The Crime Novel: A Deviant Genre*, "The detective novel generally mutes the theme of punishment, sometimes seems almost to overlook it. What matters is the detective's revelation, not the murderer's punishment, for in this myth of rationality truth takes priority over justice" (4). If we examine Cordelia's actions in *An Unsuitable Job for a Woman*, we see how she takes justice totally in her own hands, in complete opposition to the law, when she decides to make Miss Leaming's murder of Ronald Callender look like his suicide. When Leaming asks why she helped her cover up the crime, saying, "'I thought you might have acted in the service of justice or some such abstraction,'" Cordelia replies that she didn't act out of a sense of justice but for a person (391). Later when Dalgliesh is interrogating her, she muses to herself:

> Most of all, she wished that she had someone to talk to about Ronald Callender's murder. Bernie wouldn't have been any help here. To him the moral dilemma at the heart of the crime would have held no interest, no validity, would have seemed a wilful confusion of straightforward facts.... But the Superintendent might have understood [426].

In James's books, we see her constantly questioning justice and the idea of punishment. In *Original Sin*, Kate and Daniel discuss a television program on death row inmates in the USA they have both watched. Daniel asks Kate if she approves of "revenge killing" and she replies, "'I couldn't feel much pity. [The inmates] killed in a state with the death penalty and then seemed aggrieved that the state proposed to carry out what it had legislated for. Not one of them mentioned his victim. No one spoke the word "remorse"'" (283). In *Death of An Expert Witness*, the 16-year-old daughter questions Dalgliesh about the punishment of the murderer, not realizing that it is her father who is the murderer. When Dalgliesh says that he will go to prison for at least ten years, she replies "'But that's silly. That won't put things right. It won't bring Dr. Lorrimer back'" (251). Later in the same conversation Dalgliesh explains, "'Human justice is imperfect, but it's the only justice we have'" (252). Dalgliesh can say this because he is more the traditional detective. However, not all James's policemen agree with him.

At the end of the novel *Original Sin*, Inspector Daniel is clearly battling with the triangle of remorse, justice, and punishment. Inspector Daniel, who is Jewish, has discovered that it is the elderly Jew, Dauntsey, who is the murderer. Dauntsey has plotted to kill Philippe Etienne's two children, Gerard and Claudia, in revenge for the fact that 50 years earlier Etienne handed Dauntsey's wife and two young children over to the Germans because they were Jewish. Etienne had no remorse then for his action because he felt that he was justified in sacrificing a few Jews in order to stay on the good side of the Germans and run his underground resistance newspaper, which made him a hero in the eyes of France. Even 50 years later when faced by the murderous Dauntsey, Etienne challenges him, saying that his murders have been an act of revenge not justice: "Justice should be speedy as well as effective. Justice doesn't wait for fifty years" (411). In an added ironic twist, James has Etienne tell the vengeful Dauntsey that he has not, in fact, killed his (Etienne's) flesh and blood since Gerard and Claudia were adopted at birth. At this point Dauntsey reacts in horror at what he has done, walks into the marsh and drowns himself. Later when Dalgliesh and Kate arrive and ask Daniel why he deliberately let Dauntsey go, they are both angry with Daniel, and he feels "isolated in a moral quarantine" (414). Daniel obviously thinks that Dauntsey was justified in killing Claudia and Gerard in revenge because Etienne "felt no guilt, no remorse. A mother and two small children. They didn't exist. They weren't human. He would have given more thought to putting down a dog. He didn't think of them as people. They were expendable. They didn't count. They were Jews" (415). When Kate reminds him that Dauntsey hadn't limited his murders to Claudia and Gerard but had also killed the author Esme Carling because she had realized that he was Gerard's murderer, Daniel says, "'You're so confident, aren't you, Kate. So certain you know what's right. It must be comforting, never having to face a moral dilemma'" (415). Kate is obviously trying to emulate Dalgliesh here and is too professional to act like Cordelia and Daniel. Although Kate is antagonistic to Daniel's behavior, the fact that James is concerned with Daniel's motives puts her in the sphere of a feminist detective writer, at least in this instance, and takes her very far from the realm of the Golden Age mystery writers whose detectives always solved the puzzle and never questioned the morality of any of their actions.

A Certain Justice, James's recent work, is her most overtly feminist novel to date. The first victim is a successful barrister whose unpopularity with her colleagues, ex-husband, and even her daughter allows James to examine the continued difficulties women in powerful positions have juggling a family and a career. Venetia Aldridge is disliked by her colleagues because she sees their weaknesses and has no sympathy for the people. Her ex-husband wishes to have nothing to do with her because she always bullied him, and he is happily remarried now.

Her own daughter, Octavia, thinks she is selfish and unconcerned because Venetia never visited her while she was in boarding school. Indeed, in order to spite her mother, Octavia becomes involved with a young man, who turns out to be the murderer who Venetia defended in an earlier murder case. Octavia claims that she is in love with him, and he is happy to love and protect her. Hence, when Venetia, with a blood-covered wig on her head, is found stabbed with a letter opener, there are several people who are pleased to see her dead. Although this book once again uses the limited number of suspects and the closed-room type of puzzle formula, it develops Kate Miskin's character in an interesting way and demonstrates James's reservations about radical feminist views.

As stated earlier, we see Kate in this novel as a very capable detective, a crack shot and able to direct the investigation in one location while Dalgliesh holds the fort in London. When I asked James whether she would ever consider having a plot with Kate working alone, she replied:

> Well, no, I don't think so.... I'm very interested in Kate and the development of Kate's relations with the detective she works with and in both of their relations with Dalgliesh. I particularly was in [A Certain Justice] because Kate felt that for the first time there was a male exclusion here. She felt there was an understanding between Piers and Dalgliesh that somehow she had never got, and it seemed to reveal itself in an attitude to their job. Sort of detachment, sort of cynicism, whereas she had this huge commitment. She didn't sense it in them to quite the same extent. There's just a difference. For the first time she's beginning to feel educationally and socially insecure. She's never felt that before. She doesn't like that, of course. It comes out when Dalgleigh says would she have liked to have been seconded for a university education, and she says, 'Would that have made me a better detective?'—immediately on the defensive at the suggestion [personal interview July 26, 1998].

Thus, as Kate's character develops and layers are revealed, we continue to be intrigued by James's work because she always stresses her characters' psychological motivations. In her fascination with why crime occurs and how it affects all those who come in contact with it, she moved the 1960s mystery toward greater realism. According to Marilyn Rye in Kathleen Klein's *Great Women Mystery Writers*, "[James's] portraits of individual lives form a composite view of a troubled contemporary society" (168). Although there are resolutions in James's books which convey a "sense of a basic moral order underlying the universe, [the resolutions] do not dispel a lingering sense of evil and contamination" (168). However, though she still clings to certain elements of the traditional British detective story, James is a timeless novelist. She continues to move her detective fiction forward in the 21st century with settings and a style which make her not simply a great detective writer but a great writer.

Works Cited

James, P.D. *The Black Tower*. London: Constable, 1975.

_____. *A Certain Justice*. New York: Knopf, 1997.

_____. *The Children of Men*. London: Faber & Faber, 1992.

_____. *Cover Her Face*. London: Faber & Faber, 1962.

_____. *Death of an Expert Witness*. New York: Warner Books, 1977.

_____. *Devices and Desires*. New York: Knopf, 1989.

_____. *Innocent Blood*. New York: Scribner's, 1980.

_____. *A Mind to Murder*. London, Faber & Faber, 1963.

_____. *Original Sin*. New York: Warner Books, 1994.

_____. Personal interview. July 26, 1998.

_____. *Shroud for a Nightingale*. London: Faber & Faber, 1971.

_____. *The Skull Beneath the Skin*. New York: Warner Books, 1982.

_____. *A Taste for Death*. New York: Warner Books, 1986.

_____. *Time to be in Earnest*. London: Faber and Faber, 1999.

_____. *Unnatural Causes*. New York: Warner Books, 1967.

_____. *An Unsuitable Job for a Woman*. New York: Scribner's, 1982.

Chapter Two

Jennie Melville

British writer Jennie Melville (aka Gwendoline Butler) began writing in the mid–1950s. In addition to mysteries with a romantic twist and police procedurals with a male protagonist, she is particularly interesting for her series with a female detective, later a chief superintendent, Charmian Daniels. Melville's first Daniels mystery was published in 1962; her latest in 2001. Considering how much in advance of her time Melville was in the 1960s and considering the depth and range of her Daniels books, it is surprising that she is not as famous as the other great British writer whose career began in the 1960s, P.D. James. I certainly believe that Daniels is as fascinating and well-developed a character as James's Kate Miskin and far more of a feminist with a social message than Cordelia Gray. What is particularly interesting about Melville's writing is that as Daniels grows and alters, she vividly reflects societal changes regarding expectations for women in general and police-women in particular. Perhaps one of the reasons that Melville has not achieved the critical praise and interest she deserves is that the critical comments made by such magazines as *Publishers Weekly* have stressed her as a "toiler in the romantic suspense genre" which may have denied her the serious interest of detective fiction fans.

Jennie Melville is of special relevance in this book because she has very few Golden Age elements in her novels, voices many feminist messages and, especially in the early books, is surprisingly in advance of her time with social commentary. *Murderers' Houses* (1964), for example, descries the lack of interest in reading and the arts of the townspeople

Jennie Melville

of Deerham Hills. "[The town] had fewer books, fewer pictures, less time for thought than the average for the rest of the country. And the average, thought Charmian sadly, was pretty low anyway"(9). Later in this same book she is wishing that the police department felt as she did that mathematics was important in detection and that they "would buy her a computer" (102). Considering that in the 1960s it was considered unbelievably sophisticated to have an electric typewriter, Daniels' recognition that a computer would make her life easier and "the future was with statistics, mathematics and science" (102) is quite remarkable.

Gwendolyn Whitehead recommends Melville's books of the 1970s rather than the 1960s since Daniels is a more "compelling" character in the later books (qtd. in Klein's *Great Mystery Women Writers* 47). However, Daniels is a very "compelling" character in these 1960s books also because she is both completely unlike any other policewoman of the time and a far cry from the omniscient detective of earlier times. In addition, she shows that a woman, even in this period, can have some degree of self-determination. Even if equal pay for equal work is not yet in place, Daniels is still ambitious and says of herself "You have to be hard if you're going to get on in this force" (*Come Home and Be Killed* 101). This "hardness" is qualified in *Murderers' Houses* when the narrator states, "She thought she was cold and hard, but of course she wasn't, she not only cared, she wanted to interfere" (12). Thus, her desire to "interfere" or investigate makes her determined to succeed. Whereas American writers such as Katherine V. Forrest show their female policewomen suffering a great deal of sexist jokes, which in Forrest's case are compounded by lesbianism, Daniels is seen as successfully avoiding them. Melville said herself in my interview with her, "I was determined she should be a success, and I suppose in a sense I was basing her on what would have happened to me if I'd remained in academic life when on the whole in my day, even more so now, women do climb the ladder. I was in the generation that was expecting to be successful as a woman in whatever field they ventured" (personal interview July 28, 1998).

Melville is really unusual both in her criminal focus and in her main character, because, at a time when no other female writer was doing so, she wrote police procedurals with a female protagonist investigating violent crimes against women. In the books written in the early 1960s, the reader learns a great deal about Charmian Daniels, the policewoman detective who lives in Deerham Hills, a village 40 miles from London. She has many insecurities both professional and personal. Notwithstanding these, she is successful in solving crimes and eventually gaining promotions. She is described in the second book, *Burning Is a Substitute for Loving*, as "[a] brash young Scots girl with her autumnal hair and her too orange lipstick and her self-assured tread, and inside her a small empty space because she wasn't yet quite a person. But she would be" (65). As she grows in confidence and moves up the ladder of success, Daniels also learns about the importance of clothes and her "too orange lipstick" disappears. In *Footsteps in the Blood* published in 1990, we see a very different woman than the "young Scots girl":

> Learning about what to wear had been a late development in her life, and had come when she began to have enough money to spend on good clothes. Now she knew her style, and chose well-cut, simple clothes in warm colors. The girl from Glasgow, who still lurked inside her, had been surprised and even shocked at what those simple clothes cost. But she enjoyed wearing them [51].

Daniels realizes the importance of her outward appearance and uses her newfound knowledge of clothes to boost her self-confidence and enable her to impress and even intimidate the males in her life.

"The girl from Glasgow" is also unusual in that she is working class, and unlike women detectives of earlier times who were nearly always middle class, Daniels has only her own wits to fall back on. In addition, Melville does not make the mistake of making Daniels bossy and masculine, which might antagonize certain readers. Daniels is not in the least a lesbian and uses her femininity to her advantage both privately and in the workplace.

In the 1960s it was rare for a woman in British literature, as well as life, not to pursue marriage as one of her main goals. Even if she wanted to have a career, she was under a great deal of pressure from her family to be married and quickly have the requisite two children. Melville is very unusual, therefore, when she has the narrator say, "There was no place for marriage in her map of the world" (*Burning Is a Substitute for Loving* 154). However, Daniels' views of marriage do change, as we see in *A New Kind of Killer* when she is married and admits that, despite problems, she is happy: "A working wife still had problems, goodness knew she certainly had (like how to feed a husband, shop, launder and go to work, all in one day), but they were problems with a shape and a name. And when you knew the name of a problem, you were halfway to solving it" (5). Published in 1970, this novel clearly depicts the role of the woman as caretaker even if she has a career outside the home. In Daniels' marriage there is no question of a fair distribution of labor, and interestingly enough, but hardly surprisingly, her marriage has problems, and in later books we find her widowed and effectively wedded to her career. In *Dead Set* she remembers her marriage and the aftermath:

> I was married too young really. Married my boss. A good man and a good copper. Wasn't a success. If I married too young, then he married too late. After he died I had a brief kind of affair with his son by his first marriage. Not proud of that, but at least it was real, some feeling there. Then after that I was more or less celibate. On and off there were episodes [126].

Although she mourns her husband's sudden death, we see in the 1980s books that Daniels copes very well without him, and her newfound solitude allows her to follow her career path more aggressively in ways that are similar to those of the characters of the American female writers of this era.

Similar to these 1980s American hard-boiled female detectives, Daniels has no real desire to have children. In *Windsor Red* she thinks, "Not having a child made you maybe insensitive to parental love sometimes. For the first time she realized what she might have missed. But I'd have made a rotten mother, she told herself " (76). In *Footsteps in the Blood*, we are told that she once had an abortion, and now when she is having some related medical problems, she remembers: "I am ashamed.... This feeling inside me is a deep shame. I wasn't ashamed when I had the abortion, it seemed the right thing to do, but I feel shame now. No, perhaps not shame. Retrospective grief for what might have been" (166). The fact that Melville has her character have an abortion at a time when, though they were legal, few people would admit to having one, adds an unusual dimension to her novels of this period.

Daniels is not highly domesticated, and unlike characters like Patricia Cornwell's Kay Scarpetta, she is definitely not superwoman. Her deliberations as to whether she is doing the right thing or not in marrying Sir Humphrey Kent are also interesting. A part of her obviously wants the wealth and privilege, but a greater part also wants to keep her freedom and privacy. When she buys a weekend cottage in Brideswell, Humphrey is not pleased because "he wanted to be the one who chose my property. He pointed out that he had a house in Windsor and a place in the country so why, when married, did we need another?" (*Whoever Has the Heart* 18). She also worries about remarrying because she feels that Humphrey has a violent streak. Even though Daniels can give as good as she gets, she fears Humphrey's moods:

> 'Am I forgiven or are you still thinking it over?'
> Charmian frowned. 'Nothing happened, you didn't touch me. Just as well, because if you had, I would probably have broken your arm. But you thought of it, and I didn't like that' [*Death in the Family* 75].

At the end of this novel, Daniels and Humphrey seem to have weathered the storms and the relationship appears to be stable. However, it is clear that Daniels will never be subservient to Humphrey in any way, perhaps because she has struggled with inequality in her work. When she does finally marry him in *The Morbid Kitchen*, she has a very equal relationship, and Humphrey is shown as supportive towards her work and helpful around the house. Daniels is slightly surprised at her own happiness. When Humphrey tells her he wishes she'd stay out of an investigation since it was a "'bloody business'" and she replies "'Not a hope,'" the narrator comments that the pair still "[parted] lovingly; it was amazing how domestic fondness grew on you" (112). Since more policewomen are married than single, even though the divorce rate is high in the police force, Daniels' marriage is far more realistic than those of many other fictional policewomen.

In the 1960s, when the first Daniels books appeared, the place of women in the police force was definitely a menial one. Women were assigned to look after other women or children, and chances for advancement were small. In *Burning Is a Substitute for Loving* we are told that Daniels has chosen to follow a career in the police force because

> she wanted one where she believed she could rise quickly, and she wanted one where she could use her sense of justice and order. She had left Glasgow University and embarked straight away as a policewoman in Dundee and then St. Andrews, walking the beat. Deliberately she made the choice to come south and join the police force in Deerham Hills as a member of the detective force. She saw more future for herself there than in Scotland. There is only one more fearsome thing than a Scotsman on the make, she told herself with wry amusement, and that is a Scotswoman [*Burning Is a Substitute for Loving* 19].

Later Daniels explains that she was given the job in Deerham Hills to solve the numerous problems with women and children which were causing the townspeople major anxiety. Thus, at first, Daniels fits the stereotype of the policewoman which George Dove describes in *The Police Procedural*:

> She is as often as not regarded as a necessary evil. Her male counterparts gladly turn over to her the typing and filing, partly because we can do them better than men can. She is also useful for "baby-sitting" (monitoring women subjects and small children) and "matron duty" (going places where men are not permitted, like the women's powder room) [156].

In the early books, Daniels helps solve some of the "baby-sitting" problems, but her inquisitiveness creates more as she makes her presence felt with her two female assistants. In later books her skills are rewarded, and she enjoys steady promotions and far more intriguing jobs which admittedly leads to some resentment on the part of her male colleagues. In *A Death in the Family* (1994) she wants to listen in on an important questioning of a key suspect, but "She must move carefully. She was a guest, no one had asked her in, and although, because of her rank, she could not easily be moved out, still could be given the frozen treatment. She'd had this treatment several times in the past and had learnt how to survive it" (145).

The difficulties of being female in the police force are discussed in many of the Daniels books. In *A New Kind of Killer* Daniels says, "'In my job you keep emotion right out of it'" (66); and she also says, "'with a violent sick creature [one] may have to take violent action'" (66). Later in the novel, a young black policewoman claims, "'Being a policewoman takes the woman out of you'" (128). "'I'm pretty, but for this country the wrong colour.... But I'll plod on. Won't be beaten. No they'll have to kill me first'" (94). Ironically, at the end of the book, this young policewoman, Ann Hooks, does die at the hands of the killer. In *Footsteps in the Blood* Daniels thinks, "In her profession you were allowed to be a woman, but not too female" (83). This use of the word "allowed" implies the whole patriarchal order: the distinction between "female" and "a woman" suggests that a woman can be coped with since she will know her place; whereas a female, possibly hysterical, is not to be borne.

Although Daniels often tells her subordinates to beware of becoming emotionally involved, she does not appear at all cold and unfeeling with her friends or even in her dealings with criminals. When she is working with a group of female ex-convicts, she is very aware of the power of such a group, and as she analyzes this power in *Windsor Red*, we can see a definite feminist dimension in Melville's writing:

> By the end of the afternoon the strangeness of the little group and of her place in it was so overwhelming that she felt suffocated. It was a physical thing, which she could not deny. She was both attracted and pushing away at the same time, almost like a love affair that had gone wrong [56].

In the types of crimes Daniels solves as well as her empathy towards women's problems, Melville is also clearly a feminist in accordance with the description of Maureen Reddy in *Sisters in Crime*:

> Feminism is always aware of the complexity and diversity of women's lives, especially those dissimilarities arising from differences of class, race, and nationality; however, it also insists that within this pluralism is a shared core of experience that is overlooked only at peril [9].

Similarly to V.I. Warshawski and the feminist female detectives, Daniels identifies with her women friends, and many of her cases begin because she is helping a friend solve a particular problem; this leads to Daniels' more personal involvement with all of the crimes. Either it is her friends who are victims (*A New Kind of Killer*, *Windsor Red*) or she is afraid that she should have been the victim (*Footsteps in the Blood*) or the murder happens close to her house (*Whoever Has the Heart, A Death in the Family*). Daniels, on one occasion, is even the cause of a crime herself because the person is jealous of her. In *Dead Set*, Lady Mary Erskine is jealous of the love Sir Humphrey Kent has been showing Daniels and wishes to get Daniels in trouble, so she helps Daniels' secretary procure drugs, hoping to implicate Daniels in the drug scene.

Daniels is unusual as a high-ranking policewoman as we see when we compare her to protagonists in novels by other 1990s authors, for example, Lynda la Plante, who in *Prime Suspect* examines in depth the major problems a female police officer has with her colleagues. Unlike Daniels who is respected by her colleagues, Detective Chief Inspector Jane Tennison is universally disliked. Her colleagues actively resist her being in charge of the murder investigation because she is considered smug and unfeeling. Even the chief superintendent, Kernan, who acknowledges Tennison's qualifications, admits, "[h]e had never liked working with women and knew that his men felt the same way. All the same, he knew she was right. She was a highly qualified officer, it was just something about her, about all the high-ranking women he had come across. Maybe it was simply the fact that she was a woman"(*Prime Suspect* 39). Hence, women are rarely promoted to the high ranks because the males on the force feel threatened by them.

Although Daniels does not receive as harsh a treatment by her male subordinates as Tennison, she is still regarded with jealousy. This is apparent in *Dead Set* when her new position is described by the narrator: "She was head of SRADIC (Southern Register, Documentation and Index of Crime) in the whole southern police area, coordinating all documentation of crime for all southern Forces, not including London, but the Met was obliged to liaise.... She was a powerful lady" (23). She gains this position with difficulty despite her qualifications, and at first she is encouraged to be deputy head with a man as her boss. This would have suited Inspector Fred Elman who, like many male subordinates with whom Daniels has to work, believes "Women were powerful and threatening deities who could only be subdued by sexual force" (*Footsteps in the Blood* 116). This does not, of course, necessarily mean literal rape but the regular harassment experienced by women who work in male-oriented careers. As Dove explains in *The Police Procedural*, the woman detective may at first be treated as in need of protection, but later she may also become a sex object in a no-win situation (157).

Although Daniels is very different, the female sergeant as sex object is seen in *Footsteps in the Blood* in the character of Sergeant Margery Foggerty, who has been free with her favors to many of the male detectives. In addition, Foggerty is shown in contrast to Daniels since she has not risen through the ranks to gain promotion; she is "a motherly, kindly figure who was quite content to fill the policewoman's traditional role of looking after women and children in distress. She preferred it that way and had no ambitions to enter the CID" (63). However, despite the fact that Foggerty claims to have no ambitions, she is extremely materialistic and even prepared to murder her blackmailer later in the novel.

In contrast to Sergeant Foggerty is another female detective sergeant, Dolly Barstow. A protégée of Daniels and a friend of her goddaughter, Kate, Barstow is described as very intelligent and kind. "She had seen some prejudice, although she had not suffered from it herself: she was canny and knew where to put her feet" (*A Death in the Family* 198). Barstow is the new type of 1990s policewoman who is better accepted by her male colleagues, and as she admits herself, has benefited from the women who have paved the way before her. Barstow, as we discover in *The Morbid Kitchen*, is happy to walk in Daniels' footsteps and be part of her team, but is not totally reconciled to her single state and rather lonely existence. She takes all her meals in the police canteen, does laundry only when she runs out of clean clothes, and knows none of her neighbors, preferring her anonymity (89). In her love life, she is willing to have affairs even with married men and rather envies Daniels her new marriage. "How unlike Charmian, successful, married, happy, and a cat owner ... I was on the way to all that ... but I seem to have lost the knack" (89).

What makes Melville's portrayal of both Daniels and Barstow interesting is the fact that neither of these women is intimidated by her male colleagues in the way that many other fictional policewomen, such as Jane Tennison, are. Whereas Tennison has to compromise her gender in several ways in order to gain the respect of her male colleagues, Daniels does not. Daniels may receive some aggravation from her subordinates, some delaying of information, some caustic comments on the unsuitability of females in positions of power; however, when it comes to solving the crime, all the men grudgingly admit that Daniels is highly efficient, and they respect her. Because of their admiration for her abilities, Daniels never has to compromise her own quest for power. She may be tactful and careful not to offend sensibilities and fragile male egos, but she does not allow anyone to vilify her in any way. From the very first book in the series which was published in 1962, Daniels asserts her strength. "She knew that she was neither so harmless nor so neutral nor uninformed as she appeared to be" (*Come Home and Be Killed* 92). And in the same book a male informant says he "despised Charmian because his life had conditioned him to despise women and Charmian was a woman and a policewoman at that, but he quite liked her"(105). Daniels' attitude is very different from that of Tennison, who feels that she has to be masculine to be accepted. Daniels does not particularly want to be "one of the lads"; she just wants every male officer to do his job and help her do hers.

Melville fits Maureen Reddy's broader description of a feminist author in that she is especially interested in "character, with its revelation depending upon the investigation of personality and on the conjunction of the personal and the social" (*Sisters in Crime* 5). Consequently, although she lacks the didactic tone of some writers, she is similar to the latest British female detective writers, such as Val McDermid, in the element of social consciousness raising in her work. In the novel *A New Kind of Killer*, Daniels has started a degree course in criminology at the new University of Midport and is examining the increase in violent crime in the under-20 age group. She reacts with horror at the significance of the fact that "only four cases out of ten in every violent crime, like murder, are cleared up.... [W]e're creating a new kind of killer. Boyish, casual, and committing murder almost without thought" (14). Many of the victims in Melville's novels are women or children so that she is redefining the focus of the detection.

Hence, despite the fact that Melville began writing in the 1960s she has very few Golden Age elements in her novels. Unlike James, Melville does not use the closed-room technique with only a very few people involved and the detective coming in from outside to solve the crime. This convention helps create the feeling of the detective as all-powerful, creating order out of disorder, solving the puzzle, and restoring justice and morality. Rather, like the later James, Melville is mainly concerned with the mind-set of the characters instead, and the crime is a device to explore people's motivations. A great deal of each book is spent analyzing why a crime was committed as well as how. Detection is interesting, but even more fascinating are the motives for a crime. In her first novel, Melville follows the formulaic approach, also used by James, of setting up the scene before the murder, introducing us to the secondary characters and their thoughts, and only bringing the crime and the detective in halfway through the book. However, beginning in the second novel, Daniels is the main focus from the start, and her ideas and feelings are of paramount interest. In this way the character develops, and the reader begins to feel a familiarity with her. In addition, because Melville uses a cast of characters most of whom reappear in each novel, there are different layers of interest for the reader. For example, we are concerned not only with Daniels' relationship with her subordinates but also with her friends and her lover. From these relationships, she is able to draw help and information to solve crimes. As Melville said herself in an interview with me, "It's nice to create a world that's one I'm very drawn to" (personal interview July 28, 1998). By creating such a world, which also includes criminals, Daniels' detection appears more realistic than the formulaic mode of the earlier genre with the Godlike detective who comes in, solves the crime and then leaves the scene.

In the books of the 1970s, Daniels' advanced ideas and ambition have obviously paid off as we see her having a secondary, secretive job working for a group of men in London on mysterious governmental assignments. Clearly this work requires someone discreet, level-headed and intelligent; and the fact that she continues to do it even if it is not always to her liking also predisposes us in her favor. She describes in *A Death in the Family*:

> Her meeting in London, in that office off Bond Street, close to an exceedingly smart art gallery, was short. At such meetings, as always, she received certain information and in her turn, she passed some back. This side of her work was not pleasing to her, she did not like the insights she got into the lives of others whose privacy was thus invaded [225].

Daniels continues to grow and change in the 1980s and reflects to some degree the new breed of female detective in the U.S. who resembles the hard-boiled male detectives of an earlier era in their solitary lifestyle, realistic speech patterns, and willingness to use violence. Daniels, as we have seen, enjoys her own home and friends and is really not sure that she wants to get married again. However, the fact that she blames herself for many of the problems in the relationship with Humphrey and the fact that she is seriously considering him as a permanent fixture in her life, make her different from Kinsey Millhone and V.I. Warshawski.

Another difference from these two women is that she isn't victimized by her love interest. As Ann Wilson explains in "The Female Dick and the Crisis of Heterosexuality," both Kinsey and V.I. are used by the men in their lives. Kinsey is abandoned by her married lover Jonah Robb, who returns to his wife, and later discovers that a former lover for whom she still has feelings, Daniel Wade, is gay. V.I. meanwhile is abducted by her former lover, Michael Furey, who tries to kill her. As Wilson says of Robb and Furey:

> The inability of these police officers to accept women as profession-ally equal and to resist asking them to conform to a male-generated image of woman is not simply a matter of benign misunderstanding; women detectives constitute a profound threat to the officers' mas-culinity, which realizes its full potential in physical violence.... It is not difficult to understand why there is little possibility of a satisfying romantic relationship with a man [153].

This lack of a "satisfying romantic relationship" is also seen in *Prime Suspect*, where Tennison's boyfriend has a major problem coming to terms with her job and what he sees as the overly masculine side to her nature. Not only is he unable, according to her, to understand what her work entails, but he also dislikes the fact that she makes him feel "inadequate" (137). When he decides to end the relationship, he muses "if the truth was on the line, there was a side to her that he hated, that masculine, pushy side. She had never been his kind of woman, and he doubted if any man could cope with a woman who loved her career more than anything else" (204). A little later he says that his next girl "would be young, pretty and without prospects, and he'd make sure she would cook, didn't mind ironing shirts and liked kids" (204).

Daniels, meanwhile, is better understood by her lovers and indeed has a brief affair with a colleague in *Whoever Has the Heart*; later in *A Death in the Family*, she remembers how they had parted on good terms, but "[n]one of us like to think of our mistakes, the times we have not behaved well, and Charmian was no exception" (163). Here again she is obviously stronger than Kinsey and Jane since she is the one who ends the relationship and is obviously satisfied with her decision; however, she lacks the strength and liberation of Susan Moody's Penny Wana-wake because she still thinks that having a brief affair and leaving the man is evidence of "bad" behavior.

Another way Daniels refuses to be victimized is in her use of self-defense against the criminals. Kinsey and V.I. can carry a weapon and are happily prepared to use it, but Daniels does not carry a firearm, since these are only issued to certain police for specific duties. Therefore, she is forced to use her wits and limbs. In *Footsteps in the Blood* "[s]he hit the bridge of his nose so that he screamed, and before the scream was fully out, she had kneed him in the groin" (182). In *Whoever Has the Heart*, "He swayed. I kicked him in the groin and he screamed. As he staggered backwards, I pushed him into the cellar and closed the door" (217). Although this is a little tamer than the kick boxing of Val McDermid's Kate Brannigan, it is perfectly in keeping with Daniels' middle age. Also, as Glenwood Irons points out, even if 1980s hard-boiled female detectives are physically hurt, we know that they are "physically and intellectually superior to [the males]" (*Feminism in Women's Detective Fiction* xv).

One of the major differences in Melville's 1980s books from detective fiction of the pre–1960s genre is their total focus on women, including the potential of women to be criminals, even murderers. Melville is interesting because she shows women killing not because they are being victimized, but because it is expedient. *Murder Has a Pretty Face* (1981), perhaps Melville's most feminist novel, sees Daniels in charge of solving a series of burglaries, and a particularly brutal rape and murder of a man. At the start of the book, we learn that the burglaries are being committed by four women, a lesbian couple, Baby and Phil, and two sisters, Diana and Bee. Daniels' friend Kitty is full of admiration at the thought of a female gang of thieves: "'It's what we've wanted for a long time—isn't it?—the really emancipated woman criminal'" (59). As the plot develops, we see the ruthless side of Diana when she talks quite forcefully about killing the manager of the bank that they plan to rob:

> 'You are savage, Di,' said Baby uneasily. 'And a woman, too. I don't think women ought to kill women.'
> 'My dear, one way and another they do it all the time,' said Diana. 'And this is business, not a crusade.'
> 'I'm not sure,' muttered Bee.
> 'How many times do I have to tell you that I am not sexist about anything?' shouted Diana. 'This is strictly business' [77].

Far from being victimized themselves, these women are perfectly willing to victimize others, even other women and relatives. As we discover at the end of the book, Diana not only imprisons the bank manager and is about to kill her, but she also commits a vicious sexual assault with an implement on her former husband, then strangles him and throws him in the river.

The ending of *Murder Has A Pretty Face* also overturns the patriarchal, order-restoring detective novel of earlier times. Daniels joins with the gang of women in the hope of discovering what has happened to the bank manager and of preventing the gang's disappearing with all the money. Although she rescues the manager, Baby and Phil become suspicious and escape to Spain with their share of the loot to enjoy their freedom with some time in the sun. Meanwhile, although Diana is caught, she finds out that she has an advanced form of cervical cancer and so will probably die. Lastly, Bee faces her term in prison with equanimity since she believes her lover will wait for her. When Daniels' boss Walter Wing returns, he appears to have re-established the male status quo, but he hasn't because Baby is happily plotting: "'As I was so successful this time round, why don't we plan something really big, like robbing a major bank? I know I can do it, and it's time we women really showed our power'" (253). Hence, in the 1980s Melville was writing a very different novel from that of Grafton and Paretsky, yet she also had a clear feminist input which has been missed by many Anglo-American critics.

In the 1990s Melville wrote several more books with Daniels as the main character, and although she has continued her other long-running series with John Coffin as the male protagonist, these latest books show Daniels at her most complex. Daniels has risen to a position of major responsibility. She coordinates all documents relating to crime in the southern region and says of herself, "she who knows all, commands all" (*Dead Set* 23). Although at times she misses the feeling of being in the field, which is why she is always happy to help solve a crime for a friend, she realizes that all aspects of her job are important, even reading files. Thus, she enjoys her promotion and is fully aware of being in a powerful position. She additionally manages to juggle her career and private life successfully.

One way in which Melville's later books differ from those of American writers is the absence of minority characters. Although the black Ann Hood appears in *A New Kind of Killer*, no black, Indian, Pakistani or other minority character emerges in the other books. If we compare this to the burgeoning detective fiction involving minorities as their protagonists and actually written by minority female writers in the U.S.,

Melville's books appear not to be reflecting societal norms in this regard, especially considering the rise of racially motivated crimes in the Britain of the 1990s. In my interview with her, Melville said that the reason she hadn't shown ethnic minorities was that there was "an unconscious inhibition slightly because, if you're not colored or a so-called minority, you might stumble into all sorts of problems. And I do think you're in danger of being patronizing" (personal interview July 28, 1998).

Similarly to P.D. James and traditional detective novelists, Melville generally has resolution at the end of her books. However, as with the later James and the feminist detective writers, the reader is made aware that evil, criminal activity is always around the corner and will soon happen again. In *Dead Set*, Inspector George Rewley (Daniels' goddaughter's husband) says that Daniel's sense of loyalty is to justice and what she seeks is resolution (136). Daniels never states clearly what her concept of justice is, however. In fact when she asks herself this question in one of the early books, she never answers it: "What was law? Did you believe like Machiavelli, that quod placet principi legis vigorem habet: the will of the Prince has the force of law; that law and justice were, in other words, man-made. Or did you believe in a system of natural law...?" (*Burning Is a Substitute for Loving* 126).

Although Melville does not have the complex literary style of P.D. James, her books are, as one critic claims, "always elegantly written, both in syntax and thought, with never a superfluous word" (Melling 13). In addition, the early novels show female characters who are very different from the societal norms, while in the later novels, the way Daniels rises through the ranks to gain both respect and promotion makes her a role model on both sides of the Atlantic. As Lynn Pykett asserts:

> Women are the prey, the hunted, but the conventions of the detection genre also enable women, in the person of the female investigator, to become the hunter. This is not a simple role reversal in which the victim becomes aggressor, but it is a transformation, in which the potential victim, by becoming active and vigilant, avoids, and helps others to avoid, victimization [65].

Melville, far from being a "toiler in the romantic suspense genre," as was claimed by a book critic and which possibly implies a less than serious writer, has paved and continues to pave the way for the police procedural. Daniels is unique, blending the best of the American 1980s female detective traits with traditional British qualities which make her as capable of meeting the Queen at Windsor Castle as dealing with criminals in the poorest sections of town.

Works Cited

Melville, Jennie. aka Gwendoline Butler. *Axwater*. London: Macmillan, 1978.

____. *Burning Is a Substitute for Loving*. New York: London House & Maxwell, 1964.

____. *Butterfly*. Bath: Chivers Press, 1996.

____. *Coffin and the Paper Man*. New York: St. Martin's Press, 1991.

____. *Coffin Following*. London: Bles, 1968.

____. *A Coffin for Baby*. London: Walker & Co., 1963.

____. *A Coffin for Charley*. New York: St. Martin's Press, 1994.

____. *A Coffin for the Canary*. London: Macmillan, 1974.

____. *A Coffin from the Past*. London: Bles, 1970.

____. *Coffin in Fashion*. New York: St. Martin's Press, 1987.

____. *Coffin in Malta*. London: Bles, 1964.

____. *Coffin in Oxford*. London: Bles, 1962.

____. *Coffin in the Black Museum*. New York: St. Martin's Press, 1989.

____. *Coffin in the Museum of Crime*. New York: St. Martin's Press, 1989.

____. *Coffin on Murder Street*. New York: St. Martin's Press, 1992.

____. *Coffin on the Water*. New York: St. Martin's Press 1986.

____. *The Coffin Tree*. Thorndike: Thorndike Press, 1996.

____. *Coffin Underground*. New York: St. Martin's Press, 1988.

____. *Coffin Waiting*. London: Bles, 1963.

____. *Coffin's Dark Number*. London: Bles, 1969.

____. *Coffin's Game*. New York: St. Martin's Press, 1998.

____. *Come Home and Be Killed*. New York: London House & Maxwell, 1964.

____. *Complicity*. Sutton: Severn House, 2000.

____. *Cracking Open a Coffin*. New York: St Martin's Press, 1993.

____. *A Cure for Dying*. New York: St Martin's Press, 1989.

____. *A Dark Coffin*. New York: St Martin's Press, 1995.

____. *Dead in a Row*. London: Bles, 1957.

____. *Dead Set*. New York: St Martin's Press, 1992.

____. *A Death in the Family*. New York: St Martin's Press, 1994.

____. *Death in the Garden*. New York: St. Martin's Press, 1987.

____. *Death Lives Next Door*. London: Bles, 1960.

____. *A Different Kind of Summer*. London: Hodder & Stoughton, 1967.

____. *A Double Coffin*. New York: St. Martin's Press, 1996.

____. *Dragon's Eye*. New York: Simon & Schuster, 1976.

____. *The Dull Dead*. London: Walker & Co., 1962.

____. *Footsteps in the Blood*. New York: St Martin's Press, 1990.

____. *The Hunter in the Shadows*. London: Hodder & Stoughton, 1969.

____. *The Interloper*. London: Bles, 1959.

____. *Ironwood.* London: Hodder & Stoughton, 1972.

____. *Make Me a Murderer.* London: Bles, 1961.

____. *The Morbid Kitchen.* New York: St. Martin's Press, 1995.

____. *Murder Has a Pretty Face.* New York: St. Martin's Press, 1981.

____. *Murderers' Houses.* London: Michael Joseph, 1964.

____. *The Murdering Kind.* London: Bles, 1958.

____. *A Nameless Coffin.* London: Walker & Co., 1965.

____. *Nell Alone.* London: Michael Joseph, 1966.

____. *A New Kind of Killer.* New York: David McKay Co. Inc., 1971.

____. *Nun's Castle.* New York: David McKay Co. Inc., 1973.

____. Personal interview, July 28, 1998.

____. *Raven's Forge.* New York: David McKay Co. Inc., 1975.

____. *Receipt for Murder.* London: Bles, 1956.

____. *Revengeful Death.* London: Macmillan, 1997.

____. *There Lies Your Love.* London: Michael Joseph, 1965.

____. *The Vesey Inheritance.* London: Macmillan, 1976.

____. *The Wages of Zen.* London: Secker & Warburg, 1979.

____. *Whoever Has the Heart.* New York: St. Martin's Press, 1993.

____. *Windsor Red.* New York: St. Martin's Press, 1988.

____. *Witching Murder.* New York: St. Martin's Press, 1990.

____. *The Woman Who Was Not There.* London: Macmillan, 1996.

Chapter Three

Liza Cody

P.D. James and Gwendoline Butler, aka Jennie Melville, were both born in the 1920s, and though they continue writing today, their work does not fall into the category of the hard-boiled genre. In 1977 with the novel *Edwin of the Iron Shoes,* Marcia Muller created the female hard-boiled detective; later Liza Cody, Sue Grafton, Sara Paretsky and numerous others would continue and modify this genre. Why was this new genre so significant, and how did it alter forever the traditions of detective fiction? Although, as we have seen, James created a female private investigator and Melville had a very independent policewoman, neither were the tough, wise-cracking, big-city operatives involved in the tough world of corrupt institutions which are the hallmarks of the true American female hard-boiled detective. Priscilla L. Walton and Manina Jones make the point in *Detective Agency* that one of the reasons that the female hard-boiled detective was created in the early 1980s is that the conservative governments both in the United States and Britain had platforms which were threats to women and other minorities (190). They affirm that "Women's appropriation of the ambivalent figure of the hard-boiled detective opens up a site of discursive power that provides a unique space for self-conscious reflection on/of the laws of gender and genre" (194). When Cody created Anna Lee in 1980, she was the first to produce a hard-boiled type of female detective in Britain. However, Anna Lee is different from the American sleuths who immediately followed her because Cody did not see her as a feminist, the issues she examines are less far reaching, and she continues to hark back to some degree to the more traditional world of Cordelia Grey. The British world-view, its institutions, judicial system and gun laws are all very different from those of the United States. It is not surprising, therefore, that its detectives are different.

As noted, Paretsky and her contemporaries agree on the characteristics of the female detective. Anne Cranny-Francis claims she should not surrender her femininity, should involve herself totally in the action of the story, should care for herself physically, and should practice self-defense. She works alone, is openly sexual and, above all, operates differently from the male detective (166–169). She continues to say that the female hard-boiled genre is also fundamentally different from the earlier male hard-boiled genre of the 1930s and 1940s in that "the investigation of a single crime becomes the means by which the author constructs a critique of particular aspects of her own society" (170). Although the crime against the individual may be solved by the end of the novel, more usually the major cause of the crime, society or one of its institutions, is unresolved.

Liza Cody, whose first novel *Dupe* was published in 1980, was hailed by critics as the British answer to the new female hard-boiled detectives coming out of the United States at that time. However, her Anna Lee in fact preceded Sue Grafton's Kinsey Millhone and Sara Paretsky's V.I. Warshawski by two years. Although Cody has said that if anyone asked Anna if she was a feminist, "she would probably say no or that she didn't think about it" (Silet 29), Cody does evidence feminist issues and some overt social criticism; in addition, although her protagonist, Anna, reminds us sometimes of Cordelia, she is far stronger. Whereas Cordelia is in her early twenties and often intimidated by authority figures, Anna is in her early thirties, and while she is sometimes upset by her boss or people to whom she feels inferior, she actively works against these reactions. In her personal relationships she is sometimes victimized but usually succeeds in achieving her desires, even if this has to be done in a passive-aggressive way. Cordelia is scarred by her bad childhood and the death of her father, while no mention of Anna's family is found in the first novel. Anna is better adjusted socially than Cordelia, with friends and a surrogate family in the couple who share the flat below hers. She enjoys several stereotypically masculine hobbies, and is very able to look after herself in a crisis. It is difficult to imagine Cordelia coping with being kidnapped and dealing with a frightened 14-year-old as Anna does so well in *Bad Company*. Anna is an ex-policewoman and usually follows the rules regarding procedures in an investigation; however, like Cordelia, she is prepared to take justice into her own hands even if she knows her actions could cause her to lose her job. Unlike James who, before she stopped writing about her, diminished Cordelia in *The Skull Beneath the Skin* and had her regressing to finding lost pets, Cody continued writing about Anna throughout the 1980s and into the 1990s. Like Paretsky and Grafton, she successfully created a protagonist who is completely realistic simply because she is not always tough and capable and questions both her own actions and motives as well as those of male-dominated organizations.

While Anna may be tougher and more mature than Cordelia, she differs from the 1980s American detectives because she does not work for herself and, therefore, is in a vulnerable position where she can be patronized by her male colleagues, her boss, Martin Brierly, and his secretary, Beryl. She is treated as either too young or too incompetent to be successful in her work, which reminds us of the constant admonishments made to Cordelia that hers is an unsuitable job for a woman. Even though Anna spent five years in the police force, one of her male colleagues tells her in *Dupe* that she should be pleased to always get the job of finding missing children because "[she's] not big enough for banks ... [n]ot cute enough for clubs and too cute for pubs" (10). When Anna responds "'Oh don't start that again. Flipping heck. Sometimes you'd think this was a society for Victorian gents,'" Johnny retorts, "'You should learn to swear more potently if you want the Equal Opportunities Board to consider you seriously for the Man's World'" (10–11). In *Stalker*, Anna recalls an incident when a Muslim client from Qatar objected to her being part of the investigation which had resulted in a reshuffling of the work load with her at the bottom of the roster. "It had caused a lot of amusement among the men, whose opinion of a woman's ability was not much different from the Muslim one" (5). Thus Anna's male colleagues do not take her seriously because she is a woman. In *Under Contract*, Anna also comes in for some verbal harassment from the male employees of JW Protection to which she is seconded. First they survey her "as if she were a horse on its way to the starting gate" (5). Then when one asks, "'What's she doing here?'" the other replies "'Must be the spare skirt from Smallfry Security'" (5). However, Anna, like the more hard-boiled female detectives who follow her, is quick to retaliate verbally and resembles the male detectives of the 1930s in her "tough talk." In *Under Contract*, Dave from JW Protection says "'Just don't think you can give me the old eyelash treatment like you can him. Some of us don't roll over for a pretty face'" (6). Anna replies, "'Is this personal ... or are you practicing for your Charm Test?'" (6). Later, when Dave brings a BMW for her to drive and says, "'We've brought a jam-jar for our Tiddle,'" and asks Anna, "'I don't suppose you've driven anything like this before,'" Anna tells him just as haughtily, "'Well, I have, as a matter of fact'" (34).

Not only does Anna suffer abuse from her male colleagues, but her boss, Martin Brierly, continually demeans her, even in front of prospective clients. In *Dupe* when the client Mr. Jackson says that she seems rather young for the job, Brierly says that she is quite competent, but Cody states, "while Brierly appeared to be defending her, he was in fact vindicating Brierly Security. Privately, she knew that his opinion of her ability did not differ much from Jackson's" (15). At the end of the book, when Anna is injured, Brierly keeps some reward money given for Anna and even tries to fire her, claiming, "It is, of course, one of the reasons why one hesitates to employ women in this sort of work. They do seem less able to defend themselves when these stupid situations arise" (218). In *Backhand*, Brierly finally fires Anna, and she realizes just how little she means to him: "Something very like despair was boiling up inside her. He could have asked how she was, or had she been hurt, instead of 'I told you so,' and complaining about the phone bill. He hadn't even got in touch until he could do so on the cheap rate" (257).

Brierly is not only utterly condescending towards Anna but has the basic attitude that all women are inferior to men and are useful only to do menial jobs. In *Dupe*, when Beryl is out sick at one point, Anna is warned by her colleague and friend, Bernie Schiller, that Brierly is simply presuming that because Anna is female and can type, she will be willing to fill in as a secretary. The fact that two of the other male operatives can also type is not taken into consideration. Only when Anna makes sure that she has other appointments to go to and the two males create a fuss at the very idea of acting as the secretary, does Brierly agree to hire a temporary replacement. In Klein's *Great Women Mystery Writers*, B.J. Rahn says Cody clearly shows how

> [t]he calm assumption of women's incompetence and inherent inferiority is registered in numerous put-downs: from failing to introduce women to ignoring them in conversation or talking about them in the third person as if they were absent or deaf; from making denigrating

casual remarks to the habitual use of status-lowering diminutives or outright abuse; and from the universal assumption that the bottom line of a woman's worth is her sexual attractiveness [73].

However, sometimes it is not only male colleagues or bosses who victimize the female detective but other women, as we see in Brierly's secretary, Beryl, who also delights in chastising Anna more than the male detectives and obviously feels no solidarity with her own sex. Beryl is described in *Stalker* as "tough as old boots, but with all the sensibil-ities of a maiden aunt in her armoury too. On top of that, she flirted with the boys; an unnerving combination" (4). In *Dupe* when Anna calls in to update Beryl on what has been happening, Beryl immediately starts haranguing her: "'Where have you been?' Beryl's voice [is] nasal and peremptory.... 'You really should ring in more regularly. It's most inconsiderate of you'" (90). In *Head Case*, she snaps at Anna, "'You are the limit, Anna, always off somewhere, never phoning in. You'll have to pull your socks up. The Commander's getting in some bleepers to try next week'" (33). To make herself feel more important, Beryl focuses on details and complains constantly about Anna's behavior:

> 'I do wish you wouldn't perch on the edge of my desk.'
> 'It's my legs,' said Anna. 'You make such a to-do over a simple PAD search my legs get tired.'
> 'Political Affiliations Directory is not a charitable institution.' Beryl [says] primly. 'Every name we put through costs money' [25].

As Rahn states, "Like many women who have conceded power to the male gender, Beryl resents women who successfully compete with men professionally and refuses to grant Anna equal respect with the men because to do so would be to acknowledge her own second-class status" (73). Beryl's attitude is a reminder of the societal expectations of the 1970s that women should really stay at home and look after children and not compete with their menfolk by trying to have "masculine" jobs.

One of the roles of the female hard-boiled detective fiction is, thus, to depict the oppression which women suffer in different situations. They may be denigrated in the workplace, as we see so clearly in the Anna series; they may also be abused physically by family members, as we see in Paretsky's *Blood Shot* when V.I.'s client's grandmother reveals that it was her brother who raped her daughter, Louisa, and her husband slaps her hard to stop her talking to V.I. and then attacks V.I. We also see typical family abuse in *Tunnel Vision* when the successful lawyer is seen hitting his wife and verbally abusing his children after a party, and is later revealed to have raped his 14-year-old daughter.

Another form of abuse comes in the form of the victimization that so many women P.I.s experience in their sexual relationships. Unlike the investigators of the male hard-boiled fiction who fell for women who might have been attractive and available but were villains (Grella 109), their female counterparts often fall for men who could be suitable but take advantage of them and try to dominate them. Anna is typical in this regard. Although she feels that it is wrong that all the men in her life want to change her even while they may claim to love her, she blames herself for arousing their anger, rather than blaming them for their inappropriate behavior. In *Bad Company*, Gene becomes angry with Anna when she turns down his invitation to go to the coast for the weekend, saying that she has to work:

> You know this isn't the first time. Having a job is one thing, but working unreasonable hours week after week is something else. It seems to me that you get all the late hours and weekends they fork out, and you don't stand up for yourself.... You're never around when I'm free. Look I'm not possessive, but either you're my woman or you're not [35–36].

Although this particular argument ends amicably, later on, after Anna is home again after having been kidnapped, Gene says he is too busy to spend the evening with her. Immediately Anna blames herself and thinks that none of her problems would have happened if she had only accepted his invitation:

> He was going to say something else, but stopped himself. Anna was grateful. That evening she wanted to avoid even the thought of anything unpleasant. If it was bad news, it was her own fault anyway; she had refused to spend the weekend with him, she had consistently put her work first when there was any choice to be made, and she had kept him at a comfortable distance. If something exciting had cropped up for him in Weymouth it was too late to bitch about it now [193].

Anna's way of avoiding dealing with the issues which are troubling her within her relationships with men is representative of a woman who feels fundamentally unequal. In *Backhand*, the latest in the string of unsuitable lovers is Quex, a large man who towers over Anna physically and also tries to crush her spirit. As she surveys the mess he is creating with overfilled coffee mugs, she muses, "I don't want to wash the kitchen floor again because you can't keep food on dishes" (31). However, she doesn't actually tell Quex to clean up after himself. Similarly one night when she awakens sweating because Quex's arm is pinning her to the bed, she gets out of the bed "careful not to wake him" and spends "the rest of the night on the living-room sofa" (53). Throughout their relationship, even when he tries to force her to confront and discuss their problems, she will not, and at the very end of the novel, we find her still oscillating between whether or not she should make a commitment to him or return to the United States and the man she met there. When we compare Anna to Cody's 1990s protagonist, Eva Wylie, we find this ability to stand up for herself and not be victimized or abused one of the chief differences between them. If we compare Anna's relationships to that of McDermid's Kate Brannigan, we also see how Anna's liaisons are far short of the true equality shown in Kate's relationship. Although Anna is able to get her own way much of the time, she is forced either to use subterfuge or act in a passive-aggressive way. The 1990s phenomenon, the truly equal relationship, is reflective of societal changes which finally came out of the feminist movement and is really not seen in detective fiction of the 1980s or earlier.

Neither Kinsey nor V.I., for example, have a long-term committed relationship which is totally equal, and although they are not victims in the same way as Anna, they too face problems. Kinsey enjoys sex with several men, some of whom are disastrous mistakes. Her first encounter with Charlie Scorsoni is torrid but doomed, and the fact that he turns out to be a murderer harks back to the male hard-boiled fiction. Her on-again, off-again affair with Jonah Robb clearly proves that married men, even those who claim to be separated and out of love with their wives, are sure to lead to heartache. Finally when we meet Kinsey's ex-husband, Daniel Wade, in *E Is for Evidence*, we discover that their marriage had been extremely brief due in part to Daniel's drug habit but mainly due to the fact that he preferred a man to Kinsey. This ultimate betrayal may explain Kinsey's fear of committing herself to a third marriage or long-term relationship, and the whole situation reinforces the 1980s style of the loner detective.

Like Kinsey and V.I., Anna is not in a committed relationship. Cody has given the reason for this as "She is claustrophobic, for instance, and she doesn't like being kissed.... [S]he is probably quite bad at intimacy herself" (Silet 31). Perhaps this is how Cody wishes to see Anna, but she, too, never explicitly describes Anna's sexual encounters, unlike the way Grafton does Kinsey's. In *Backhand*, at the end of one chapter, Anna is bemoaning the fact that Quex has left the kitchen in a mess, and the next chapter begins "At eight-thirty on Sunday morning..."(31). The implication is obviously that they have spent the night together, but nothing is actually described. This is a far cry from Grafton's description of Kinsey's torrid night with Charlie:

> At first, there was too much hunger, too much heat. We came at each other with a clash, an intensity that admitted of no tenderness. We crashed against one other [sic] like waves on a backwater, surges of pleasure driving straight up, curling back again. All of the emotional images were of pounding assault, sensations of boom and buffet and battering ram until he had broken through to me, rolling down again and over me until all my walls were reduced to rubble and ash. He raised himself up on his elbow then and kissed me long and sweet and it began all over again, only this time at his pace, half speed, agonizingly slow like the gradual ripening of a peach on a limb [*A Is for Alibi* 148].

This is an overt portrayal, but we note that the pace is still the man's.

Linked to their inability to form suitable lasting sexual relationships is the female detectives' loneliness in another sphere. The traditional male hard-boiled private investigator of the 1930s and 1940s is always unmarried, childless and without family, and some of the 1980s female hard-boiled detectives imitate this tradition. Accordingly, Anna, like Kinsey, is without a close family and so makes her neighbors her surrogate family. Bea and Selwyn Price live in the apartment below hers in a house off Holland Park Avenue in London. Although Bea has a job, Selwyn stays at home ostensibly writing poetry and enjoying his artistic temperament. Because of his flexible timetable, it is he who has most contact with Anna and makes use of her abilities to fix anything electrical or mechanical. Thus, after a long hard day, Anna may enjoy one of Bea's special meals as she mends Selwyn's bicycle or watches cricket with him on the television she has just fixed. Unlike Cordelia Gray, who is still troubled by her poor childhood and the death of her father, Anna rarely mentions her family, and only in *Bad Company* do we learn of the existence of Anna's mother and sister. When Anna is kidnapped, her colleague, Bernie, visits Bea and Selwyn to tell them what has happened. When he asks what he should do if her mother calls her apartment, Bea says, "'We'll tell them as little as possible.... Anna hates them fussing unnecessarily.'" And Selwyn adds, "'Bea and I are more of a family than they are'" (89). When Anna reminisces about her childhood, it is usually in a tone of regret that she was obviously not understood or warmly cared for. In *Dupe* she describes her childhood home in Dulwich:

> She could remember the house in Dulwich clearly. The small rooms. The doors always shut. The piano no one played. The collection of china ornaments. It had always been a crime to break something, but to break one of those was a sin. More than anything else, they symbolized the restrictions and repressions of that house [36].

In *Bad Company*, she talks about the grownups in her life. "She had not admired the adults she knew and so she had not been eager to imitate them" (22). Perhaps it is because she had such an unsatisfactory childhood that she is able to empathize with the concerns of her teenaged assignments and not become frustrated and angry with them.

Moving from the traditions of the early male hard-boiled detective fiction to the ethics of the 1980s female detective fiction as critique of societal mores, we learn that many of Anna's jobs are to find missing teenagers or to deal with parents who have difficulties with their children. In this regard her work resembles that of the real policewomen of the time. In *Dupe* she is hired to discover why Deidre Jackson died in a horrible automobile accident. In *Bad Company* while shadowing one teenager, Claire Fourie, she is kidnapped with the friend of that teenager, Verity Hewit, and spends most of the book incarcerated in very unpleasant circumstances. In *Head Case* she is hired to find a missing gifted 16-year-old, Thea Hahn, who is acting in a deranged fashion; while in *Under Contract* she is subcontracted to another firm to protect pop star Shona Una. Finally, in *Backhand* what begins as an investigation into some wrongdoings in the fashion world ends as an attempt to track down a nubile 18-year-old, Cynthia Garden, and return her to the safety of her distraught mother. This focus on teenagers and small-scale investigations makes Anna's detection different from that of the characters of the American authors.

V.I.'s cases, for example, often focus on corporations and institutions, and Kinsey's often have her solving old murders which were wrongly detected. While their cases often lead to clear criticism of patriarchal institutions, Anna's do not. This is the biggest difference between the 1980s British hard-boiled female detective and the American. Cody may criticize the treatment Anna receives from the males in her life, but she is not saying that their behavior is caused by the institutions for which they work. It is not Brierly Security which is corrupt, but Brierly himself who has no respect for women.

Because V.I. Warshawski and Kinsey Millhone both work for themselves, they often pursue cases concerning friends or family at the same time as cases for high-paying clients. Since Anna is given cases by her male boss which he thinks are suitable for her, as a woman, not only does she feel less personally involved than Kinsey and V.I. but her motives for the detection do not become an issue. Whereas V.I. and Kinsey often have family who question their motives for continuing to search for the truth after they may have been told to stop, and who also question their authority to act, Anna does not have. By their actions Kinsey and V.I. draw the reader's attention to inequities caused by dominant institutions, whereas Anna's cases and her position allow for less overt criticism of social injustices. V.I. explains why she became a private investigator saying,

> I got tired of seeing poor innocent chumps go off to Stateville because the police wouldn't follow up our investigations and find the real culprits. And I got even more tired of watching clever guilty rascals get off scot-free because they could afford attorneys who know how to tap-dance around the law [*Dead-Lock* 35].

Kinsey also has a similar reaction to insurance companies who allow clever rascals to get away with scams. When she sees Marcia Threadgill, the woman she is watching in *A Is for Alibi*, lifting up a heavy plant when she is claiming a large sum of money for a hurt back, Kinsey tells California Fidelity Insurance that Marcia is a fraud; however, they will not take her to court since they feel the sum of money is too small to warrant their effort. This angers Kinsey, who feels that the company is acting immorally. However, since the company is paying her to act for them, Kinsey is unable to do anything except complain.

Anna is even more constrained than Kinsey because she can only rectify situations to which she objects by going behind Brierly's back and possibly endangering her own future in the firm. At the end of *Bad Company*, she goes to the mother of the girl she has been hired to investigate and informs her that it is her ex-husband who hired Brierly Security to find evidence that she is an unfit mother and her daughter, Claire, is running with a bad crowd. When the mother, Janet Fourie, tells Anna she is pleased to know the truth about Claire, Anna is relieved but asks her not to tell her boss: "This sort of conversation just isn't the done thing in my trade. I could lose my job" (199). Cody, thus, does question inequities, albeit in a different way to American female hard-boiled authors.

In the Anna Lee series we are also aware of the lack of justice, and Cody questions its efficacy as do all the authors in this survey. In an interview with Richler she said: "'When I finish a book I very rarely finish on the note that a wrong has been righted and somebody brought to justice because quite frequently they aren't. A lot has been explained, but not a lot will be done about it'" (qtd. in Walton & Jones 212). In *Bad Company*, Bernie says that the villains haven't yet been caught, but "'They'll be coming out of the woodwork soon enough'" (188). He presumes that they'll be captured, but this is by no means certain, and Anna is not praised for what she did. In fact the mother of the kidnapped Verity will not even allow her to see her again because "'it'd be better for her to forget all about it now'" (194). In *Dupe*, although Anna discovers how Deidre Jackson died, no one is charged, and Brierly tells her "'I doubt if they will be in the future. Both Eady and Brough blame that poor idiot who committed suicide, of course. And even if that was not the case, there were too many mitigating factors'" (217). And in *Backhand*, Lara is probably not going to jail since she suffers a stroke when Anna is accusing her. Anna herself thinks, "Had she won? It didn't feel like winning. Or if it did, winning wasn't very pleasant" (269). At the end of the same book she discovers that a man whose good credit rating she proved did not get a promotion, despite her earlier investigation. "'Typical,' Anna [says], depressed. 'That is so effing typical. Everyone standing foursquare behind their mistakes. That is so small-minded. Everyone, all the way from the garage to the client with Brierly sodding Security in between'" (274).

In the traditional British detective novel, the idea was that the world was a just place, and the detective, police force or the judicial system would remove the criminal and reestablish the status quo, but in the female hard-boiled novels, as noted, this restoration does not happen since the detectives all question the worthiness of the justice system and the establishment in general. We are shown how in several instances the villains do not get their just deserts; they escape; they do not serve a sentence, or they even commit suicide rather than allow themselves to be captured. In *G Is for Grafton*, for example, the authors describe how out of 20 murderers in the Kinsey series, ten are dead, eight get away with their crimes or Kinsey doubts they will be punished, and only two are definitely being prosecuted, which implies a frightening indictment of the failure of the judicial system (Kaufman & Kay 259).

Another criticism of the justice system is implied in the fact that Anna, like Kinsey and V.I., was once a policewoman and had reason to leave the force. In *Stalker* she describes why she disliked being on it. When she joined, she thought the job would bring excitement and adventure, but very quickly she discovered that typing and filing were the keys to success. However, the thing she hated most was the uniform. "She abhorred the fact that everyone knew at a single glance what she did for a living, but worse than that, everyone felt they could make assumptions about who she was, what she was like, and what she thought about. There was something in her nature that rebelled against being so easily and sometimes wrongly identified" (16). Thus, she felt that the job had not given her the opportunity to demonstrate her true abilities, and the prejudice she encountered in and off the force was unacceptable. Linked to this, and one of the interesting aspects we see in much hard-boiled fiction, is the relationship between the detective and the police. Both V.I. and Kinsey at one time have a sexual relationship with one of their local policemen, which both helps and hinders their investigations. V.I.'s lover, Conrad, spends a lot of time chastising her for not telling him in advance the dangerous steps she is going to take, which annoys her because it is clear that he doesn't understand her job and yet does succeed in making her feel loved and cared for. Kinsey, meanwhile, after her affair with Jonah Robb is over, is able to call on him for information which is useful to her. Anna, on the other hand, has no such relationship with the police, and it is Brierly, as the male authority figure, who tries to keep on good terms with them. It is clear that the authoritarian nature of the police is at variance with the female private eye and even more with feminist detectives. As Maureen Reddy tells us:

> Most feminist crime writers doubly problematise authority: on the one hand, they question the entire concept of authority, while on the other they assert the female detective's authority. Traditionally, authority—the power to judge, the right to command, the power to persuade based on knowledge or experience—inheres in the masculine role, with that role part of a social structure based on male superiority. From a feminist standpoint, authority based on such a structure is necessarily illegitimate ["The Feminist" 177].

Linked to the relationship of the private detectives with the police is their relationship with the villains and the treatment of violence in the novels. Like Kinsey and V.I., Anna is able to defend herself, and we see the physical and psychological effects of her encounters with villains. In *Dupe* when she is attacked on the stairs, she manages to inflict some damage on her assailant, but the element of realism is apparent in the description:

> Trying to capitalize on a very small advantage, she swung again and trod sideways on to his instep with as much force as she could muster. This time he protected his head with his arm and shoulder. In theory she should have been able to hurt his feet quite considerably, but in fact his shoes were more substantial than hers, and besides, she was not heavy enough. He responded by lifting her off the ground and throwing her against the wall [199].

When later she faints from her injuries, ends up in the hospital and has to have all her front teeth replaced, we gain a far more realistic portrait of the consequences of a fight than in the early hard-boiled novels by male authors.

British novelists, such as Cody, do, however, have a tonal difference in their descriptions of violence because of the lack of guns. In *Backhand*, Anna is shocked that the male detective in Florida is packing a weapon: "Before he shut the compartment Anna saw a short black handgun. She began to feel uneasy.... Anna was thinking about the handgun and American detective books. Maybe one man's fiction was another man's reality. If that was so, she was in the wrong place at the wrong time with the wrong company" (170). In contrast, the American writers have tougher female protagonists and a harsher tone. When Kinsey kills Charlie Scorsoni at the end of *A Is for Alibi*, we are told she "blew him away" (214). She is affected by her actions as she says, "'The day before yesterday I killed someone and the fact weighs heavily on my mind'" (1). However, if we take into consideration that this is the man with whom she slept twice and with whom she was considering having a serious relationship, her toughness is amazing. Later in *B Is for Burglar* we see that some of this toughness is an act. After she has tried to justify what she did by telling her neighbor Henry that "'All this talk about women being nurturing is crap. We're being sold a bill of goods so we can be kept in line by men. If someone came after me today, I'd do it again, only this time I don't think I'd hesitate,'" she asks him, "'I'm still a good person, aren't I?'" (83–84). For all her hard exterior, Kinsey is still vulnerable inside. This is also true of V.I. who, though she often carries her gun to protect herself, rarely uses it, and when she does, is relieved if she hasn't actually killed the villains. As Ann Wilson asserts:

> [T]he heroines never initiate the violence, and respond violently only when it is clear that inaction on their part would result in death either for themselves or for someone who is defenseless. Their violent actions, cast as the only possible actions if lives of the innocent are to be preserved, seem to involve an almost maternal instinct to protect those incapable of protecting themselves [149].

Hence, although the American women have created the female detective who is able to use a weapon but never glories in violence like her earlier male counterparts do, she is still tougher than her British colleagues, who follow the national expectation that handguns are to be avoided at all costs and have no wish to see a time when all the police will be armed as a matter of course. Cody has spoken at some length about the differences in violence on both sides of the Atlantic.

> 'British sleaze just isn't the same as U.S. sleaze. The same goes for violence. It's harder, in the UK, to achieve a reasonable level of tension and danger. Ours is altogether a tamer society. The danger seems to begin and end at street level. After that, there's a layer of supposedly polite society through which violence is not supposed to pass. When the Brits write tough, we write street talk. What we don't get are industrialists and politicians who are physically just as tough as villains. I'm thinking particularly of Sara Paretsky's novel, *Tunnel Vision*, where that sense of violence actually goes all the way through society' [Silet 33].

Even though Anna does not carry a gun, some of the situations in which she finds herself are both violent and terrifying, but despite feelings of intimidation, she copes remarkably well. In *Bad Company* when she is abducted along with Verity Hewit, she manages to calm Verity, stand up for both of them against her captors, and even make valiant attempts to escape. While Verity does not want to do anything which might antagonize the three thugs, Anna reasons with them, makes her demands clear, and is not afraid to harangue them if necessary: "'You should sort something out between yourselves. I mean is this the punishment wing, and if so, what for? Or is it business? In which case it wouldn't hurt you to stop trying to intimidate us and start treating us properly'" (92). Later she embarrasses the leader by saying, "'[I]f you haven't concluded your business by tomorrow, will someone bring me a packet of Tampax?'" which has the result of having him say, "'Women are nothing but a bloody nuisance'" (92). When Verity is angry with her for having upset the men, Anna points out to her that being passive is tantamount to condoning the men's behavior:

> 'You don't care do you?' Verity said at length. 'You're just rude to them and shout and get their backs up. You don't care what happens to me.'
> 'Nothing's happened to you so far,' Anna said quietly, 'and the noisier I am, the less notice they take of you' [93].

Anna knows that it is only by making their wishes felt that they have any chance of keeping fit and well and perhaps of even escaping. Although she is not able to use her straightened bedspring to unlock the door to their prison, Anna keeps her own spirits up by continually shouting for help and plotting ways to get out. Cody's own commentary on the situation is clear at the end of the novel when Verity in a newspaper article describes her captors. "'They weren't too bad really. One was quite friendly. Some people just don't deserve respect or good manners. But I don't bear them a grudge.'" Anna reacts, "'Blimey'" (190).

While much urban detective novels of the 1960s had large cities like Los Angeles, New York and London as their settings, the 1980s female authors moved their locations to different cities. However, Cody continues to use London as she obviously feels completely at home there, and both Anna and her second series protagonist, Eva Wylie, are distinctly urbanites, experiencing a real culture shock when they have to go to a country location. In *Stalker*, Anna travels to Frome and Exmoor, and when the local policeman says "'We aren't all turnip heads round here, you know,'" she replies "'If anyone feels stupid and under-informed, it's me'" (124). This same novel has a most amusing description of Anna's attempt to catch a little girl's pony on Exmoor, which causes her major difficulty and annoyance so that at one point she tells the horse: "'Come here, you poxy, sodding cow.... You stinking fat lump of dog meat. Come here or I'll boot you from Porlock to Minehead'" (94). In her second series Cody continues this trend with Eva commenting in *Bucket Nut*, "'In the country, things are either dangerous or dead. People may not be much better than animals, but at least people don't leave other people dead on the roads'" (8). Later, when recollecting her enforced childhood foster situation in the country, she says "'Nature is supposed to be good for you. But it isn't. It bites, stings or poisons you at the drop of a hat.... No London's the place to be, and don't let anyone tell you different'" (9).

Paretsky called Eva Wylie, the heroine of Cody's second and most recent series, "A breathtaking tour de force ... a staggering achievement ... talk about grit, going to the bone—what a brave and brilliant creation" (*Bucket Nut* back cover). She is indeed gritty, breathtaking, and unique. With the creation of Eva, Cody achieves another first, the portrayal of a very different type of amateur from those of the Golden Age. Eva is a junkyard night-watchwoman and a wrestler who, as an amateur, is obviously less restricted than professionals; however, if we compare her in speech and behavior to Val McDermid's Lindsay Gordon, we realize how different she is. Eva is based on a real person, Klondyke Kate, who Cody watched wrestle and described as "a barrel in leotards, ... a villain. The more people hate her the better she is doing her job" (Silet 36). Having seen Klondyke Kate in action, Cody re-evaluated her own writing and decided to create a woman who was totally different from the caring women private investigators of the 1980s who are always thinking about the victim and trying to solve all ills. She felt that with a character like Eva she could "deal with anger ... deal with the way people are treated because of the way they look" (Silet 36).

Unlike in her treatment of Anna, Cody tells us numerous details about Eva's past and present life, her likes and dislikes, and her ambitions from the very first few chapters of the novel. Since Cody also uses first person narration, and Eva appeals constantly to the reader, "I'll give you some advice for free ... you have to admit" (*Bucket Nut* 3–4), we are involved both in her thought processes and her actions. In her raw energy, toughness and lack of conventional morals, Eva is more an antihero than a role model for the average female reader.

According to Anne Cranny-Francis:

> [O]ur contemporary amateurs are sexually autonomous, economically independent, intelligent and courageous and on those grounds alone offer a fundamental challenge to the traditional role.... And sometimes they simultaneously expose the myth, the patriarchal discourse which so seriously limits the range of activities available to women and which accordingly structures their fictional representations [165].

Eva, for all her uniqueness, does fall into the conventions of this new feminist detective. She is not sexually active but this is through choice, as is her financial situation. She is very courageous and is at pains to persuade us that her lack of education does not imply that she is unintelligent. It is particularly in her choice of career, however, that she challenges the "patriarchal discourse" since she sees nothing strange about being a female wrestler and junkyard night-watchperson. Unlike Kinsey, who may do some breaking and entering but meticulously keeps her receipts and never overcharges her clients, and Anna, who may pad her expenses but only a little if she feels the ever-vigilant Beryl won't notice, Eva steals cars, has never obtained a driver's license, and has a police record. Although she is adamantly against drugs, she is willing to steal people's wallets from a club since, according to her, if they are stupid enough to leave them in their jackets or handbags unattended, then they deserve to have them stolen. Thus, Eva is by no means the typical "good guy" private investigator. Cody said that she gained a sort of power when writing about Eva since "books try to make something reasonable of life, whereas I don't actually believe that life is reasonable. When you're using an unreliable narrator, which Eva is, she's not reliable at all, you can say and do all sorts of unusual things" (Silet 37).

Cody has made in Eva a voice for all the women who feel themselves disadvantaged because of their looks, social class or lack of education. As Eva comments on and retaliates against all the slights, real or imagined, that she receives from the people around her, she may make us smile, but she gives vent to the feelings of frustration we may all have felt because we did not have the nerve or ability to counter the insults or injuries we experienced. In looks she is very different from Kinsey, V.I. and Anna. In her own words she is big, strong and ugly, so masculine-looking that the owner of the nearby convenience store thought she was a man and called her "sir" the first time he met her. She admires beauty, envies it, and comments on how the world treats attractive people differently from ugly ones: "I never would have thought girls like her had to pay the rent. Someone always looked after them. Right? And why not? Beauty is something you pay for, isn't it?" (*Bucket Nut* 52). However, she also realizes how her looks, and especially her strength, can be advantageous. When she sees her mother being hit by the current lover, she remarks: "'If you are strong, men won't take liberties. Nobody hits me any more—not unless I'm paid for it.... Take a tip from me—if you want respect in this world—get rid of the wobbly bits'" (*Bucket Nut* 23).

Part of Eva's strength has been caused by her major desire to be different from her mother. Cordelia's mother is dead, as is Kinsey's and V.I.'s, but they were all good women, and their daughters remember them fondly. Anna's mother is alive, as is Charmian Daniels', but has little contact with her daughter. Eva's mother is very much alive but is an extremely unpleasant character. In *Bucket Nut* we learn that she is a drunk and a prostitute whose own behavior placed her two daughters in miserable foster homes. On one occasion when they ran away from the home just before Christmas, they were not welcomed back. Eva says of her mother that she always thought of Eva as a "thorn in her flesh" (62). In *Monkey Wrench*, Eva remembers the time when her mother shut both children in a cupboard under the stairs so that they would not disturb her activities with her client, then fell asleep with a cigarette in her hand and set herself and the room on fire. "So we did what small weak people do—we screamed and cried and wet ourselves. And still Ma did not wake up. Well she couldn't, could she? She was sotted out of her brain-box, and even before that, she'd forgotten all about us" (46). Eva despises weakness in an adult because she so clearly remembers how her own weakness as a child limited her. What is also interesting in this quotation is that although Eva has no desire to imitate her mother, she does not condemn her, and in *Bucket Nut* she constantly excuses her because she has had a hard life. In addition, at the end of *Monkey Wrench*, she is furious with Bella, the prostitute, who says that Eva's mother is just like her. "My ma is not like Bella. She isn't! Bella's a dirty, filthy, shitty liar. My ma has a hard life and gets by as best she can, but she is not like Bella. I won't stand for it" (211).

Eva's ambivalence towards her mother is also reflected in her relationship with her sister, Simone. In the first two books Simone doesn't appear, but she is fondly remembered by Eva as the pretty older sister whom she looked after since she was the stronger of the two. In *Musclebound*, she is an integral part of the plot and shown in sharp contrast to Eva. While Eva is stealing a car, she discovers a bag filled with thousands of pounds of paper money. Thrilled at her unexpected fortune, she takes a bundle and hides the rest in the dog house in the junkyard. Later, after she has paid her mother's rent with some of the money, her troubles begin. Her mother sends two of her lovers to kidnap Simone in the hope that Eva will pay a large sum in ransom for her life. Unfortunately, Eva kills one of the men when she hits him overly hard, and Simone, who at first promises to help get rid of the body, takes off in fear. Eva is angry that Simone has left her to take care of the body, but after she has dumped the man in the Thames, she accepts Simone's weakness, and the news that the dead man was sent by her mother, with the same equanimity that she did other revelations throughout their childhood. "'Don't cry, Simone,' I said. 'It ain't no big surprise to me. She ain't a proper ma. Never was. Never will be. She's a toad and she laid spawn in a puddle. That's us. You and me. She never thinks she got to care for us. That ain't what toads do. We got to take care of ourselves'" (110). So instead of admonishing Simone for having left her in the lurch, Eva, yet again, takes on the role of protector.

Eva's determination to take care of herself makes her a very different protagonist than Anna, and we see in her attitudes towards men a strength, a ruthlessness that is missing in most hard-boiled female detectives. One of the few men she admires is Harsh, a fellow wrestler who has technical skills which make him superior to the other male wrestlers whom Eva knows. Harsh, an Indian, is described as always warming up properly and having beautiful balance (*Bucket Nut* 5). Eva emulates him in her fitness program and often quotes what he has told her; however, when his words of wisdom and calm demeanor don't suit her, she does what she wants. Although Eva admires Harsh, she despises most men, especially those who want to have a sexual relationship with her. In *Bucket Nut* she asks, "Does everyone want to be wanted? Do all women want to be touched—even by a greasy-handed dip brain? Well, I don't know the answer to that, but then, I'm different" (3). Eva's difference is a key component of her character, and with this topic, Cody moves the genre back again to the total loner detective. Unlike Anna who has her neighbors and colleague Bernie as her support system, Eva really has no one. As we discover in *Musclebound*, her dreams of having in Simone a soul mate, or at least someone she can rely on, are unfounded. Whereas Simone needs men to lean on, Eva hates this aspect of men. In *Musclebound*, Keif, whom she has accepted as a personal trainer, says he wants to look after her. Her reaction is to tell him to go away, and she claims, "Blokes make complete pillocks of sensible women" (96). Later her attitude is contrasted to Simone's reaction when Greg, the owner of the money Eva stole, comes to get it back. Simone tells Eva to be nice to him: "'Eva, he's a big, dangerous man. It doesn't matter if he's got a gun or not. Even when you had the gun, he was calling the shots. Can't you see that? Big dangerous men always win'" (208). Simone claims that she doesn't want to have to keep "placating" (209) the men in her life, but at the end of the novel, she goes off in the car with Greg because he has promised to set her up in business. Hence, having wanted a strong relationship with Simone at the start of the novel, Eva is shown at the end realizing that Simone is too different from her to really be a friend, so once again she ends up totally alone.

Another way the Eva Wylie series resembles the early male hard-boiled detective fiction is in its colloquial speech. For the non–British reader much of the slang will be difficult to understand even within context; however, it gives to the plot a raciness and immediacy which is appealing. Similarly to McDermid's Kate, Eva uses working-class vocabulary which is not standard. For example, she uses the words "dosh," "jack" and "wedge" for money, and in *Bucket Nut*, she hires a middle-class sculptor to call some lawyers because she knows that she doesn't have the vocabulary to speak to professional people.

Linked to her inability to communicate in standard English, Eva is shown as often losing her temper inappropriately and shouting whenever she becomes frustrated. In this respect she is very different from the cool-headed Kinsey and V.I. and the very controlled Anna. Cody is turning the detective novel on its head, by having a detective whose behavior we not only may have difficulty relating to, but would not want to emulate. She seems to be creating in Eva a protagonist who harks back to the early American hard-boiled fiction of Dashiell Hammett, whose novels, according to George Grella, had a "penchant for the marvelous, the sensational, the legendary, and in general the heightened effect" (104).

What is the future of the British hard-boiled detective novel? Will it continue in the Anna Lee tradition or move even further in the Eva Wylie mode? Since the opportunities for women have changed so much since the early 1980s, I believe we may well see more protagonists like Eva. These amateur detectives may well have jobs which would once have been considered the province only of males and follow to a tough way of life which needs no male protection. With the advent of more detective fiction set in northern cities, it follows that we shall also have hard-boiled female amateurs and private investigators who speak in regional dialects and have strong working-class roots.

Works Cited

Cody, Liza. *Backhand*. New York: Doubleday, 1992.

____. *Bad Company*. New York: Scribner's Sons, 1982.

____. *Bucket Nut*. New York: The Mysterious Press, 1995.

____. *Dupe*. New York: Scribner's Sons, 1980.

____. *Head Case*. New York: Bantam Books, 1990.

____. *Monkey Wrench*. New York: The Mysterious Press, 1995.

____. *Musclebound*. London: Bloomsbury Publishing, 1997.

____. *Rift*. London: Collins, 1988.

____. *Stalker*. Bath: Chivers Press,1986.

____. *Under Contract*. New York: Bantam Books, 1990.

Chapter Four

Val McDermid

Val McDermid, who, like Gwendoline Butler, gained her degree from Oxford University, began her writing career as a journalist before writing her first novel in 1987. Eleven years younger than Liza Cody, she departs radically in her writing from the traditional detective fiction. She has three series at present: the first with an amateur lesbian sleuth, journalist Lindsay Gordon; the second with a professional straight private investigator, Kate Brannigan; and the third with a criminologist, Tony Hill, aided and abetted by police inspector, Carol Jordan. In an interview in Melbourne, Australia, with Sue Turnbull, McDermid analyzed her motives for writing three very different series. Lindsay was her alter ego, but since it was impossible to make a living writing lesbian crime novels, she created Kate Brannigan: "'I wanted to see if it was possible to write a private eye novel within the Chandler/Paretsky tradition, that could be thrilling, exciting, tense and scary, but still maintain the wise-cracking, smart-mouth private eye'" (4). She moved from the first two series to the Tony Hill books because she wanted to "'stay fresh'" (20). "'I think of imagination and writing techniques as muscles, the more you use them, the more you stretch them, the stronger they get'"(20). McDermid is innovative in her writing in several important ways. In all three of her series, her settings, urban cities in the north of England, depart markedly from those of the traditional detective novels which, as has been mentioned, were usually set in London or an idyllic countryside. Furthermore McDermid is similar to such writers as Paretsky in that she discusses social ills, especially those linked to working-class urban backgrounds. As such she takes the detective genre ever further from the genteel settings of the Golden Age. In addition, the attention paid in her novels to the sexual habits of her protagonists makes her very different from earlier works. Lindsay Gordon is an exceedingly out of the closet lesbian; Kate Brannigan enjoys a monogamous relationship with her lover but is very much his equal; and Tony Hill is a highly disturbed, some might claim dysfunctional, sexually impotent profiler. All of these innovative aspects of her novels make them of great interest to the modern reader.

In her initial series with amateur sleuth Lindsay Gordon, who is in her own words "a cynical socialist lesbian feminist journalist" (*Report for Murder* 3), McDermid reminds the reader, sometimes in a mocking tone, of the sleuths of Christie and Sayers. In her first novel, *Report for Murder*, her setting is a private girls' boarding school in Buxton, Derbyshire. Lindsay is called to use her journalistic skills to report on a gala, fund raising weekend being promoted by the school which is in dire financial straits. After the murder of the key guest musician, Lorna Smith-Couper, and the arrest of her friend, housemistress Paddy Callaghan, Lindsay is retained by the headmistress to find who the real murderer is. However, what might appear to be a classic whodunit is altered irrevocably by the one major difference—Lindsay's lesbianism. Although lesbian author Nancy Spain created many detective novels in the 1940s with male and female homosexual characters, her lesbian detective is by no means as sexually overt as Lindsay Gordon. Hence McDermid is the first British detective writer to have an overt lesbian as a protagonist. She places Lindsay's lesbianism right at the forefront of her plots as she openly comments on her lustful feelings for various characters, demonstrates her sexuality, and shows the reader the implicit and explicit prejudices to which lesbians are subjected. McDermid told Sue Turnbull:

> When I was writing Lindsay Gordon, I was very aware that she was the first British lesbian detective. I felt the strong sense that she had to be some kind of every-dyke, which is why she's never physically described. I wanted readers not only to identify with Lindsay as the detective protagonist, but for her to be a fantasy figure, either someone they'd like to be in a relationship with, or have as a friend, or even hate to have living next door [22].

Although the Lindsay Gordon series uses a traditional amateur sleuth tracking down a variety of villains, it is chiefly of interest for the lesbian and other issues it depicts. Like the other 1980s detective writers, McDermid used the medium of the detective novel to address societal problems and to broaden the scope of the genre. Having an openly lesbian sleuth, who shows her lustful feelings for different women, attempts to normalize the gay experience. McDermid cleverly realized that many readers would move from the Kate Brannigan series to the Lindsay Gordon novels, and she would achieve the unusual feat of getting straight readers to buy lesbian novels (Turnbull 4). In *Report for Murder*, Lindsay lusts after the novelist, Cordelia Brown, as she remarks to her friend Paddy: "How do you expect me to sleep knowing she's only the thickness of a wall away?" (23). Later in the same book, McDermid is not afraid to write about Lindsay's and Cordelia's first sexual encounter:

> She kissed her suddenly and hard. Lindsay tasted cigarettes and whisky and smelled shampoo. And was lost.
>
> Glued to each other, they performed a complicated sideways shuffle into Lindsay's bedroom. Because it was the first time, the clumsy fumbling to undress each other lost its ludicrous edge in mutual desire. They tumbled on to the duvet, bodies burning to the other's touch. Lips and hands explored new terrain, hungry to commit the maps of each other's bodies to memory [72].

These descriptions of sexual encounters may have made the books appealing to their initial predominantly lesbian readers, but may prove unpalatable to some straight, older readers. However, these types of descriptions are, according to Pauline Palmer, part of the convention of the crime novel as escapist literature (21).

In McDermid's second Lindsay Gordon novel, *Common Murder*, Lindsay's relationship with her partner Cordelia is portrayed as fraught with the same frustrations as any heterosexual relationship. "Much as she loved and needed Cordelia, Lindsay had begun to sense that her initial feeling that she had found a soul-mate with whom she occasionally disagreed was turning into a struggle to find enough in common to fill the spaces between the lovemaking that still brought them together in a frighteningly intense unity" (5). In *Final Edition*, the third Gordon novel, the complexities and interweaving of lesbian relationships are illustrated as Lindsay tries to help a friend of hers, Jackie, who has murdered her lover, Alison, who also happens to be Lindsay's past lover. Jackie's lawyer, and also former lover, Claire, meanwhile is now having an affair with Cordelia, again a past lover of Lindsay's. The fact that

McDermid inhabits the same world as Lindsay makes her depiction of the gay lifestyle very realistic. As one critic stated, "[McDermid] invests her ... series featuring Lindsay Gordon with something like a soul, an internal world that consistently rings true" (Phillips 2).

The discrimination to which lesbians are subjected is seen throughout all the books. In *Report for Murder*, the lesbian music teacher at the school recognizes that if her sexual orientation becomes known, she will never again be allowed to work in an all-girls boarding school. In *Common Murder*, Ros, the daughter of the murdered man, Rupert Crabtree, is given money by him to open a restaurant, but we are told, "Rupert Crabtree would never have put up money for her restaurant if he'd thought for one minute she was gay. He'd have killed her!"(78). In *Union Jack*, Lindsay is told, "Let's face it, no normal person's going to shed a tear because there's one less dyke on the planet" (51).

Although the lesbian theme is very clearly stated in the Lindsay series, these novels explore other issues too. In *Report for Murder*, Lindsay's working-class background causes some problems for Cordelia, who has inherited money, as well as wealth from her writing, films, and television series. Lindsay remarks to her:

> 'You really are one of the obscenely privileged minority, aren't you? ... I don't know what I'm doing with it all. In my job, I see so much poverty, so much deprivation, so much exploitation, I can't help feeling that luxury like this is obscene. Don't you want to change things?'
> Cordelia laughed and replied lightly. 'But what would you have me do? Give all I've got to the poor?' [108].

When Lindsay sees Cordelia's home, she says she never really feels comfortable there because "It's like living in a page out of *House and Garden*" (107).

McDermid's own background and former career as a journalist are also reflected in the way Lindsay is prickly not only about her working-class origins but also about her work as a journalist. In *Report for Murder*, Lindsay finds Lorna murdered and later discovers the supposed murderer, a student called Sarah, with her wrists slashed most gruesomely. At the same time, however, she is able to file her copy to her editor and make sure she also gets a lead story in three other papers. She asks Cordelia, "'Bet you think I'm a real shit, don't you?' Cordelia looked at her. 'I couldn't have done what you've just done.' Lindsay shrugged, her face a mask. 'It's a way of dealing with what's happened. A way of hiding, a way of postponing'" (163). Thus Lindsay's job is shown as hardening her yet freeing her from having to acknowledge her own emotions.

Another issue which first appears in the Lindsay Gordon series is the role of women and motherhood. In *Report for Murder*, Lindsay's editor asks her to do a feature on a woman who has finally given birth to twins after doctors told her she couldn't have any children. Lindsay's reaction to the editor's assignment of a real tearjerker needing a woman's touch to present the woman as a heroine who has "triumphed against all odds" (75), is to retort "'You'd think after thirteen miscarriages she'd have realised there's more to life than babies. There are plenty of kids up for adoption who need love and affection'"(76). This criticism of motherhood is also seen in the Kate Brannigan series where Kate makes it clear she feels no need to be a mother in order to achieve fulfillment.

Even though Lindsay may criticize some mothers, she really values motherlike support in true feminist fashion. In *Sisters in Crime*, Maureen Reddy states "The feminist movement on the whole values female community, mutual support, and collective action for social change, but lesbian feminist crime novels illustrate the special significance of such community for lesbians" (130). The female community in *Common Murder* is based on the peaceful protest at Greenham Common. Although the women are not the threat the local men claim they are, they are targeted as much for their sexual orientation as for their political stance. The novel describes the plight of a woman, who is part of the group protesting at the siting of U.S. cruise missiles at the American airbase at Brownlow Common. The woman, Deborah, a past lover of Lindsay's, is first accused of breaking the nose of Rupert Crabtree, the leader of the Ratepayers Against Brownlow's Destruction, a pressure group which aims to remove the protestors. Later when Crabtree is found murdered, Deborah is arrested, and Lindsay is asked by the protestors to try to discover the truth. When bikers roar into the camp one night, throw blood and animal entrails at the women's tents, and cut and bruise many of the women with sticks and heavy chains, Lindsay cries, "We must call the police!" (17). Another woman replies:

'It's a waste of time calling the police, Lindsay. They just don't want to know. The first time they threw blood over our benders, we managed to get the police to come out. But they said we'd done it ourselves, that we were sensation seekers. They said there was no evidence of our allegations. Tyre tracks in the mud don't count, you see. Nor do the statements of forty women. It really doesn't matter what crimes are perpetrated against us, because we're sub-human, you see' [17].

Similar to American detective fiction writers of the 1980s, McDermid goes beyond women's issues to more general social problems. In *Common Murder*, she turns her anger toward retail developers who have transformed the British high street into ever similar malls. In *Crack Down*, she mocks the very wealthy in posh Prestbury, just outside Manchester. "They don't have sweetie shops run by Asians in places like Prestbury. They don't have anything that isn't one hundred per cent backed up by centuries of English Conservative tradition" (153). And in *Booked for Murder*, she examines the practice of companies which deduct bribes from their income, claiming them as commissions, so they don't have to pay as much tax.

Also like Sara Paretsky, McDermid attacks British patriarchal society by probing specific institutions in her novels. For example, in *Common Murder*, MI6 is implicated in the murder of one victim and the attempted murder of another. We learn that the intelligence agency has bugged the phone of the police superintendent, Rigano, and proposes to allow the murderer, Simon Crabtree, to remain free and act as a very possible threat to Lindsay's friend Deborah. When Rigano questions the MI6 chief and protests "I still don't bloody see why you people want Crabtree free. He's a bloody spy as well as a murderer," he is told, "He has uses at present. He will eventually pay the price for his activities" (171). At the end of the novel when Lindsay has exposed both Crabtree and MI6, Crabtree suffers an unexpected motorbike "accident," and that patriarchal institution, the intelligence agency, is once more off the hook.

In *Union Jack*, trade unions are criticized. One character most vividly describes the problems unions are facing as he tells Lindsay that the reason unions are having trouble is

> because when people like you were our union reps back in the eighties you were too busy playing politics and screaming about AIDS and sexism instead of fighting for jobs. Youse all just stood back and let Thatcher and Tebbit kick the union movement to death. Youse said yessir, no sir, to the Maxwells and Murdochs and Carnegie Wilsons while they decimated our jobs and wrecked our industry. And then you buggered off to a cushy number in the sun while we run about the country like headless chickens, desperate for casual shifts anywhere that'll pay our bus fare [99].

In the same novel, the unions are also criticized indirectly since the murderer is also implicated in a scheme to defraud the unions of thousands of pounds, and she is able to do this because of inadequate safety checks of members' expense reimbursements.

Similar to Grafton and Paretsky, McDermid's interest in social inequities is supported by her ultimately feminist views on the efficacy of justice, which are highlighted in the endings to some of her books. The ending of *Final Edition* is reminiscent of Melville's *Murder Has A Pretty Face* because the murderer, Cordelia, is not turned over by Lindsay to the police, but allowed to escape. Lindsay gives as her reasons the pity she feels for Cordelia and the knowledge that incarceration would kill her. However, she realizes that,

> [d]iscovering the truth about Cordelia was going to change her life in ways she couldn't even imagine yet. Her trust in her own judgment was only the latest casualty of Cordelia's monstrous course of action. To preserve Cordelia's good name, Alison Maxwell had had to die and Jackie Mitchell's life had been destroyed. But in spite of her 'finely honed sense of justice', Lindsay prayed that Cordelia would escape [207].

Similarly, in the end of *Union Jack* we learn that Pauline, a black administrative worker for the AMWU, was being sexually harassed by the union secretary, Tom Jack, whom she killed by accident when she pushed him towards a window on the tenth floor of the building where they were staying, and he fell through it to his death. Pauline had been writing and distributing the scurrilous *Conference Chronicle*, a broadsheet filled with gossip designed to avenge Pauline and all the workers who had been badly treated by the union. Knowing that Tom's death was an accident, Lindsay decides not to turn Pauline into the police because "justice wouldn't be served by taking her away from her kid and locking her up in Holloway" (*Union Jack* 262).

As McDermid said in the interview with Sue Turnbull, her reasons for beginning a new series with a straight private investigator were to try something new and to reach a wider audience. Kate Brannigan is every feminist's dream, a woman totally of the '90s. She uses Thai kick boxing in order to keep fit and protect herself, is single because "married is for mugs, masochists and mothers"(*Kickback* 207), none of which she is, and has been to university at Oxford, although she never finished her law degree. Kate is indeed a far cry from P.D. James's Cordelia Gray but McDermid also says she wanted to make her very different from the other hard-boiled private investigators:

> I can't think of one who's married. It's one of the things I wanted to make different about Kate Brannigan, who has a nexus of close women friends with whom she does normal things like shop and gossip, and a man with whom she has a permanent, close relationship which mirrors reality in its emotional swings [Turnbull 4].

In addition to several close women friends, Kate has a number of male friends like Josh, the financial broker, Gizmo, the computer whiz, and Dennis, the ex-burglar, to whom she can go for help or advice. Hence, Kate appeals to those readers who prefer their P.I.s to resemble their real-life counterparts rather than the early male hard-boiled loner investigators. In fact Kate closely resembles the investigators whom McDermid interviewed for her nonfiction work, *A Suitable Job for a Woman*, where she discovered that most women P.I.s were in relationships, and many were mothers. Kate has a committed relationship with her boyfriend, Richard, even though she doesn't live with him but lives next door to him, with a conservatory linking both their properties at the back. As she says, the conservatory allows them to cohabit when they both want it, but also allows her the privacy she desires away from Richard's noisy rock band friends and his young son, Davy, who sometimes comes to visit. Kate is always shown as very strong in her relationship with Richard as is seen in *Clean Break* when he is helping her to follow a suspect. Richard gets jealous and frightened for Kate's safety, and she gets angry when he tries to stop her from continuing her work. She says: "I was inches away from completely losing control, but I had enough sense left not to flatten him. That would be one move that our relationship wouldn't survive. 'Trust me, Richard,' I said quietly. 'I know what I'm doing'"(*Clean Break* 179).

As well as being strong, the fact that Kate openly says she doesn't want to marry, or be encumbered by a child, makes her a contemporary contrast to other sleuths who seem to need to prove they still have maternal instincts. Kate analyzes her attitudes with a marvelous self-deprecating humor. In *Blue Genes* she says :

> I've never been smitten with the maternal urge, which means I always feel a bit bemused when my friends get sandbagged by their hormones and turn from perfectly normal women into monomaniacs

desperate to pass their genes on to a waiting world. Maybe it's because my biological clock has still got a way to go before anything in my universe starts turning pumpkin-shaped. Or maybe, as Richard suggests when he's in sentimental father mode, it's because I'm a cold-hearted bastard with all the emotional warmth of Robocop [41].

It is clear, however, that Kate is not "Robocop" in her relationships with friends. Like other hard-boiled female investigators, she enjoys a great deal of support. Glenwood Irons says V.I. Warshawski "turns to other women because she is aware of her own vulnerability, because she is smart enough to be afraid when the odds are against her (which they always are true to generic form), and because she is aware of the power that the community of women offers against 'the system'" (139). Kate also turns to a friend, Alexis, the lesbian crime reporter for the *Manchester Evening Chronicle*, whenever she needs help.

The fact that Kate's best friend in this second series is a lesbian allows McDermid to continue to analyze many of the major concerns of lesbians: disapproval, discrimination, and even procreation. *Blue Genes*, for instance, explores the possibility of illegal experimentation in female fertility and the mixing of the nuclei of two female eggs to create a girl baby which is then planted into the womb of one of the women of a lesbian couple. McDermid's discussion of these topics makes her something of a rarity in crime fiction. If we compare her to Patricia Cornwell, for example, we can see how McDermid has been much bolder. When Cornwell began writing in 1990, Kay Scarpetta's niece, aged 11, had not yet defined her sexuality. Later as Cornwell herself came out of the closet more and more, the niece's gay character engaged in discussions of the difficulties of being a lesbian in a committed relationship and working in the FBI, that predominantly masculine enclave. However, unlike Alexis's problems in McDermid's novels, the lesbian focus is rarely central to the mystery being solved in Cornwell's novels. In addition, unlike Kate, the heterosexual Kay is a rather unrealistic figure, since she cooks her own pasta, draws up her own architectural plans for her very modern house, scuba dives, and rejects her male lover's desire to marry her after he has finally obtained a divorce. Unlike Cornwell, McDermid, also writing in the 1990s, openly examines the lesbian agenda from the point of view of a protagonist who is straight and not so perfect that she intimidates the reader. Kate also has a totally equal relationship with Richard but admits her own sexuality and seems to have the best of both worlds. Thus, Kate Brannigan is the first British female private investigator who is not dominated by men, like Anna Lee, and enjoys a relationship with a man on her terms. She does not feel that he will limit her career, like Cordelia Gray, and she can admit to her own sexuality in a healthy, open way which allows her readers to empathize with her.

McDermid's Kate Brannigan series also reflects the works of Grafton and Paretsky in that she tackles crimes other than murder. The fact that she investigates "fraud, missing persons, theft—and the murder happens almost incidentally, and usually a long way down the road" (Sykes 314), makes the books, like those of Liza Cody, very realistic and less outside the reach of most readers' lives. At the beginning of *Kickback*, Kate is hired to look into the reason why a builder of conservatories has been prevented from extending his credit by his bank and several of his conservatories have been removed from their houses. At the same time, Alexis discovers that the plot of land where she hoped to build her new dream home has been sold to someone else and the owner of the land has taken her 5,000 pounds and disappeared. These are two simple white-collar frauds which should be easy to solve and not involve too much mayhem; however, as we discover, this is not, in fact, the case.

In *Crack Down*, Kate is also called upon to solve two unrelated crimes. The first involves proving a car-sales fraud. While Richard is helping Kate find out how the car dealers are defrauding the manufacturers, he is arrested by the police because the car he is driving is found to be full of drugs. As she is trying to prove Richard's innocence, Kate starts working on the second crime, finding out who is lacing children's transfers with drugs and how this is related to a child pornography ring. Once again these white-collar crimes prove to be a real challenge to Kate.

In the Kate Brannigan series, a racier McDermid uses a first person narration which allows us greater insight into Kate's character. Stylistically throughout the series, McDermid displays a wry sense of humor and has some apt descriptions. The spa town of Buxton is described as having a "magnificent Georgian crescent that ought to blow your socks off, but it's been allowed to run to seed, rather like an alcoholic duchess who's been at the cooking sherry" (*Kickback* 78). When told that Alexis plans to live out in the country, Kate remarks that "if you're more than ten minutes away from a Marks & Spencer Food Hall, (fifteen including legal parking), ... you're outside the civilized world" (*Kickback* 22). When she goes to interview a possible witness:

> I made my way back round to the front and rang the doorbell, which serenaded me with an electronic 'Yellow Rose of Texas'. The woman who opened the door looked more like the dandelion clock of Cheshire. She had a halo of fluffy white hair that looked like it had been defying hairdressers for more than half a century [*Kickback* 24].

Another of McDermid's stylistic quirks is her use of "the irregular verb theory of life." In *Kickback*, Kate says, "I am a trained investigator, you have a healthy curiosity, she/he is a nosy parker" (135). In *Crack Down*, it is "I am creative, you exaggerate, he/she is a pathological liar" (29). In *Blue Genes* "I have considered opinions; you are prejudiced; he/she is a raging bigot" (183).

Not only is McDermid typically English in her language, but she follows British conventions in her portrayal of violence. Though it is harsher than it is in Cody's novels, it differs from that of the American novelists because of the lack of guns. In *Kickback*, when the villain tries to push Kate's car off the road into the Manchester Ship Canal, she doesn't immediately leap out of the car, rush after him and shoot out his tires. Having been rescued by the police and cut out of the wreck, she decides in the casualty department of Manchester Royal Infirmary to buy a cell phone and admits, "I was shaken up. To hell with the tough guy private eye image. I was trembling, my body felt like a 5' 3" bruise, and I just wanted to pull the covers over my head" (69). In *Crack Down*, when she is hit over the head and tied to a water pipe by one of the villains, first she manages to get free, then she kicks him in the crook of his knee, and finally she rescues him from the encroaching flood of water so that he won't drown. "Call me a wimp, but I couldn't do it. I crouched down, grabbed his hair and hauled his poleaxed head out of the water.... I'm too nice for my own good" (205).

As in the Lindsay Gordon series, McDermid's Kate Brannigan exposes general social ills. As mentioned, in *Crack Down* Kate exposes a child pornography ring which is linked to juvenile drugs. When she finally finds the house where many of the videos are being shot, she says, "I'd have been fairly revolted to see adults in some of those poses, but with children, my reaction went beyond disgust. At once I understood those parents who take the law into their own hands when the drunk drivers who killed their kids walk free from court" (200). In *Kickback*, McDermid's description of the Manchester housing situation also clearly shows her concern:

> Modern concrete boxes and grimy red brick terraced shops were mixed higgledy-piggledy along almost every street, a seemingly random and grotesque assortment that filled me with the desire to construct a cage in the middle of it and make the town planners live there for a week among the chip papers blowing in the wind and the soft-drink cans rattling along the gutters [155].

This criticism of social ills is also tied in with her descriptions of the region, since for McDermid one of the major relevancies of detective fiction is its use of place. McDermid is one of the earliest British writers who depicts a working-class, regional urban side of Britain in her novels, which in some respects links her naturally with the early American hard-boiled P.I.s who depicted similar "mean streets." In an interview with Jerry Sykes in *The Armchair Detective* she says, "The best crime fiction always [paints] a picture of its society and its landscapes ... its focus on social history and the relationship between people and their landscape is one of its great claims for ... relevance and significance" (315). It is strange, therefore, that Gerald Bartell claims that *Final Edition* lacks "a strong sense of place.... Lindsay embraces Glasgow as 'the only truly European city in Britain' yet McDermid never lets us see much of what Lindsay sees—or hears, tastes, feels or smells—walking its once mean streets" (1).

In 1996, McDermid moved into a totally different area with a new police procedural, *The Mermaids Singing*, which was the first of a harsher series. In the acknowledgments at the start of the book, the author states, "It is always disturbing when life seems to imitate art" and recalls serial killings of gay men in London which happened after she had begun the novel in 1992. This tragic coincidence obviously disturbed her greatly since detective fiction, after all, is supposed to entertain. It is, however, not surprising that with her journalistic background, McDermid chose to write about a type of crime that is currently on the rise. In an interview, she discussed her attitude toward violence. "I've always tried to avoid glamorizing or trivializing violence.... I write about it in a way that I hope makes the reader uncomfortable, because violence defiles those who use it and those who are its victims" (Forshaw). *The Mermaids Singing* indeed makes the reader feel uncomfortable, yet it is fascinating with its detailed analysis of the hunting of the serial killer, its descriptions of the killer's motivations from his own perspective, and its meticulously accurate research on the psychology of serial killers and the work of profilers. The blend of the main narrative in the third person and the killer's narrative in the first person in the form of a diary gives the reader insight into both worlds and allows the full horror of the tortures used by the killer to be more vividly portrayed. In fact, it is this move toward a blend of familiar police procedural and innovative, more lurid type of horror story which gives this new series its appeal.

McDermid's protagonist, too, is unusual as he is a mix of the totally knowledgeable professional in his public persona with the sexually inadequate failure in his private. McDermid arouses our interest and even fear by making Tony Hill parallel the killer in many aspects. While Hill admits that he hides behind a mask when he has to speak in public and wears a suit that is hopelessly out of date, it is his penchant for phone sex and his impotence which make him completely removed from the American male hard-boiled heroes, even the modern ones. Although Robert Parker's Spenser might on occasion be sick when he has to kill someone and insensitive to many of his girlfriend's needs, he is hardly likely to pay for sex or enjoy phone sex. At one point when Hill is first working with Inspector Carol Jordan, he says: "Why was it that, faced with a woman any normal man would regard as attractive, something in him closed down? Was it because he refused to allow himself to feel the first stirrings that might lead him to a place where he was no longer in control, where humiliation lurked?" (*The Mermaids Singing* 99). The use of the word "normal" implies that there is something abnormal about Hill which, coupled with the very abnormal crime, makes the reader even wonder on occasion what type of link there might be between Hill and the killer. While Adam Dalgliesh may sometimes question the nature of his work and its effect on the innocent, Hill questions his own personality in a disturbing lack of self-confidence:

> The worst of it was, he recognized his own behaviour. How many times had he sat across the table from a multiple rapist, arsonist or killer and watched them reach the point in their reliving of events where they could no longer face themselves. Just like him, they closed down.... Part of Tony prayed that Angelica knew enough about the theory and practice of psychology to stick with him till he too could break down the barriers and stare into the face of whatever it was that had bred this sexual and emotional cripple [124].

We learn later in the book that Hill, like some of the female detectives described in earlier chapters, had a sad childhood: abandoned by his father, neglected by his mother, and punished by his grandmother. This inadequate upbringing, similar in profile to those of many serial killers, forces Hill to confront his own weaknesses constantly as he analyzes this particular killer.

In addition to creating such an innovative protagonist, McDermid also depicts a new type of policewoman in the form of Carol Jordan, who follows in the steps of Charmian Daniels since she is efficient, hard-working and very ambitious. However, she differs from her and Kate Brannigan in that she does not have a committed relationship and appears to find it hard to find suitable men. Her last liaison was with a doctor in London, who, when she moved to Bradford, had "no intention of wasting any of his valuable off-duty time putting unnecessary mileage on his BMW just to go to a city whose only redeeming feature was Carol" (65). Now, Carol lives with her brother. The love interest between her and Hill is a salient factor in the plot. According to Penny Burgess, the newspaper reporter in the novel, Carol is "CID's most glamorous officer" (313). However, her colleague Kevin Mathews disagrees, saying she is "'totally bloody ruthless. She wants to go all the way, that one, and she'd drop me in it soon as look at me if she thought it would take her a rung up the ladder'" (313).

It is true that Carol is ambitious and, like other fictional and real-life policewomen before her, she is not always taken seriously by her peers. Even Hill is not willing to follow her ideas regarding the killer, Handy Andy. When she suggests to him that the killer could be a transvestite, and it is by dressing up as a woman that he gains the trust of his victims, Hill agrees that "it's a possibility," but he doesn't want to include it in the profile sent to the rest of the police because it is "only a bit of kite-flying" (323). Hill's own desire to be in control and make the important decisions makes him at this point similar to the more close-minded Brad-field police.

Stylistically, *The Mermaids Singing* is also a very different type of police procedural, far more akin to a horror story. With the use of the killer's first person narrative diary, McDermid is able, as noted, to give us gruesome details of the tortures used, which causes the tension to mount. Some readers of detective fiction have found these details too disturbing and skipped these portions of the novel. This is a mistake, since without these diary extracts, we cannot fully know the killer and cannot understand his similarities to Hill. Stylistically, too, McDermid continues to celebrate language in clever similes: "Popeye's going around with a face like a melted wellie" (131) and unusual imagery: "Cross stopped momentarily, with the slightly baffled air of a dog who can hear the fly but can't see it" (43). Hill's use of slang when he profiles the killer can be criticized, however. His report to the police does not sound formal enough or even technical enough:

> He believes he's absolutely justified; he thinks that in his crimes, all he is doing is actually committing the actions that everybody else wants to but lacks the bottle for. He has a big chip on his shoulder and feels that the world has conspired against him; how come, since he's so bright and talented, he's not running the company instead of doing this poxy job?" [282].

The use of the phrase "lacks the bottle" and "chip on his shoulder" and the word "poxy" all seem to be too informal for a written report by someone who is a doctor. On the other hand, McDermid's informal style serves her well when it comes to dialogue, and her characters speak convincingly, including in the use of the odd swear word.

The ending of *The Mermaids Singing* also combines aspects of the detective genre with that of the horror. Hill's capture, torture, and subsequent killing of the murderer suggests an ending akin to that in Grafton's *A Is for Alibi*, and like Kinsey, Hill is wracked with guilt which continues into *Wire in the Blood*. However, unlike Kinsey, Hill continues to be damaged sexually since Angelica was to be his savior and cure.

In *The Wire in the Blood*, McDermid's second book in this series, she continues to create innovations, especially in the plot. Two departures from the normal detective novel are apparent: in her telling the reader who the villain is quite early in the story, so that this book is clearly not a whodunit but a "whydunit" and a "howdunit," and in her killing of one of the key characters. This last is particularly interesting and unusual, since the detective novel is a genre which usually depicts clear-cut good and bad characters, with good main characters never dying.

Jacko Vance, the villain of the novel, is plausibly drawn as an important media star who was once a top athlete who lost the use of his arm in a heroic rescue of a truck driver whose vehicle had been involved in a multiple pile up on a foggy highway. Vance is a likely serial killer having had a poor childhood, having been rebuffed by his fiancée after the accident and, above all, being a total control freak. As we learn not only why Vance commits the murders but how in gruesome graphic detail like in *The Mermaid's Singing*, we are drawn into a world of horror and violence. McDermid doesn't shy away from violence, unlike Patricia Cornwell who, to quote one fan and up-and-coming writer of detective fiction, "is always in the middle of gruesome, horrible crimes, yet takes on this 'Oh the humanity' attitude and doesn't really delve into the violence. She backs off very quickly from anything that might offend the grandmothers and Baptist churchgoers who make up a great deal of her fan base" (Slaughter).

The death of Shaz, the brilliant profiler of whom Hill says, "She was driven, her need burning inside her and consuming any trace of frivolity" (*The Wire in the Blood* 52), is a compelling tour de force on the part of McDermid. To build up such a sympathetic, intelligent character, and then have her die basically because she acted in a way that most ambitious women might well have acted is powerful plot manipulation. When Shaz discovers that there is a cluster of girls all of whom were in the vicinity of Jacko Vance the day before they disappeared, carrying only their best outfit with them, it is understandable that her instinct is to tell her teammates of her possible discovery of a serial killer, albeit a very famous one. Only when the group mocks her idea and makes her feel stupid, does she foolishly decide to confront the man herself. Her demise with the message "hear no evil, speak no evil, see no evil" is graphically described: "Then his prosthetic thumb was over her eyeball, pushing down and out, rending muscles, ripping the hollow globe free from its moorings. The scream was only inside Shaz's head. But it was loud enough to carry her over into blessed unconsciousness" (200).

The two themes of the efficacy of justice and police efficiency which are apparent in the other authors' novels are also much in evidence in this latest McDermid series. Since the murderer is killed by Hill at the end of *The Mermaids Singing*, there is no trial or traditional justice. At the end of *The Wire in the Blood*, justice also is not served, since we are left with the idea that because the killer is so clever and rich, he will get away with the crime. His fame and attendant wealth will enable him to buy a witness who will swear that the vise which mutilated the arms of his victims was not bought many years ago, effectively ruining the prosecution's strategy.

The efficiency, or more accurately inefficiency, of the police and their relationship with Hill's group is also examined at length. In *The Mermaids Singing*, the police are shown in many lights, nearly all of them bad. Carol Jordan's immediate superior, Tom Cross, nicknamed "Popeye," is the stereotypical loud-mouthed, chauvinistic old-fashioned P.C.

Plod whom Carol classes as a "Neanderthal" (13). His immediate boss, the assistant commissioner, John Brandon, is at first sight far more willing to take advice from the experts and be open-minded about the crime solving; however, even he is not above a little illegal breaking and entering of the suspect's house to see if he can find any clues. Hence, when Cross later is found planting evidence in this suspect's house in a desperate attempt to gain a conviction, Brandon is both furious at his action but also a little guilty that he too behaved illegally.

The problems which women face at the hands of their male colleagues are examined most fully in *The Wire in the Blood*. Both Shaz and Di Earnshaw die because they are not privy to the male camaraderie, not "one of the boys." Shaz is embarrassed by the mockery which she receives from her male peers and feels she has to prove her theories on her own, which leads to her horrific death. Di, meanwhile, is not told by her colleague with whom she is watching the arsonist, that he is going to go to a club, and so finds herself alone without backup and dies at the hands of the arsonist. When Carol asks one of the team why Taylor did not tell Di where he was going, he replies, "'He wouldn't have told Di. Not one of the lads, was she?'" Carol's dismayed response to this is: "'You're telling me I've lost one of my officers because of traditional Yorkshire male chauvinism?'" (447). Not only do the women find trouble at the hands of the male police, so do Hill's group, in particular, Simon. When Shaz is killed, Simon's prints on her French windows coupled with his having asked her out on a date, make him a primary suspect in the eyes of the local police. No matter how many times they are told that he is not the killer type and that Vance is a far more likely candidate, they will not budge in their views. When they finally interview Jacko Vance, they are overawed by his smooth performance and tell Hill that he can't possibly be guilty. Hill responds: "The blindness of the human animal never ceased to amaze him. It wasn't that Wharton was a stupid man; he was simply, in spite of years in the police service, conditioned to the belief that men like Jacko Vance could not be violent criminals" (300). Because of this lack of vision on the part of the police, we are made to feel frightened that Vance will not get his "just deserts" because he will be able to manipulate the system to his best advantage, and there will be many on the force itself who, even when faced with irrefutable evidence to the contrary, will not want to believe that a famous person could be anything other than good.

McDermid's *A Place of Execution* heralds yet another change of style and plot. In this book she is not exploring the mind of the serial killer but the way the police tackle a murder hunt. The plot concerns the disappearance of Alison Carter from her home in a tiny isolated hamlet in Scardale, Derbyshire, and the writing of a book about this crime by Catherine Heathcote who was a schoolgirl in Buxton at the time of the crime. Alison's disappearance from Scardale Manor comes at the same time as the infamous Moors murders of 1963, and there is some question as to whether or not her disappearance might be linked to those of John Kilbride and Pauline Reade. The policeman in charge of the investigation is George Bennett, a newly promoted detective inspector who heads the search because his chief inspector is incapacitated with a broken ankle. Bennett is portrayed in a most sympathetic way, which is very different from the portrayal of the police in McDermid's other works. Throughout the investigation both Bennett and his second in command, DS Clouth, are shown as thorough, painstaking and sensitive. Indeed it is these very qualities which allow the villagers to perpetrate the amazing crime they do.

The first part of the book is a rather slow read, albeit very interesting in its detailing of the interviews of the villagers by the police and the depiction of the 1960s lifestyle. McDermid's attention to detail makes this early part of the book a fascinating portrait of the police methods of the time. In comparison to the onslaught of horrors in *The Mermaids Singing* and *The Wire in the Grass*, *A Place of Execution* is tame and might not appeal to those who are expecting McDermid to continue in the detective-horror genre; however, those readers who reject the novel and do not read to the end will miss a book with a superb twist along the lines of Agatha Christie's famous *Murder on the Orient Express*.

After many red herrings, Alison's disappearance is revealed not to be linked to the crimes of Myra Hindley and Ian Brady but as the work of her stepfather, Philip Hawkin. Hawkin, who has been sexually molesting Alison ever since his marriage to her mother, Ruth, a year previously, has taken several photographs of himself and the girl performing unnatural acts, and at one point in the investigation these photos, along with a gun of Hawkin's wrapped in his shirt stained with Alison's blood, are found by the police. Although Alison's body is never found, the police are able to get a conviction of Hawkin based on the precedent of two earlier crimes where a body was never discovered. He is sentenced to death and hanged.

Is this all there is to the novel? Surely not! Catherine Heathcote is just about to get her book of the crime published when she meets Bennett's grown-up son and learns that he is going to marry a friend of hers, Helen. Amazingly enough Helen's sister, Janis, lives in Scardale Manor. George Bennett agrees to visit the sister and the village, which he thought he'd never see again. Having met Janis, he writes an extraordinary letter to Catherine, telling her that she must halt the publication of the novel since it is based on lies, and then suffers a massive heart attack. Reading the letter and having visited a still-unconscious Bennett in the hospital, Catherine decides to see Janis herself and discover what could possibly have caused Bennett's reaction.

She is horrified by the sight of Janis and decides to ask the retired Clough to return to the manor and confront Janis for the true story of Alison's disappearance. The truth is that Alison never died but is, in fact, Janis. In a superb complex ending to the novel, McDermid reveals what the villagers of Scardale had learned from other photos that Hawkin had taken. The man had been a sadistic monster who had preyed not only on Alison, but also on all the children in the village, sexually seducing them and terrifying them out of their childhood innocence. At first the men in the village had wanted to arrange a farming "accident" to befall Hawkin, but knowing that, since he is the squire of the village, this would arouse the suspicions of the police, they decided to perpetrate an amazingly complicated crime. Alison, who was in fact pregnant with Helen, would "disappear" to her relatives in Sheffield. The villagers would fabricate a crime scene in a little known disused mine on the moors and plant evidence, which could be found by the police. They would only leave the photos of Alison, which were horrendous enough for a definite conviction of Hawkin on a rape charge and would persuade the sensitive Bennett and Clough that Hawkin was a monster who, even without Alison's body, was deserving of death. They succeeded.

Thirty years later, Clough and Catherine, viewing photos of the other village children which Alison/Janis had kept, could not but agree that the villagers had acted correctly:

> Catherine could not resist the conclusion that the villagers of
> Scardale had had right on their side when they turned their sleepy
> backwater into a place of execution. They had known that nothing but
> death would stop Hawkin and save the other children he would lure
> into his grasp. Even sending their own children away would not have
> prevented him from continuing. He would have found other children
> to destroy; he had both the power and the money to do what he

would with witnesses who would not be believed even if they bring themselves to speak [400].

Hence, with the ending of this novel, McDermid returns to the ending of *Wire in the Grass* and the problem of the rich and powerful being able to twist the law to their own advantage. By making the villagers successful in their entrapment of Hawkin, we feel that justice has been served in *A Place of Execution* just as it was all those years ago in *Murder on the Orient Express*.

Thus, McDermid continues to move the detective novel in innovative directions. Very aware of the changes which have occurred in British policing in the last 20 years, her different series reflect those changes and the ever more violent Britain of today. In addition, as she told Barry Forshaw, "'The best of contemporary crime fiction reflects an awareness that there are other crimes than the ones codified in the law'" (13). Her move to an examination of the serial killer answers the desires of those readers who are fascinated by the highly intelligent professional man who can commit sadistic crimes and possibly get away with them, and shifts the detective story into the realm of the horror genre. At the same time, her ground-breaking treatment of both protagonist and victim adds a new dimension to the novel's conventions.

Works Cited

McDermid, Val. *Blue Genes*. New York: Scribner, 1996.
____. *Booked for Murder*. London: The Women's Press, 1996.
____. *Clean Break*. New York: Scribner, 1995.
____. *Common Murder*. London: The Women's Press, 1989.
____. *Crack Down*. New York: Scribner, 1994.
____. *Dead Beat*. London: Gollancz, 1992.
____. *Final Edition*. London: The Women's Press, 1991.
____. *Kickback*. New York: St. Martin's Press, 1993.
____. *The Mermaids Singing*. New York: Harper, 1995.
____. Personal e-mail interview October 13, 1998.
____. *A Place of Execution*. London: Minotaur Books, 2000.
____. *Report for Murder*. New York: St Martin's Press, 1987.
____. *Star Struck*. London: Collins, 1998.
____. *A Suitable Job for a Woman*. London: HarperCollins, 1995.
____. *Union Jack*. Sutton: Severn House, 1993.
____. *The Wire in the Blood*. London: HarperCollins, 1997.

Chapter Five

Joan Smith

Since the changes the feminist movement brought to British society by the early 1980s were significant, it is not surprising that all the authors examined in this book and their female protagonists have been affected to a greater or lesser extent by feminism. One author in particular has chosen to have as her main character an amateur detective who is also a professor of English and an avowed feminist. Joan Smith, whose first novel appeared in 1987, has a very different protagonist than Liza Cody's Anna Lee. While Anna is beset by all the males in her life and victimized constantly, Professor Loretta Lawson, Smith's protagonist, is a strong woman, able to hold her own both in the workplace and in her private life. Smith's novels straddle the two subgenres of detective fiction—the cozy and the hard-boiled. As Susan Leonardi claims, "The academic-woman-as-detective novel falls more easily into the British cozy than into the hard-boiled tradition, predictably enough, since these heroines are by profession more inclined to research and deduction than to chases, break-ins, and more than one brush with death per novel" (112). However, Smith herself, is similar to Paretsky in that she examines patriarchal institutions and in particular how power corrupts. In the hard-boiled tradition, Smith also challenges the traditional Golden Age view of justice, and as an amateur Loretta Lawson demonstrates that the forces of professional order are often inept or even corrupt.

As an English literature professor, Loretta's concerns involve numerous feminist topics which are linked to academia. A professor at London University, Loretta moves from Islington, London, to live in

Oxford where a number of her friends teach at the university. This move is important in that it makes Loretta constantly aware of the vast gulf which exists between universities, such as Oxford, and others such as her own London University. Although her friends in Oxford rarely make disparaging remarks about her degree or place of work, Loretta is quick to be on the defensive and justify her existence. In *What Men Say*, when she is asked by her friend, Bridget, to cover her courses while she is on maternity leave, Loretta says, "'I'm not an Oxbridge sort of person'" (101). Her remark implies that she would feel uncomfortable teaching at Oxford or Cambridge because she gained her undergraduate degree from Sussex University and her doctorate from Royal Holloway, London. Bridget inadvertently adds to Loretta's inferiority complex by recalling where she received her Ph.D. saying, "'I know—Egham. Very suburban'" (101). This use of the word suburban reinforces Loretta's ideas that London University, however good it might be considered, will never be equal in stature to Oxford or Cambridge. Because she has obviously felt inadequate at times, Loretta is particularly thrilled when her major critical work on Edith Wharton is very well-received, and she is invited to lecture at the University of California at Los Angeles. In Smith's last novel, Loretta receives a part-time lectureship in Oxford, so she is able to leave the London University job, which pleases her immensely.

Although an amateur, Loretta becomes involved in crimes in completely plausible ways. In *A Masculine Ending* she finds bloodied sheets in a friend's Paris apartment at which she is staying and realizes that the man she saw sleeping there earlier was probably dead, not asleep. In *Why Aren't They Screaming*, she is renting a cottage on the land of a woman when that woman is murdered. In *Don't Leave Me This Way*, an old friend, Sandra, is staying with Loretta when she mysteriously disappears only to be discovered a day later dead in a car wreck, while in *What Men Say*, a body is found in the barn of Loretta's friend, Bridget. Finally, in *Full Stop*, Loretta herself is the victim of harassment, and there really isn't a body until the very end of the novel. Hence, although Loretta is involved with the five deaths, the reader's credulity is not stretched beyond belief by an amateur protagonist who is continually "falling over corpses." In addition, most of the crimes take place at the beginning of a new academic term. Thus, initially Loretta has time to become embroiled in the situation and later makes time to continue to investigate.

Similar to other female protagonists like Kinsey Millhone, Loretta has a very detailed persona with which it is extremely easy to empathize. Here, clearly, is a strong woman who is successful at balancing her professional career demands, her love life and her friends. Although she is not a professional private investigator like Kinsey Millhone and Anna Lee, Loretta investigates crimes even as she deals with her family's demands and continues to have contact with her ex-husband and past lovers. However, though Loretta is involved with her family members in *A Masculine Ending*, they do not impinge at all in the later

Joan Smith

books. We do not feel that Loretta resembles V. I. Warshawski in her need to be continually solving her family's problems. In this first novel, Loretta travels to Kent to help her mother before her surgery the next day, but does give vent to her "feelings of irritation" (21) toward her sister. These are caused by the fact that, in Loretta's opinion, the sister, Jenny, could easily have helped with the mother but felt that "her role as a wife and mother excused her from anything she didn't feel like doing, and Mrs. Lawson happily went along with her" (21). Loretta often feels obliged to defend her chosen single state whether by reminding people to call her Ms. or Dr. Lawson rather than Miss or by making such remarks as, "for women, marriage was at best an irrelevance and at worst a shackle" (24).

Her ex-husband, John Tracey, an investigative reporter who works for the *Sunday Herald*, also plays an important part in Loretta's life. In *A Masculine Ending*, he is always trying to help her, telephoning people to gain information for Loretta, since she feels he is able to produce more plausible sounding excuses than she can, and is even trying to get back into bed with her. In *Why Aren't They Screaming*, he helps Loretta with research and is so obviously concerned about her safety that he makes the new lover, Robert, feel he should not become involved with her, at least at this time. In *Don't Leave Me This Way*, John does not appear in the novel, and Loretta is disconcerted to receive his news that he is going to marry a Greek girl half his age, possibly because she has been rather comfortable with their separation status and is not that pleased to learn that he has found someone to replace her. Later in *What Men Say*, John returns from Romania, never having married, still worrying about her and willing to help her.

In her relationships with other men, Loretta also follows the pattern of the new hard-boiled female detective since she does not appear to want a committed sole relationship, but she is not totally able to "love them and leave them" without a backward glance. She has sex once with the young Jamie Baird in *A Masculine Ending* and is upset when he rushes off the morning after the event, thinking that he either has found her ugly in the cold morning light or is, in fact, homosexual and has been trying to prove that he isn't with her. When she finally learns that he is the murderer, she makes a point of asking him whether he went to bed with her to gain information and is relieved when he admits that he could have left earlier in the evening and did not feel coerced by her. "Loretta closed her eyes and forced back tears. Was he telling the truth? Perhaps it didn't matter" (180).

In *Don't Leave Me This Way* her friend, Sandra, criticizes her relationship with her lover, Robert, saying that he reminds her of Loretta's ex-husband and appears bossy (15). "'It's the effect he has on you; ... when he's around you seem—subdued'" (16). Later on Loretta remembers these words, and when Robert argues with her about her proposed new detective fiction course, she is disturbed at his lack of sensitivity and leaves the restaurant and him in anger. Later when he sends her some photos taken on Christmas Day, she remembers with regret, "They had been getting on well that night,...—as well as they'd ever done, which wasn't saying much" (198). Loretta's relationships with males are similar to those of Susan Moody's Penny Wanawake and a reminder of how different women in the 1990s are from the timid Cordelia Grey, who wanted a relationship to resolve her problems with "Daddy and the landladies."

In *What Men Say*, Loretta is not involved with any man at the start of the novel, and many of her comments about her best friend Bridget's marriage and her rather 1950s-style relationship with her new husband clearly point to Loretta's own dislike of inequitable relationships and men who do not take feminist issues seriously. When Bridget says that Sam Becker wants to have their baby take his last name and she respects his feelings, Loretta thinks: "This, from a woman who had been outraged by her younger sister's decision to change her name when she got married the previous year, was more than [she] could bear" (8). At one point she talks to a mutual friend about Bridget's personality change since she married: "the way she's retreated into this ... this parody of the nuclear family.... It's as if, all these years, it was all second-best and she really wanted a husband—just like my *sister*. I thought we were different, I thought our generation—" (67). Loretta not only misses the old confiding Bridget but feels that a relationship with a man should not alter the fundamental woman, should not be one of need. Later in the novel, Loretta reinforces her difference from Bridget when she has a brief relationship with Christopher Cisar, and, as with Robert, she is able to thoroughly enjoy the sex without becoming emotionally involved.

This aspect of being able to enjoy a sexual, albeit short, relationship with a man makes Loretta closer in temperament to V.I., Kinsey, or Penny Wanawake than Kate Brannigan. At the very heart of these relationships is the notion that women, too, have physical appetites just like men and can enjoy them and assuage them without feeling a need for a long-term emotional commitment. At the very end of *What Men Say*, Smith reinforces the novel's feminist concerns for women in inequitable relationships by revealing the true nature of Sam Becker. Sam is an abuser of women and a man who uses S&M to enliven his relationships. Bridget reveals to Loretta that at one point early in their relationship he went "too far" with the S&M (234), and she broke up with him. At this point she has sex after a drunken party with the very married Stephen Kaplan, and when Sam begs her to continue their relationship and marry him at the very time she discovers she is pregnant by Stephen, she does what so many women before her have done and agrees, thinking that Sam will change his behavior. When Sam learns that the baby is not his, he reacts, as he has always done, with violence, and hits Bridget. Shortly after, she understands the full extent of his viciousness, which is worse even than hitting his wife, when he implicates her in his murder of his former lover, Paula. Loretta's horror when she discovers the full extent of Sam's perfidy becomes a comment on the ever-growing trend of wife abuse by well-educated men who society believes could never act "that way." Thus, Smith, like other authors such as Susan Moody and Minette Walters, uses her novels to indicate that violence in sexual relationships is a universal social problem, not an individual aberration.

Although it is implied that Loretta would never be so foolish as to marry a man like Sam Becker, in the workplace her relationships with her male colleagues, and some female ones, are shown as problematical, linked as they are to concerns for job parity and the need for professional respect. In *A Masculine Ending*, Loretta's first problem concerns her fellow members of *Fem Sap*, the international feminist literary criticism journal on whose editorial board she sits:

> A group of feminist literature teachers from universities in the United States, backed by a handful of French academics, had come up with the proposal that the editorial policy of *Fem Sap* should challenge the inherent sexism of French and Italian, two of the three languages in which the journal accepted contributions, by refusing to use masculine endings of any sort [3].

While her colleagues bicker about this issue and finally form a new group of their own, Loretta knows that on her return to her college at London University, she is also going to have to defend her feminist and radical views to the members of her department, most of whom are male. Here her problems are caused by her permanent fears that she will lose her job because of the educational cutbacks which always affect women before men since more women are part-timers or untenured. To counteract this fear, Loretta is shown as having written a considerable tome on Edith Wharton, as mentioned earlier, and then immediately starting on another on Charlotte Brontë. Interestingly her scholarship is well received in the United States but seems to gain little respect from her own department. In *What Men Say*, Loretta's department chairman wants all the faculty members to provide a description of each course they teach, the numbers of students who take the course, the degrees they obtain, and the "relevance of the subject in the light of current educational parameters" (134–5). Smith's description of what amounts to an attempt to make all educational courses useful to the business world and to eradicate what are considered esoteric or old-fashioned courses such as Chaucer, is a contemporary issue to which all academics can relate.

What is interesting regarding Loretta's problems at work and the feminist messages of the novels is the suggestion that, though Loretta may be criticizing the patriarchal institution which employs her, she also desperately wants to belong to it. As Sandra Tomc discusses in her article "Questing Women: The Feminist Mystery after Feminism," several women's crime stories published in the early 1990s depict a situation with a narrative that "highlights the virtues of submission and conformity" while aggressively critiquing patriarchy (47). With *Prime Suspect* we see Jane Tennison thrilled to be accepted by "the lads" at the end of the first novel, and Loretta too, despite criticizing her department chair, would love to be a tenured full professor, utterly accepted by all the "good old boys." As Marion Frank affirms, Bridget and Loretta are liberal feminists who "use their positions as lecturers and writers to gradually bring about change in society" (97); however, the key word is gradually.

While Loretta's relationships with men are filled with problems, those with her women friends are close and nurturing. Bridget Bennett, the most important one, appears in the first novel and again in *Why Aren't They Screaming,* where it is her friendship with Clara Wolstonecroft which enables her to find Loretta accommodation outside London after Loretta has been ill. In this novel, Bridget is described as always wanting to rescue her women friends from their problematical predicaments and help them with their love lives (3). Bridget is sorely missed by Loretta in the third novel when she is out of the country and unable to help her. However, in *What Men Say* Bridget's problems take center stage. From the first novel we learn that Loretta used to belong to a feminist group, with some of whose members she stays in touch. Although Bridget is her closest friend from those days, she also keeps in contact with Sally Wilkins who was also close to the fateful Sandra Neil, the victim in *Don't Leave Me This Way.* While the males in Loretta's life, especially her ex-husband, may mock her involvement with the group and with the editorial staff on *Fem Sap,* these women are the very people who help her solve every crime and act as her support system.

Unlike Val McDermid and Liza Cody, Smith does not examine white-collar crimes like fraud but always has a murder in her novels and usually follows the traditional formula of having a small group of possible suspects and more of a whodunit slant than a whydunit. However, the victims of the crimes are very different from one another. In *A Masculine Ending,* Hugh Puddephat is unveiled as a closet homosexual who marries into the aristocracy and encourages a female student to fall in love with him to hide his true nature. Sally Munt in her critical work *Murder By the Book? Feminism and the Crime Novel* describes Hugh as a "manipulative, egocentric, preying, pompous, unscrupulous, duplicitous, misogynistic, hypocritical, promiscuous, priapic pederast," whose gay male sexuality is blended with "anti-feminist, anti-social behaviour" (55). While it can be said that Hugh is a totally unattractive individual with almost no redeeming traits, we are still intrigued to discover who killed him and why. As Loretta learns more and more about him, we ascertain more about her character by her reactions to the information she learns about him. His ex-wife, Veronica, informs her of a plan Hugh put to her, that she would agree to have sex with both him and his male lover at a suitable time in the month, carry the baby to term, and then give it to both men so they could enjoy being parents. Loretta's horror is described:

> Loretta sat in appalled silence. Of all the things she had ever heard about Hugh Puddephat, this was unquestionably the worst. She had never encountered selfishness on such a grand scale. He must have been mad, she thought. And what about the lover, what would he have thought about it? Puddephat had apparently taken his acquiescence just as much for granted as Veronica's [166].

Smith continues to have unattractive victims in her other novels. Sandra in *Don't Leave Me This Way* is a moody, bad-tempered, lying, thieving, conniving adulterous woman for whom we feel, like Hugh, minimal sorrow when she is dead. Smith does not change this victim pattern in *What Men Say*, where the murdered woman is a 19-year-old bank robber who has betrayed her fellow robbers to the police. Although Clara and Peggy, the victims of *Why Aren't They Screaming*, have numerous redeeming qualities, they both have major faults which make them acceptable as victims. Clara has deliberately agreed to have the peace camp on her land, antagonizing numerous people in the village as well as the members of the American air base. In addition, she has married a much younger man with whom she has a strange relationship. Peggy, meanwhile, is shown to be a convicted thief as well as having a problem marriage. Interestingly in *Full Stop*, there are two victims. The murdered man turns out to be Jamie, the murderer from *A Masculine Ending* who, we feel, deserves to die since he has become a drug dealer as well as the stalker of Loretta. However, the other victim, of course, is Loretta herself, who, in a major way, turns the idea of the victim in some way deserving her fate on its head.

Although Smith's depiction of the crimes and the victims in her novels harks back to more traditional detective fiction, similar to the other writers in this survey, she also takes a long hard critical look at the British police and the justice system in general. In an e-mail, Smith told me that "not trusting the traditional forces of law and order is central to the novels" (personal e-mail February 14, 2001). Thus, in every novel, she has some major criticism of the way the police handle investigations, their general ineptitude and their mishandling, especially of women witnesses. In *A Masculine Ending*, Loretta does not report the blood-soaked sheets and the disappearance of the corpse to the French police because she is afraid of their scorn and the likelihood that they won't believe her story. "The French authorities, famous for their orderly minds, might construe her vagueness as highly suspicious. And wasn't there some peculiarity of French law which said you were guilty until proved innocent?" (15). Later, at the end of the novel, she asks herself why she had set out to find the murderer:

> She supposed it had come about almost by accident, like the murder. In the first place, she hadn't been sure enough to go to the police—and she had had a pressing reason for going back to England in the shape of her mother's hysterectomy. Then the evidence had disappeared. By the time the body was discovered, she had been too afraid for her own skin to go to the police. It wasn't a sense of justice that had involved her in the investigation, it was straightforward guilt [185].

It is also Loretta's sense that justice will not be served if Jamie is arrested by the police, which causes her, like McDermid's Lindsay Gordon in *Final Edition*, to allow him time to escape. Her feeling that Hugh Puddephat deserved to die is sufficient reason to let his murderer go free. As she explained in the e-mail:

> [T]he unresolved endings in several of the books were deliberate, as well as a tease in terms of traditional expectations of the detective novel. In the UK, crime fiction was for a long time a right-wing and conservative form—eg Agatha Christie's rants against Bolshevism, and the way in which the social fabric is always repaired by the end of her novels—and I wanted to appropriate it as a radical form [February 14, 2001].

In *Why Aren't They Screaming*, the murderer also gets away with his crimes but not because Loretta feels justice is better served this way. Colin

Kendall-Cole successfully evades a jail term because of what and who he is. As a formerly successful solicitor, one of the upper-middle class, and presently a Conservative member of parliament, Colin is held in some awe by the local constabulary and even Scotland Yard. Conversely Peggy, whose last name is never given, is poor, ill-educated and a convicted shoplifter. Even if she could prove that Colin murdered Clara Wolstonecroft, who would believe her? She describes how she believes the police would react to her accusation of Colin:

> I'm a shoplifter, right? A thief! The only time the Old Bill's ever been interested in me was when they was arresting me!.... So when Clara's lying there dead and the only people in the house's me and a posh bloke like him [Colin], who're they gonna believe? [181].

Later, when Colin kills Peggy and steals the evidence which she had linking him to the illegal abortion of his girlfriend while he was at Oxford University, Loretta is fully aware that if she goes to the police at this juncture and accuses Colin, she, too, will not be believed and might even be in danger because he has more power and authority in this patriarchal society. Thus, Colin effectively gets away with not one murder but two, simply because he has the clout and charm to persuade the police that men "like him" just can't be murderers.

In *What Men Say*, Smith makes some particularly harsh criticisms of the police both as to their utterly insensitive dealings with the pregnant Bridget and about their complete ineptitude in solving the case. On several occasions, when the police wish to interview Bridget, Loretta is quick to remind them that she is pregnant, and they should not act so belligerently towards her. In a postscript to the novel, Loretta thanks John Tracey in a letter for all his investigating which has brought numerous witnesses to light who are willing to testify against Sam Becker and whose evidence should effect the release of Bridget from prison. The fact that she is incarcerated for several months due to the police's unwillingness to spend time or money on ascertaining the true facts of the case, reinforces the criticism of justice in Britain as inadequate. The old adage of "being thought innocent until proven guilty" is clearly not a truism any more. According to Marion Frank, "By leaving it unclear whether Bridget will be convicted of a murder she did not commit, the author conveys her message about the unfinished state of feminism" (106).

Smith's novels clearly examine some of the same feminist issues as those of the other novelists in this survey. However, these issues are not allowed to become tracts which the author is pushing down the readers' throats. Unlike Carolyn Heilbrun aka Amanda Cross's Kate Fansler, Loretta does not push her views as lectures from a soap box. Nor do we obviously have a feminist dilemma as the focus of a crime. Whereas Cross's books have changed radically from her prefeminist novel *In the Last Analysis* to her *Death in a Tenured Position* (*Death in the Faculty*, in Britain) and *The Puzzled Heart*, Smith's novels have grown in complexity but not in ways which antagonize the reader. As was pointed out at a Popular Culture Association conference by Dr. Nancy Barrieua, Cross communicates her views to the reader in ways which make us nervous: "Instead of ideas forming a backdrop for a well-constructed mystery, the mystery plot has become a thinly-disguised vehicle for feminist polemics." Indeed, Barrieua continues to say:

> I suppose this attitude—that a mystery novel can "sum up neatly" and didactically the concerns of a contemporary feminist—is what bothers me. Instead of applauding, I find myself annoyed, wondering, "Is this a mystery novel?" "Am I being entertained?" "And whom, pray tell, does Heilbrun expect to convert?" Certainly her opponents would not read beyond the first chapter. And even readers (like me) who largely agree with her politics must surely get bored and even offended by outright indoctrination [6].

Smith, despite the fact that her protagonist is an English professor facing many of the same problems as Kate Fansler, does not forget that her primary task is to use the detective novel to entertain.

Perhaps because Smith started writing after the feminist movement was fully established, her novels do not, like Heilbrun's, reflect her own growth as a feminist. In the Cross novels, we are keenly aware that the author is discussing feminist issues which pertain closely to her own position. While Cross had for years to hide the fact that she was writing detective fiction under a pseudonym for fear of censure at her place of work, Columbia University, this is not true of Smith. In addition, Cross is particularly vituperative about women professors being given posts as the "token female" because this was a situation in which she too had found herself. In *Death in a Tenured Position*, the major problems of Janet Mandelbaum are shown to be the patriarchal society which allows her brothers to belittle her academic achievements in the face of her lack of children, a university search committee which does not include even one woman, and, finally, a male graduate student who plays a prank on Janet which makes her look both incapable of holding her liquor and exposes her lesbianism. According to the article "Amanda Cross" by Steven R. Carter, "The crime in [*Death in a Tenured Position*] is not the act of an individual driven by personal motives; it is the spiritual harm done by ingrained social attitudes that need to be changed" (294). As Carter goes on to say, although Kate stays within patriarchal institutions, she can "recognize that the power structure does suppress women, and she is willing to bond with other women against this suppression" (295). Certainly *Death in a Tenured Position* is Heilbrun's strongest academic feminist novel, where she combines "classical and hard-boiled detective conventions as vehicles for an increasingly broad and wise social vision" (295). Although in later years, Heilbrun may have become overly didactic, her earlier works, certainly, were ground-breaking regarding the feminist movement.

Things have progressed since that time, however, and Joan Smith, a former journalist, has not had to face the same problems as Cross and approaches her feminist concerns with greater equanimity and less passion. She avoids the danger of making her novels more of a tract than a mystery by having the convoluted plot of the cozy and examining numerous issues which are not obviously gender-based. In both *A Masculine Ending* and *Don't Leave Me This Way*, Smith analyzes literary concerns, in particular those linked to English departments. In *A Masculine Ending*, the murder victim, Hugh Puddephat has written a book filled with innumerable quotations from American academics in the forefront of the deconstruction movement. The woman who lends Loretta the book says that she understands little of the arguments it contains, while Loretta dismisses the movement saying, "The very name of the movement offended her. She imagined the English departments of various American universities converted into huge breakers' yards in which was being dismantled the edifice of world literature" (46). Later in *Don't Leave Me This Way*, she discusses the formation of a new course on crime fiction with her boyfriend, Robert. While trying to explain to him that the reason so many women turn to writing crime fiction is that "the rules make them feel safe" (138), he asks her if by having such a course she is in effect comparing Agatha Christie to the Brontës (138). At this point Loretta sharply criticizes him saying, "It sounds to me like you're defending the canon—the idea that you can draw a line and say this is literature and everything else is rubbish" (139). Since this is Robert's belief and one which Loretta clearly decries, she leaves the restaurant soon after, knowing that they will never agree on this, among other topics. Because her own views on literature are fundamental to her very being, she also faces the fact that this relationship is doomed.

Another aspect of Smith's novels which is similar to Heilbrun's and rather different from that of most of the other authors in this survey, is her criticism of specific contemporary political issues. While the Cross novels critique such things as the Vietnam War and Watergate, *Why Aren't They Screaming* analyzes the morality of the Americans using British bases from which to fly and bomb Libya. In the novel, one of the women protests the existence of the base itself:

> 'Those blokes over there'—she gestured, presumably in the direction of the base—'if they can bomb one place we're not at war with, they can bomb another. I don't want my kid to die 'cause the Americans decide to attack Russia. They're welcome to their atom bombs and their missiles—if they like them so much why don't they keep them in America' [29].

Smith also examines the use of violence towards women who protest at such bases and the opinion of the general public toward them. As in McDermid's novel *Common Murder*, the women in *Why Aren't They Screaming* are disliked and feared by both the police and the local residents. After the local council evicts the women from their tents outside the base, Clara Wolstonecroft allows them to set up camp on her land close to the base, which causes half the village of Flitwell to stop speaking to her. Next, when the residents and some Americans from the base throw stones at the women and even try to set fire to their tents, the police say that they do not have enough men to guard the women, and there is nothing they can do to protect them. The women are considered by most men to be, in the words of the Conservative MP Colin Kendall-Cole, "misguided" and in need of "protecting from themselves" (57). In addition, their nuisance factor makes them fair game as victims of physical abuse.

Smith's latest Loretta Lawson novel, *Full Stop*, continues the examination of violence towards women in a highly charged, fast-paced style with Loretta in New York for a weekend. A great deal more suspenseful than her other books, the plot has Loretta staying at a woman friend's apartment on the Upper West Side and experiencing, first, several obscene telephone calls and then the fear that she is being followed. When Loretta informs the police of the phone calls, she is told to either call a counseling hot line, the Annoyance Call Bureau, which unfortunately is only manned Monday to Friday 9 A.M. to 4 P.M., or the telephone company. The policeman tells her they just don't have the manpower to help and implies that unless a real crime has been committed, they aren't interested. Loretta's immediate response is to feel utterly rejected. Later she recounts the event to her ex-husband, and her feeling is reinforced as he, too, does not take her plight seriously and tells her, "'You have got an unusually vivid imagination ... and maybe you're ... not exactly *imagining* things. Jumping to the wrong conclusion. You're an attractive woman'" (84).

John goes on to recall a situation which happened ten years previously in Rhodes when she accused a waiter of touching her breast, and he, John, was mortified by the whole event.

This verbal violence from the obscene caller followed by the lack of sympathy and understanding from John shows the type of abnegation which is prevalent in women's relationships with men. However much Loretta may persuade herself that she is really in no danger because obscene callers are usually timid men, not prone to violence, the fact that she is in a strange city, noted for its high crime rate, fills her with a sense of not being able to control her situation. As she says, "A resigned acceptance to crime seemed to be woven into the fabric of everyday life in New York, so much so that even the TV weather forecast she had watched before leaving Toni's flat was squeezed between live news reports from a siege somewhere in the East Village" (*Full Stop* 109). Typically when she finally does discover who the telephone caller is and tells him that she knows all about him, he pretends that he is just an actor trying to get into his part and that she has taken his harmless prank in totally the wrong way. "'I was rehearsing, you were helping. You've heard of the Method. I have to get into a part, really live it'" (184). Later she fires this accusation at him: "'You really like manipulating people, don't you? This isn't about sex, it's about power.'" His rejoinder is "'Wow. A feminist'" (184). Thus, the implication is that feminists are humorless and antimen.

Because this last book does not follow the usual mystery format of having a murder victim early on in the plot, Smith is able to make the reader analyze and empathize with Loretta as victim and enjoy what the critics have called "'a chilling story about pursuit, about being alone in a strange city where every news bulletin reports another violent crime, about the fine line between danger and paranoia'" (book jacket).

Smith's book *Misogynies* is nonfiction, but it is relevant to this survey for the light it casts on her attitudes in all her novels. The book examines misogynistic attitudes throughout time and is a clear statement of Smith's most deeply felt feminist beliefs. Whereas in her detective fiction she does not want to preach, in this work she can give full rein to her feelings of anger and bitterness against the treatment women have suffered. In her introduction, Smith states that the starting point for the book was her own work as a journalist on the Yorkshire Ripper case. Sent to interview George Oldfield, who was head of the West Yorkshire police squad investigating the case, she was "dismayed by his masculine bluster ... and doubted the police's strongly held conviction that the murderer's prime target was prostitutes" (xv). The police's horrific ineptitude in solving the case quickly led to numerous murders which could have been avoided. Peter Sutcliffe was interviewed not once but nine times, in connection with evidence concerning the murders, and afterward the only excuse that Ronald Gregory, the Chief Constable of the West Yorkshire police force throughout the time of the murders, could make was to blame his force's inefficiency on chaos in their filing system, which had caused many of the police to think they were interviewing Sutcliffe for the very first time (119). What Smith goes on to prove in *Misogynies* is that the police's attitude regarding Sutcliffe's victims was, in fact, the cause for their lack of insight into the murder. Their labeling of some of his early victims as prostitutes, even though they were women who simply went for a drink at the pub without their husbands, caused them not to step up the hunt until an "innocent" 16-year-old middle-class girl, victim number five, was killed. Smith claims, concerning the police in the Yorkshire Ripper case and in history throughout the ages, it is men's misogynistic attitudes which cause an individual man to behave horrifically and other men not to admit that such behavior is vile:

> Peter Sutcliffe was always different, but not by a wide margin: the world is full of men who beat their wives, destroy their self-respect, treat them like dirt. They do it because they hate and despise women, because they are disgusted by them, because they need to prove to themselves and their friends that they are real men [150].

Smith fears our very culture "is not simply sexist but *occasionally lethal* for women" (xvi). As she claims, "Misogyny wears many guises, reveals itself in different forms which are dictated by class, wealth, education, race, religion and other factors, but its chief characteristic is its pervasiveness. So powerful is it that society is organized along lines which sanction the separation of the sexes to an extraordinary degree" (xvii).

By reading Smith's detective fiction in the context of *Misogynies*, we learn how her deeply felt concerns with social inequities, especially those toward women, make her another author who is shifting the detective genre from the optimism of the conventional earlier fiction, where crime was shown as an aberration of an individual, to the bleakness of a much more inherent social plague. As Margaret Kinsman says, Smith is noteworthy because of her "ability to establish a sense of menace and danger without the use of excessive or graphic violence" (940). Her nonfiction work aside, Smith tempers the earlier feminist concerns present in Heilbrun's novels and blends social criticism with a more entertaining plot, since she does not feel the need to be as didactic.

Works Cited

Smith, Joan. *Clouds of Deceit*. London: Faber, 1985.

____. *Different for Girls*. London: Vintage, 1997.

____. *Don't Leave Me This Way*. New York: Charles Scribner's Sons, 1990.

____. *Full Stop*. New York: Fawcett Columbine, 1995.

____. *Hungry for You*. London: Chatto & Windus, 1996.

____. *A Masculine Ending*. New York: Charles Scribner's Sons, 1987.

____. *Misogynies*. London: Faber & Faber, 1989.

____. *What Men Say*. London: Chatto & Windus, 1993.

____. *Why Aren't They Screaming?* New York: Charles Scribner's Sons, 1988.

Chapter Six

Susan Moody

Of all the protagonists critiqued in this book, perhaps the one who is most different from her American counterparts is Susan Moody's black character, Penny Wanawake. The differences in her portrayal are caused not only by societal dissimilarities between the United States and England, but predominantly by the fact that Moody herself is white. Most of the blacks in Britain came either from the Caribbean at the end of World War II or from former colonies in Africa at other times, and although some of the Caribbean blacks were the descendants of former slaves, the memories of slavery do not give rise to perennial issues as they do in the United States. In addition, since Moody is white, she does not write with the empathy towards her protagonist's problems concerning race and color that authors like Barbara Neely, Valerie Wilson Wesley and Grace Edwards do, to name but a few African-American authors. Obviously there is a greater involvement when a black author writes about race issues, as we see in Neely's books when Blanche talks about race and color discrepancies; however, in the Penny series this involvement is apparent when Moody deals with the issues of class and colonialism. In her novels Moody moves the cozy to a more questioning genre without losing the intricacies of the old-fashioned convoluted plot. She, therefore, will appeal to readers who still want a mystery, a "whodunit," while also attracting readers who want more social commentary in their detective fiction.

The daughter of Lady Helena Hurley and Dr. Benjamin Wanawake, and granddaughter of Lord Drumnadrochet, Penny Wanawake fits in

Susan Moody

well in the tradition of aristo-cratic amateur sleuth. Penny finished her education with a year in Switzerland, a year at the Sorbonne and a year at Stanford; and at six feet tall and weighing 126 pounds, she is strong as well as intelligent and beautiful. She combines her detection with fast-paced action reminiscent of the James Bond novels and is defi-nitely a larger-than-life hero-ine, richer, sexier and prettier than anyone could really be. She becomes sexually involved with at least one good-look-ing male in every book in the series and also wins our admi-ration for her tough-talking, self-confident ability to over-come even the roughest of sit-uation. However, Penny is not the conventional protagonist for one main reason—she is Britain's first black amateur detective, with skin like oil and hair braided in cornrows. Her choice steady boyfriend, Barnaby Midas, shares the same sympathies, but goes much further in acting on them. South African Barnaby, educated at Eton and Oxford, is a white professional antiques dealer, cat burglar and Robin Hood. Having spent some time at Parkhurst Prison in England, he now runs a business which places hired help in the homes of the very rich and possibly famous. Once he has taken the time to check out the mansions, he steals jewelry and paintings and sends the proceeds to the starving millions in Africa. So far he hasn't been caught again, nor has he left the country for good on the proceeds, which is Penny's greatest fear. The fact that Penny has a white boyfriend led to Moody's books being banned in South Africa, and she told me this made her "extremely proud." When asked why she had chosen to have a black protagonist, Moody wrote to me and said:

Penny was always intended to break new ground, to say something political. Black women at the time were almost invisible in fiction, not just in crime fiction. I'd spent nearly 10 years in Tennessee in the 60's, and taken part in the civil rights movement, seen the Ku Klux Klan, even had a cross burned on my lawn and having grown up in liberal Europe, I was absolutely appalled [personal e-mail January 19, 1999].

However, even though Moody may have felt "appalled," her depiction of her protagonist clearly shows that she herself is not black. While she has a great deal of serious analysis of contemporary concerns in her detective novels, Moody does not focus on challenging the societal image of the black woman in the way Neely does. As Natalie Kaufman states in her article "A New Look at African American Domestic Work in Literature: Barbara Neely's Blanche White," "Neely chooses to imbue Blanche with clearly black physical features and to celebrate them, but Blanche is neither Mammy, Matriarch, Welfare Queen, nor Hot Momma" (8). In Neely's work, the issue of being very dark-skinned is seen as a major limitation both in the way white people perceive Blanche White and even the way other lighter-skinned blacks treat her. In the novel *Blanche among the Talented Tenth*, for example, Blanche mentions color as an issue numerous times just in the first chapter. As Blanche says: "She assumed there must be some black-black rich women in the country, but she'd never seen one; so she wasn't expecting to find her egg-plant-black self mirrored at Amber Cove" (10). As a black woman, Neely imbues her work with all the rejections she probably has felt herself. Since Moody is white, this is not relevant to her, and it is not so relevant to Penny either, who, after all, is particularly privileged, supported as she is by her father's important position as Senangaland's permanent ambassador to the United Nations and her mother's aristocratic background. Thus, although Moody does examine numerous societal ills, the tone of her books is very different from Neely's and other African-American female authors'. Interestingly enough, the reason why Moody stopped writing about Penny is because, with the emphasis on political correctness today, she felt many publishers would not be willing to publish books with a black protagonist written by a white author (personal e-mail January 19, 1999).

Penny Black, the first novel in the series introduces us to Penny and the murder of an old school friend, Marta Lund. Like V.I. Warshawski, many of Penny's cases begin at the request of a friend, and although she is very efficient, she often compares herself to fictional private investigators, claiming that she does not have the resources they have. Although Penny does at times show up the local police force as inefficient, she does not, like Loretta Lawson, spend a lot of time criticizing them. Both this novel and the one which follows, *Penny Wise*, are less overt in their social criticisms. Moody told me that she felt Penny "started out ... as something of a fantasy figure, [but] became more serious in subsequent books" (personal e-mail January 19, 1999). Barnaby Midas is described in all the books in increasing detail. We are told in *Penny Black* that Barnaby first met Penny when he was attempting to burgle her jewels from her apartment in Paris. In *Penny Wise* "She told him that his education was incomplete. She offered to complete it. She persuaded him to turn his considerable brain to the problems of the Third World. Like starvation. Like disease. Like death. The R.H. Domestic Agency was born, fronted by the impeccably antecedented Miss Ivory" (10). Barnaby continues to hone his talents as a cat burglar, robbing the homes of the wealthy to which Miss Ivory has sent staff. However, from his hauls, he keeps only a few works of art and the funds realized from the jewelry and antiques are sent, as mentioned, to all the deserving poor which Penny finds in Africa. Despite the fact that Barnaby may feel no guilt in robbing the rich, Penny obviously has some concerns about his playing Robin Hood since she finds it necessary to justify his actions in *Penny Black*, saying that the owners who were well insured did not suffer financially and often did not even notice the loss of a small, though valuable *objet d'art*.

Penny's relationship with Barnaby might appear unconventional to many readers but does follow the new tradition of the female sleuth as free agent, able to enjoy many sexual relationships just like a man does. Moody told me, "The original intention was that, like James Bond, Penny would engage a new sexual relationship in each book. However, AIDS caught up with us, and promiscuity was suddenly not an acceptable message, so I drastically reduced the 'sleaze factor!'" (personal e-mail January 19, 1999). However, in most of the books, as noted, Penny becomes involved with a good-looking male. In *Penny Black* it is Aaron Kimbell, a black private investigator hired by Marta's father to solve her murder. However, in *Penny Dreadful* it is the white Charles Yeoman, who, in fact, turns out to be the murderer. Whomever she turns to during the case, at the end of each novel either Barnaby rescues her in the nick of time, or she simply returns to him, and neither seems to feel that an explanation of her behavior is called for.

In her close relationship with both her parents, Penny is also very different from the American hard-boiled detectives of the1980s and those of Liza Cody and Joan Smith. In *Penny Wise* when she fears that her mother may have been murdered because she knew too much, she says, "'Mother ... you can spill ash all over the whole damn house if you want. Just don't get tangled up with whoever it is behind all this. Just don't get yourself killed for something you maybe saw and didn't tell'" (221). Similarly when her father is kidnapped in *Penny Pinching* and she rescues him, he manages to shoot the murderer and disable him. When Penny says it is lucky that her father is a good shot and that it was a good thing that his eye was in, he replies: "'That's right, sweetheart, ... But then it would have been. It's called the eye of love'" (228).

In her relationships with other women, or her lack of relationships, Penny is very different both from other female hard-boiled private investigators, and especially from such amateur sleuths as Neely's Blanche White or Grace Edward's Mali Anderson. Both these African American authors comment on the power of friendship between women and the feminist idea of sisterhood. Penny, meanwhile, although she has some female friends, enjoys no major close relationship with any woman, and in this respect, too, she resembles more the fantasy superwoman figure than the real-life V.I. Warshawski type.

In her use of a gun, Penny follows the cozy tradition, not the hard-boiled one. In *Penny Pinching*, Penny gives the explanation for why she does not like to use a gun. In Africa one time, she was attacked by three men one night in her tent and in self-defense she shot one of them. When the other two ran away, she decided, "If it was kill or be killed, better to die herself than take another life" (61). Like McDermid's Kate Brannigan, Penny defends herself quite effectively with kick boxing and feels a gun is unnecessary.

Moody's novels contain social criticism of institutions as well as individuals. She has claimed that although she wishes to make certain statements about issues, she "doesn't feel didactic about them, nor [does she] have any overt 'message' to impart" (Bailey 134). I would agree that for the most part she is not didactic, but there certainly is a clear message in all her works, even in the first one, *Penny Black*, where she has comments to make about many institutions. The right wing, Bible Belt, "holier than thou" group come under fire, for example, when Penny reveals why Senator Lund may have killed to avoid having Congress and his constituents discover that he was having an affair with a black girl young enough to be his daughter. This is reminiscent of the scandal with President Bill Clinton. Penny points out:

> If the senator *did* kill Marta, it'll be because he's scared shitless of being found out doing something ordinary and human, like screwing someone who's not his wife. The Silent Majority will pull him down and tear him apart if they find out, half of them because they're doing it too and know they shouldn't. The other half because they'd like to and haven't got the guts [271–272].

One of the issues which is analyzed in numerous books is that of the plight of the African people. Since Penny feels most strongly about her roots in Senangaland, she spends a considerable time in Africa documenting the famine, poverty and man-made disasters and bringing aid. She says of a three-week trip to the Sudan:

> She'd travelled across country, dodging roving bands of mercenaries and guerrillas, to distribute the supplies she'd brought with her from London: medicines, blankets, sacks of beans and rice, gasolene to power the jeeps. And watching men with nothing left but dignity wrap their families in grey rags and scratch them into the dry ungiving earth, she felt hopeless, cast-down, despairing. You could save ten lives, twenty, a hundred, even. But thousands died for every one saved. It was the death of children she couldn't handle [*Penny Saving* 8].

Hence, Penny is not simply a rich daughter of an African with a social conscience, she actually faces the dirt and squalor and puts her own life in jeopardy to bring aid.

However, Moody takes pains to make clear that the problems of Africa are complex ones and cannot all be blamed on colonialism. As she states in *Penny Pinching*, "[T]he whites could be blamed for exploitation, for greed, for the imposition of an alien culture and the desire for goods it spawned, but not for the lack of rain. Not for the way the desert shifted southwards every year. Not for everything" (95).

Penny Pinching is the novel which most closely examines the problems of the fictitious Senangaland which is representative of many of the poorer countries of the continent. In the novel, Penny's father is kidnapped along with his friend, Pilot Whitman. Pilot lived for many years in Senangaland and married a black woman while out there. From that union there was one son, Leo, who lived and another who died along with his mother in the house fire she had set. Later Pilot had an affair with another black woman and had a daughter, Susannah, who is the first murder victim. When Penny discovers the history of Pilot and the fact that Susannah has fallen in love with Leo, she immediately thinks that the murder is somehow linked to the past. Her ideas are reinforced when she also discovers that Whitman has a priceless collection of old Senangaland artifacts which the Senangan Minister for Arts, Nkasa, helped him smuggle out of the country and now wishes to have returned to help him win the upcoming presidential election. When the murderer is discovered to be a boyfriend of Susannah with no ties to her home country, we are reminded of one of the most essential characteristics of a cleverly constructed convoluted plot: that man is often forced to weave ever-increasing webs when he decides to kill.

Since Penny has an entree into the British upper class, there is also social satire in many of the novels. In *Penny Saving* not only is the upper-class attitude toward money mocked, but their lifestyle is also shown as "outmoded ... [dependent] on an outdated social structure" (367). One aspect of this lifestyle, which is ironically, yet also seriously, depicted as causing major problems, is the British nanny. According to Penny in this novel, "the loss of Empire and the slide in industrial output might well be attributable to habits acquired by the managerial classes in the nursery" (272). While Penny has cause to remember, usually fondly, many of the aphorisms taught her by her own nanny, Nanny Simpson, Fiona McIntosh's nanny, Nanny Campbell, is shown in her full horror as a bigoted, sexually repressed, and repressing, verbally abusive woman. In her younger years, she was responsible for the welfare of the boy, Gordon McIntosh, who became Dr. McIntosh. It is implied that the way she treated him may have led to his inability to form a satisfactory relationship with his wife, Katrina, or his daughters, Fiona and Dymphana. After Katrina flees the marriage to marry an attractive, loving, albeit womanizing South American, Dr. McIntosh refuses to let her have custody of the girls and abuses Fiona in an incestuous relationship. Nanny Campbell, continuing as nanny to the two young girls, poisons their minds as to the true nature of their mother and fails to protect Fiona from her father. Fiona, meanwhile, learning to equate sex with attention becomes ever more promiscuous as she grows older. Finally she realizes that sex can also be used to gain power and money through blackmail, and she begins the dangerous habits which lead to her eventual death by strangulation. Ironically it is through her own job as a nanny that

Fiona successfully makes a great deal of money, blackmailing the father of the child in her care after she has seduced him.

Ludovic Fairfax, the unwilling heir to Wrestebury in Norfolk, is likewise satirized in *Penny Saving* for his desperate attempts to keep up the house. Having decided to rent most of it out to a summer language school, he still doesn't have enough money to make essential repairs to the house. His love for Fiona McIntosh cannot lead to marriage since as he says: "'When I get married, it'll have to be to someone with lots of the stuff [money]. Jesus, it's like the Middle Ages. I've got to make an economically sound alliance. It's the only way I can retrieve the family fortunes'" (364). Although Penny sympathizes with his situation, she feels most strongly that "she wasn't even sure [one] could admire him for his struggle to fulfill ambitions that were so limited" (367). For Penny, money is a means to help other people, and although she is the first to admit she enjoys buying designer clothes and eating quails' eggs, she is equally at ease and able to cope in poverty-stricken African countries.

Moody also scrutinizes the type of school the rich go to and the value of the education they receive there. In the novel *Penny Dreadful*, Penny goes to a private boarding school in Canterbury as a favor to a friend, returning his cousin, schoolmaster Max Maunciple, to his apartment. While she is enjoying the end of term festivities, Max is murdered and the question is posed as to who would most benefit from his death. Since Max was a totally unpleasant and unscrupulous man, author of a series of novels which aimed to reveal the darkest secrets of the rich under a thin veneer of being fiction, there are many suspects. Once back at the scene, Penny discovers that the beautiful surroundings of the abbey school disguise the fact that many of the students are not gaining the superior education for which their parents are paying huge sums. Max himself was detested by one parent, Ken Sumnour, whose son was not tutored satisfactorily by Max, which led to his failing his A levels. As a result of his poor exam results, Jeremy was unable to go to university so joined the Rhodesian police force. Having been expelled from the force because of his drunkenness, he married a black woman and had numerous children. Ken continues to blame Max for Jeremy's failures and feels that the education the school is giving to his other son, James, is equally inadequate for the demands of the modern world. Another teacher at the school, poet-in-residence, Dominic Austen, author of numerous erotic poems, also demonstrates the inadequacy of the teaching staff. Hired to add creativity to the English department, Austen spends most of his time ogling the sixth-form girls and writing scurrilous verse. When he reads some of his poems to the parents at the end of term ceremonies, most are shocked, disgusted and angry that this man has been teaching their privileged offspring.

When it is finally revealed at the end of the novel that Max was murdered by Charles Yeoman, the brother of a girl who committed suicide after Max had seduced and then left her in America, we feel that revenge is sweet and justice has been served. We cannot help but sympathize with Penny when she allows Charles Yeoman to get away. When she questions her actions, Barnaby reminds her that "'The name's Wanawake, not God'" (231).

Despite what I have said earlier, Penny's color means that the issue of racism occasionally arises in these books, though it is far less in the foreground than it is in their American counterparts. Although the books mention that, despite her color, Penny has always been accepted by Britain's aristocracy, it is implied that it is not because the members are broad-minded but because her mother's ancient lineage is more powerful than prejudice. In many of the novels, references to Penny's blackness and the supposed inferiority of black people are shown as offensive. In *Penny Post* for instance, one of the main characters, Rupert, says he wants to marry the widow Emerald, who, like Penny, is black, and the murderer, Kate, says, "'You can't possibly marry her ... she's a Negro'" (384). Often Penny mocks bigoted attitudes by speaking in an exaggerated form. When justifying her efficiency to the less than efficient Detective Inspector Anthony Pritchard, she jokes: "'Honkie.... You just jealous cos we're such a colourful, fun-lovin' crowd with a natural sense of rhythm'" (396).

Male chauvinism is also an issue in these books, and it can be linked with racism. In *Penny Post*, Penny is approached by two male reporters in search of information about the widow, Lady Sartain:

> One of the men called to her. Much of his beer-belly was covered by a pale-blue V necked sweater with a pair of hockeysticks embroidered on it in gold.
> 'Hel-lo there,' he said. He used the sort of tones that are supposed to make a woman's blood leap in her veins. He was the sort of man who'd call her frigid if it didn't.
> Penny turned. 'Yeah?' Cold but polite. Just. 'Do you want something?'

'Depends what's on offer,' said Hockeysticks. He uncovered his teeth. They were tobacco stained. Hair grew out of his nose. What gives a slob like that the right to make suggestive remarks? [175].

Moody has been told by black women that they especially identify with passages like these in her books.

Although Moody has said that her later books became more serious than the earlier ones, it is not that there is more social criticism but that the topics criticized are more ground-breaking. For example in *Penny Royal*, Penny is describing how one of the characters, Drusilla, has used sex as a weapon. She justifies Drusilla's behavior: "However bright a woman might be, and whatever the feminists liked to pretend, in a patriarchal society it was still the best weapon. Born to be exposed on hillsides, clitorectomised, burned alive for not bringing enough dowry to a marriage, women often hadn't got a lot else going for them" (169). The very fact that she mentions female circumcision takes the book far beyond the usual boundaries of "escapist" detective fiction. By doing so, Moody is effectively saying no subject is outside the province of this fiction and that a genre which reaches millions of people, both male and female, might as well be used to increase people's awareness of the world.

The Penny Wanawake series certainly marks an intriguing departure from the usual British amateur detective. In her youth, color and vibrancy, Penny brings an element of "exotic adventure and fantasies of female derring-do in familiar locales" (Huntley 237). However, the books also make several pertinent and searching criticisms of societal inequities which make them far more than just escapist literature. Although Moody writes to some extent in the cozy tradition, she can better be described in Dorothy Davis's terms as a topical mystery writer, determined to turn "an escape fiction into an involved one" (74).

Moody's second series introduces another amateur sleuth, bridge-playing Cassandra Swann, possibly the most engaging sleuth of all those profiled in this work. The books are innovative not because of the convoluted whodunit plots, which are definitely reminiscent of Agatha Christie, but because of Cassie herself, whose complex character is slowly revealed from one novel to the next. Unlike other modern sleuths, Penny especially, Cassie is not slim, lithe and athletic; instead she is overweight and makes her living giving bridge lessons. She has had a difficult upbringing which continues to impact forcefully on her present life. Her mother, who gained a double first degree from Cambridge, was all set to have a career in law when she met and married handsome Harry Swann, a publican who owned a pub in the Hackney area of London. Sarah's father, a judge, and her sister, Polly, married to a rector, never reconciled themselves to this unfortunate marriage, and their relations with Harry, and later with Cassie, are horribly strained because of their feelings that Sarah married far beneath her. Still, the real traumas were the death of Cassie's mother when she was six, and the murder of her father when she was 11.

The last event is one which, naturally enough, like Kinsey Millhone's memories of her parents' car crash, continues to haunt Cassie from novel to novel. Like Kinsey, we learn about different aspects of Cassie as the series goes on, which makes her character development as interesting as the particular mystery. In the third book in the series, *King of Hearts*, she has the courage to search for the truth regarding the murder and discovers that it was not a random act of violence outside the pub, as had been the verdict of the police 20 years earlier, but in fact a killing planned by Harry's mistress, a horse trainer, who he had discovered was fixing horse races.

Another event which occurred when Cassie was 13 also has a lasting effect on her psychologically; this is the unexpected death of Gran, Harry's mother, with whom Cassie lived at the pub after Harry's death. Following Gran's death, Cassie was taken by Aunt Polly to live at the vicarage. Years later at her Uncle Sam's birthday party, Cassie recalls life at the vicarage as one with "this sense of imprisonment, of wings clipped and spontaneities stifled. Of enjoyment denied" (*King of Hearts* 182). Not only was her aunt Polly a stifling influence, but her cousins, Rose, Primula and Hyacinth, petite, unbelievably thin, unintelligent and conformist to a degree, also made life for the young Cassie a living hell.

Used as she was to the robust and unconventional life of a pub which was utterly working class, the 13-year-old Cassie, who spoke with the flat vowels of "Souf" London and already had a size 38D bust, could not fail to be the weed in the family of flowers at the vicarage. She remembers numerous occasions in the course of the novels, but perhaps the most pathetic is her arrival at the vicarage wearing her best dress:

> Her best dress. Why should she think of that now? Gran had taken her up West to buy it and they'd found something in C & A. Gran had loved it. 'You look a real treat in that,' she'd said. 'A real treat.'

> When Cassie had pulled it out of the plastic carrier bag in which
> she had packed her few possessions, Aunt Polly had fingered it with a
> hateful expression on her face which made Cassie want to be able to
> put her arms round Gran again and cry. 'But it's made of polyester,'
> her aunt had said [*Grand Slam* 106].

Not only is Cassie's polyester dress completely unacceptable in her new
lifestyle, but so too is her lack of grammar. She is quickly made aware
of the huge gulf which exists between classes in Britain.

Moody told me that the Cassie books "were conceived as a means
to look lightheartedly at different aspects of current British society, and
class is an issue which very much permeates the novels" (personal e-mail
March 25, 1999). In *Grand Slam*, we learn that for Cassie, "[t]he tug of
different values, working-class on the one hand, middle-class on the other,
was one which even now she had not yet fully resolved" (106). Because
of the change of circumstances which occurred at a very difficult age,
and because she was forced to turn her back on her working-class origins
both at home and at the boarding school to which she was sent, Cassie
finds in later years that she is often offended, even repulsed by the brash-
ness of working-class people. In *King of Hearts* when her father's lover,
Brigid Fraser, refers to a friend of Cassie's as "very NOSD ... Not Our
Sort Dear," Cassie's "egalitarian hackles lifted briefly then sank back
into place as she reminded herself that this crude piece of snobbery more
or less reflected her own feelings about Charlie" (177). On other occasions she is overtly critical of the rough diamond who is Charlie Quartermain. She despises his "non–BBC voice and ... lack of basic academic
qualifications" (27). In *Grand Slam* when he says to her, "'one day I'll
share that bed with you,'" her response is, "'No!' It came out like a shriek
of pain. Talk about bloody nightmares" (83). For all Charlie's help in
the crises of her life, and even though he brings her a degree of comfort
and a feeling of safety which she has not known since her father died,
Cassie at first rejects Charlie totally out of a sense of snobbishness and
an unreasonable fear that her friends might look down on her if she
dated him. In *Doubled in Spades*, she finally turns to Charlie for help with
solving the question of who is stalking her and ends up going to bed
with him. Although she has had quite a lot to drink, she does admit to
herself that she enjoyed the experience and certainly was not coerced.
However, she still has a problem admitting her feelings towards him:
"His voice came back to her, urgent but gentle, speaking words not in

the throes of passion but as he held her quietly in the safety of his huge embrace. 'I love you, I love you.' Over and over again. ... Oh, she thought. If only I loved him back'" (226).

Having been married once to a man, for whom at the end of the six years she felt only "amicable resignation," Cassie is in no hurry to get married again (*Death Takes a Hand* 206). She has a slightly jaundiced view of marriage: "Coping with the trivia of daily living was bad enough one on one [*sic*]: scuffed heels, stray hairs, crumbs on the table, dirty knickers. To choose voluntarily to assimilate someone else's trivia as well, made as much sense as booking into Norman Bates' motel" (*Grand Slam* 79). However, she enjoys a healthy sex life as, despite her own angst about her looks, she is obviously attractive to men. Both Charlie and her other boyfriend, Detective Inspector Paul Walsh, often tell her she is beautiful and sexy. Like McDermid's Kate, Cassie too has strongly held opinions on having children. In *King of Hearts* when the pregnant Primula regales her with descriptions of her ever-increasing bust size and early morning sickness, Cassie comments: "Despite the occasional weakness, at the moment the idea [of pregnancy] had all the charm of an invitation to share a cell with Hannibal Lecter" (129).

Although Cassie is very much her own woman, relishing her financial independence, single state and freedom to please herself, she is less aggressively a feminist than Smith's Loretta Lawson. For example in *Grand Slam* when an old friend of her father's calls her "sweetheart," Cassie says, "[she] knew she was supposed to feel indignation at this patronizing endearment which demeaned not just herself but all womankind. Hard to do—Jimmy was a nice old boy who intended no offence and would be mortified if challenged on it" (224). However, in the same novel she objects to Lord Wickham calling her "good girl" and contemplates what kind of husband he may have been:

> Had he been one of those husbands who used the small cruelties to undermine? Had he told her she was putting on weight, asked aloud if she was going through the menopause, openly wondered if she realized just how like her bloody mother she was getting? Stuff like that. Men's weapons, designed to humiliate a woman precisely because the answer is nearly always yes, however much she wishes it was not [131].

Moody may not be discussing women's rights in the workplace or certain other feminist issues, but she makes perspicacious remarks about marriage and its "small cruelties."

This second series of Moody's is thus far more than a set of amateur sleuth whodunits. Like the other authors in this survey, and as in the Penny series, Moody uses this series to comment on and criticize the numerous inequities which she sees in British society. Like American authors, Grafton and Paretsky, she examines not only feminist agenda issues but several political ones, although hers are naturally particular to Britain in the 1990s. Her concern with one such issue, the efficacy of the justice system, reflects the views of all the authors in this dissertation. However, Moody is far more specific in her criticism than the other authors as she places Cassie in her local prison as a teacher of bridge. There Cassie gains first hand experience of hardened criminals like Steve:

> He was young, vicious, angry. And completely without a conscience, any ability to recognize the needs of other people.... He was serving too short a sentence for persistent attacks on women. His last victim, a twenty-year-old who had foolishly accepted his offer of a drink in her local pub one Saturday night, had subsequently spent five months with her jaw wired up; her knife-slashed face had needed more than a hundred stitches just to keep it from falling off the bones beneath [*Grand Slam* 17].

Having first felt sorry for the inmates of Bellington Prison, as so many claimed that they were innocent and the victims of miscarriages of justice, Cassie is faced with the reality of the tough British criminals when she meets Steve. Later, when he is released after his short prison term, he continues to frighten her with harassing telephone calls in the middle of the night which make her forever scared that he might slash her face one dark night.

Although Steve is obviously an example of someone who deserved his prison term and should have probably received a far longer sentence, Cassie is fully aware of how society short changes so many people who end up taking to a life of crime:

> Society itself was unfair to these men. They were given no standards, taught nothing, abused by parents, employers, each other. The system ignored them until they finally took it on and then champed down with little or no interest in the precipitating factors, none whatsoever in seeing that they were given a chance to change their lives [29].

Later in the next novel, *King of Hearts*, she challenges her boyfriend, Paul's, views on all criminals being evil and thinks: "Nonetheless, villain and cop, what were they but two sides of the same coin? The disloyal thought crept into her head that if Walsh's attitudes were typical of the police as a whole, then the government's plans to arm them could be the first step on the road towards legalizing death squads" (117). Hence, Cassie is divided in her liberal "bleeding heart" attitude towards criminals because she has been personally exposed to the full horror of the pointless violence committed by so many young males in Britain.

Although Moody's novels all feature at least one murder, there is very little violence perpetrated by Cassie herself. Unlike Eva Wylie or Kate Brannigan, Cassie is not prepared to wrestle or kick-box her way out of tough situations, although she does become tougher as the series continues. In the first novel, *Death Takes a Hand*, she puts up little resistance to the villain, Felix Ryland. When Ryland manhandles her into a chair and winds tape across her mouth, she "mewed like a kitten, gazing up at him, pleading, begging" (287). In *Grand Slam*, she does make a dive for the gun which Chilcott, the murderer, had just dropped, but it is Paul Walsh and his force who overpower Chilcott and rescue her. In *King of Hearts*, although accompanied by the large presence of Charlie, she confronts Brigit with the truth and manages to get a confession out of her.

The villains of this latest series of Moody's are interesting because many are people who kill to prevent a "dark" secret from their past from being discovered, and the victim is often killed because they happened to be at the wrong place at the wrong time. In *Death Takes a Hand*, Sonia Wetherhead, despite her head being bashed in with an alabaster obelisk, is not the target of the crime, even though this was the original conclusion to which both Cassie and the police came. In fact it was the elderly colonel and Mrs. Plumpton who were the targets since she recognized Ryland as the criminal she once knew. In *Grand Slam*, similarly, Cassie is, in fact, the intended victim, but in the rain and dark, Chilcott kills Lady Portia Wykham in error. Finally in *King of Hearts*, far from being an innocent victim of husband abuse and hate mail, Dr. Vida Ray is the writer of all the poison-pen letters and the unbalanced murderer of her long-suffering husband.

This last villain is interesting since, once again, Moody uses an ethnic minority character in an unusual way. At the start of the novel, the Rays are depicted as the stereotypical Pakistani couple with the husband who does all the talking for the wife. Vida captures the interest of both Cassie and her half Sri Lankan friend, Natasha, because she has bruises on her neck and shoulder and what appears to be a cigarette burn on the back of her hand. Later when she confides in Natasha that she is receiving hate mail and has had dog feces and a burning rag pushed through her letter box, Natasha and Cassie are naturally worried. When the husband, Sammi, is found garroted outside the apartment of Jessica Tennant, who the police discover was having an affair with Sammi, Vida seems even more of the victim. However, Cassie discovers the truth about the psychotic murderer Vida and as she says, "Men had such a poor press these days, it wasn't difficult to convince people there was abuse when in fact there was none" (309). She also comments on how crime affects all the members of a family. "And looking at the faces of Vida's children, she had felt strongly that in this particular dysfunctional family, the victims were those left to carry their burdens with them into the future, rather than this woman, or the man she had killed" (301).

This idea of the children also becoming victims is developed most strongly in the novel *Doubled in Spades*. Here Moody tackles the highly emotive topic of child molestation by a close relative, in this case by a stepfather. Cassie's bridge partner, Naomi, is found dead in the trunk of her car, a supposed victim of suicide. Asked by her husband, John, to discover the truth as to why she should have taken her life, Cassie begins very quickly to suspect that Naomi's death might be murder. When a youngish man, Philip, appears, claiming to be Naomi's lover and that she was planning to run away with him, it looks even more certain that Naomi was murdered. Finally Naomi's illegitimate daughter Lucy arrives on the scene, saying that Naomi was going to change her will in her favor which would have badly affected John's already precarious business position. Everything points to John having murdered his wife and making the death look like suicide. However, Lucy tells Cassie a great many facts of her childhood including the horrific one that from her eighth birthday her adoptive father sexually molested her and was even now continuing to stalk her, demanding that she return to live with him since her adoptive mother had died. Lucy's description of the molestation is powerfully written:

> It hurt like hell. God how it hurt. I was pushing him off, trying to scream, but he put the pillow over my face. It seemed to go on for hours. I was bleeding, there was blood on the duvet cover. When he'd finished, he didn't look at me. He said that if I told Mummy, she would cry, she'd be so sad she might go away and leave us. He knew

that after that, I'd never do a thing which might leave the two of us together [*Doubled in Spades* 177].

As the plot unfolds, we learn that not only was Lucy a victim of child abuse, but so was Naomi. In fact, Lucy is the child of the rape of Naomi by her own stepfather. It is when Lucy tells her mother the full horror of her childhood which Naomi obviously thought had to be better than the baby remaining in a household where she herself was being molested, that Naomi takes drastic action. Driving to Northampton with Lucy, Naomi first murders the stepfather whom she hoped she would never see again, and then, after dropping off Lucy, drinks a quantity of whisky, takes pills and shuts herself in the trunk of her car. The knowledge that it was her graphic disclosure which caused her mother to act brings Lucy great feelings of guilt. However, the further knowledge that her own adoptive father, who turns out to be the man who has been stalking Cassie, is on his way to prison for a long term brings relief.

The fifth novel in the Cassie series, *Sacrifice Bid*, is possibly the weakest in terms of style. In this work, Moody appears to have forgotten Paretsky's advice that a detective novel must entertain rather than preach, and her tone is most didactic in places. The novel examines the death of a 72-year-old bridge player friend of Cassie's, Lotty Haden-White. Interspersed among the search for clues as to who could possibly have killed the seemingly innocuous Lotty, are major criticisms of society's unfeeling treatment of the elderly and the dilemma of putting the aged into homes. At one point Cassie goes to visit a friend of Lotty's, Bettina Maggs, whose son has put her in such a place and graphically describes the lounge in it:

> High-backed chairs upholstered in shiny uncomfortable-looking green leatherette were ranged all round the walls of the long room. A variety of elderly people sat or slumped or slept in these chairs, their faces vacant, their hands idle except in the case of a grey-haired lady who picked continuously at the sleeve of the overwashed pink cardigan she wore over a pea-green nylon blouse [92].

As she walks down the hall, Cassie asks a nurse where to find Mrs. Maggs's room and is told that "'Betty's in Number 89.'" When she queries that she thought her name was Bettina, the nurse replies "'Oh well, Betty's near enough.'" This reply causes Cassie to protest, "if someone's name was Bettina, then calling them Betty simply didn't do" (93).

Later still in this description of the home, Cassie paints a vivid picture of the treatment by the nurses of an old incontinent man as nothing short of cruel. "Cassie was appalled. Should she intervene, ask them what they were doing, why they were bullying an old man who clearly wasn't quite sure which day of the week was Tuesday?" (96). She decides "cravenly" to do nothing but reflects:

> A smell of loss permeated these antiseptic corridors. Loss of status. Loss of choice. Loss of a future. With shame, she recognized a conspiracy at work, society colluding to homogenize the elderly into a single group whose members felt nothing, were worth nothing, whose minds were as feeble as their bodies. And there was little she could do about it [94].

Although Moody has no problem focusing on many of life's "gritty" situations, most of her books avoid the danger of being treatises more suited to a sociology course. The main reason for this, of course, is her heroine, Cassie.

Cassie is easy to empathize with since she is so very far removed from the Godlike detective of traditional Golden Age mysteries and also very different from the glamorous Penny. Not only does she feel a victim due to the early death of her father, but her own inadequacies endear her to all readers who sometimes feel overwhelmed by life. Cassie is a haphazard housekeeper, incapable of keeping her house plants alive and especially incapable of sticking to a diet. Being constantly reminded by her cousins of the ugliness of being overweight, Cassie has a complex about her weight and size to which many readers can relate. Sometimes comic, sometimes pathetic, Cassie's comments on the difficulties of dieting pepper the novels. Like the cartoon cat, Garfield, Cassie is constantly standing with one foot off the bathroom scales in the vain hope that she will have lost some weight having starved on celery for a few weeks:

> Standing on the scales in the bathroom, she squinted down at the register. *What!* Surely some mistake. Bending closer, she watched the needle waver on either side of the impossible total. She stepped off, removed her pearl earrings and clipped her toenails then stepped back on again. Not a blind bit of difference. Despair gripped her. This really wasn't fair. All those weeks of celery, all those hours of abstinence, and for what? The hell with it all. She went downstairs and cooked eggs and bacon, found an English muffin at the back of the freezer

and toasted it, spread butter and jam generously over the two halves, and felt a kinder gentler woman for it [*King of Hearts* 161].

This wonderfully humorous portrayal of the tribulations of trying to be thin makes Cassie far more attractive to many readers than the jogging fitness fanatics of so many hard-boiled detective novels. As she so aptly says herself:

> There's something wrong with a society which asks half its members to aim for the impossible ... which sets the nagging thorn of inadequacy squarely on their weight, then sits back and lets them suffer, while at same time happily ignoring such faults as beer bellies and balding heads, varicose veins, and hair growing unchecked out of ears and noses.... No one asks men to go on diets: it wasn't fair [*Death Takes a Hand* 224].

Moody said, when asked about her depiction of Cassie's size as an issue:

> I wasn't talking about size as such. I am much more interested in the way women are socialized into perceiving themselves. To be a size 16 is to be overweight but not hugely so. Yet Cassie worries about this constantly. Had I made her much larger, I would have been into a different ball game, where health and mobility would have to become issues. My aim was to critique the way society insists that we are somehow not valuable if we don't look like stick insects. I wanted Cassie in Book 8 (Which I haven't written) to finally accept that she is beautiful, witty, brave and worthy, even if she bulges [Personal e-mail March 25, 1999].

In this second series, Susan Moody has created a detective who is unusual in ways which make her extremely attractive. Cassie's personality, along with the issues she criticizes, reflects the 1990s where women are coming to terms with the impossibility of being superwoman and are more determined to be content and accepting of themselves. Examining Cassie, it is easy to see that Moody is moving the female amateur detective in a very realistic direction. A far cry from Miss Marple, Cassie is a totally well-rounded individual who evinces many of the problems and dilemmas of women of today. She is far from perfect in her personal or professional life, which makes the reader easily able to identify with her. Although Moody is as effective at analyzing topical issues in this series as she was in the Penny series, it is in her characterization that she excels.

Works Cited

Moody, Susan. *Death Takes a Hand.* New York: Macmillan, 1994.

____. *Doubled in Spades.* New York: Scribner, 1996.

____. *Dummy Hand.* London: Headline, 1998.

____. *Falling Angel.* London: Hodder & Stoughton, 1998.

____. *Grand Slam.* New York: Simon & Schuster, 1995.

____. *House of Moons.* London: Hodder & Stoughton, 1993.

____. *Hush-a-bye.* London: Coronet, 1993.

____. *The Italian Garden.* London: Hodder & Stoughton, 1994.

____. *King of Hearts.* New York: Scribner, 1995.

____. *Misselthwaite.* London: Hodder & Stoughton, 1995.

____. *Penny Black.* Anstey, Leicestershire: F.A. Thorpe Ltd., 1984.

____. *Penny Dreadful.* New York: Fawcett Gold Medal, 1984.

____. *Penny Pinching.* New York: Fawcett Gold Medal, 1989.

____. *Penny Post.* Anstey, Leicestershire: F.A. Thorpe Ltd., 1987.

____. *Penny Royal.* New York: Fawcett Gold Medal, 1987.

____. *Penny Saving.* Anstey, Leicestershire: F.A. Thorpe Ltd., 1993.

____. *Penny Wise.* New York: Fawcett Gold Medal, 1988.

____. Personal e-mail interview January 19, 1999, and March 25, 1999.

____. *Playing with Fire.* London: Macdonald, 1990.

____. *Sacrifice Bid.* London: Headline, 1997.

____. *Takeout Double.* London: Headline, 1993.

Chapter Seven

New Voices

Which of today's authors I should include in this chapter was a difficult choice. In keeping with the rest of this survey, I picked writers who had won prizes, or who were recommended to me by my other authors, or who had already started a series with a female protagonist and were in some way original either in their setting, content or in the protagonist herself. In addition, I wanted to examine one of each kind of amateur, private investigator, and police officer so readers could see how these types of detectives have evolved. The following authors are both interesting and innovative.

Having read so many detective novels of the 1980s and early 1990s which depicted a clear social consciousness raising and overt criticism of the justice system in Britain, it was a surprise to read the first in a series by Judith Cutler published in 1995. *Dying Fall* is a strange mixture of the forward looking and the old-fashioned cozy. While the subject matter of this first novel in the series along with the location of the books is innovative, the protagonist, Sophie Rivers, is a traditional amateur, and the police are shown as kindly, gentle types in marked contrast to those of the other authors in this work.

Dying Fall concerns the death of a Pakistani student, Wajid, and the subsequent death of Sophie's friend, the musician George. Although certain undercurrents of tension between the Pakistani community and the white are mentioned, this is not a book about racism. At one point in the novel, Sophie is told by a group of Pakistani youths not to interfere in family matters, but all her other encounters with the Asian students

Judith Cutler

are friendly. When she becomes concerned about Manjit, a 16-year-old girl who appears to be suffering from sexual abuse by her brother, the girl is willing to take her advice and speak to a counselor, and her boyfriend's family happily talk to Sophie about the possible future marriage between the two young people despite their different religions.

In *Dying to Write*, the third book in the series, there is a brief mention of tension between black and Asian and white youths, but again Cutler does not analyze the reasons behind the tension, nor does she appear to be trying to raise our social consciousness about the situation. In an aside while Sophie is giving evidence at the police station, the woman police officer says, "[T]hey've just brought in a kid who got caught up in that affray down the Lozells Road. Asian girl, fourteen. Gang of skinheads found her on her own. Gang-bang, they call it. And she was too ashamed to go back home. Thought it would bring disgrace on her family" (418–9). The conversation continues with Sophie giving her evidence, and we learn nothing more about the girl or the skinhead violence. The lack of anger on the part of Sophie and the calm presentation of these facts suggest that this behavior is an ordinary feature of life in parts of Britain today. While African-Americans like Barbara Neely have protagonists who are bitter about racist behavior towards them, and other British authors, like Susan Moody, also voice dismay and anger at racism, in these early novels Cutler is markedly dispassionate in her portrayal of race relations in Britain in the mid–1990s.

Racial issues also appear in *Dying for Millions*, the fourth book in the series, but are also not in the foreground of the novel. Sophie is busy finding job opportunities for her students, including one of her Sikhs, Gurjit. Although Gurjit's father claims that he wants every opportunity for his daughter and is very modern in his attitude toward her, when she is late handing in one of her college assignments, he arbitrarily tells Sophie that Gurjit may no longer work one evening a week because he says so.

On another occasion Sophie takes a group of Asian students on a day trip:

> It's Ramadan! The poor little beggars won't be able to have lunch.
> Not even a hot drink when we get back to the minibus.
> 'So long as they don't expect us to fast with them,' Carl muttered.
> I bit my lip: how could anyone possibly eat in front of people who'd
> not eaten or drunk since daybreak? And shouldn't we have made some
> arrangement for them to pray [151].

Again, this is simply an aside in the plot and not shown as significant.

On the other hand, in the fifth book, *Dying for Power*, numerous racial issues are shown as important. In essence a great deal of the plot hinges on a group of white youths who are coloring their faces brown, dressing like Palestinian Muslims and targeting different ethnic groups for a variety of purposes. The ringleader is "getting Asian youths a bad name by attacking people. Fostering extreme—and therefore unacceptable—anti-women views in susceptible, ignorant youths who already hold a grudge against whites" (244). Another youth, a Muslim follower of the ringleader, criticizes Sophie in one of her classes for wearing a short skirt and tells her, "'There's to be a motion before the Students' Union tonight that, in future, classes must be segregated ... by race and gender'" (54).

The issue of women's dress comes up again later when an Afghanistani cab driver friend of Sophie comments on a skimpily dressed white woman. "'Asking for it! Asking to be raped. Now you can see why people want to see women veiled'" (67). An additional aspect of the treatment of women is also seen later in this same book when another friend of Sophie's discusses Afghanistan:

> [The Taliban] wish to confine women absolutely to the home. They
> are not allowed to work, to have any education: they've already sent
> women home from where they work, from schools and universities.
> Because no male doctor is permitted to touch a woman, they will be
> denied health care—for women, of course, cannot be doctors. Because
> women may not be seen in the street, children will not be taken to the
> doctor [69].

All the different racial issues and tensions come to a head at the end of the novel when we learn that the new female principal of Sophie's college is "[a] fully fledged partner to the British National Party, EFE:

England for Ever" (259) who is being groomed as a parliamentary candidate as she is in a position "to manipulate vulnerable black and Asian
people ... into doing things that will bring them into disrepute" (260).
Thus, although the earlier books in this series do not focus on racial
issues, this last one does and is certainly the most interesting to date.

Dying Fall, like the second novel, *Dying on Principle*, describes cyber
crime and, as such, this whole series is helping to move the detective
genre in a new direction. Wajid, the victim, works for the International
Commercial Bank inputting and retrieving information from their computers. During some of his personal hacking activities, he discovers a
drug ring and is killed by one of the main traffickers. In *Dying on Principle*, Sophie has become much more computer literate and learns of a
scam by the principals of her new college to gain money from nonexis-
tent students. In addition, the chief executive of the college, while wired
up to a computer, dies as he is watching pornographic material. His corpse
is described: "Mr. Blake was sitting in front of a state-of-the-art computer, wearing a virtual-reality headset and overalls from which emerged
clusters of wires, apparently connected to the rear of the headset via a
tube an inch and a half or so in diameter" (168). The varied possibili-
ties for cyber crime are clear in Cutler's books and add a dimension to
crime fiction which will be interesting to witness.

Although she may be computer literate, unlike most of the other
protagonists in this work, Sophie is not tough or sexually bold. She is
never called upon to defend herself with a gun or even by kick boxing,
and when she is attacked, she tends to run away. She leaves all the macho
moves to the police and is so far removed from Kate Brannigan that one
feels that one has slipped back in time to the gentle 1950s. In addition,
her amorous adventures are very few and those mostly unsuccessful. In
Dying on Principle she remembers with fondness a long-term relationship
she had with a Japanese man called Kenji, who kept rabbits in her house,
but when her faithful policeman friend, Detective Chief Inspector Chris
Groom, makes it quite clear that he'd like to sleep with her, she dithers
about the decision for ages. Finally they do get together, but the whole
event is rather unsatisfactory. After sex, Chris is being particularly quiet,
so Sophie asks him:

> 'Chris? What's wrong?'
> He muttered something.
> 'Guilt? Why guilt?'

Again no response.

'Chris, we're adults. Unattached. Came here of our own free will, both of us. Where's the guilt in that?'

For answer he shook his head; and all I could do was speculate on what his upbringing had done to him [226].

Here Sophie seems to be implying that it is Chris who is holding back, but later in *Dying to Write*, she talks about the problem of Chris's loving her: "We'd formed two sides of an eternal triangle in the spring, and I liked and respected him too much to want to stir up hopes I knew I couldn't fulfil" (63). It is clear from these words that Sophie is ambivalent about forming a relationship with Chris, but she is willing to sleep with more unsuitable men. In this same book we learn that she has just finished an affair with a married man and has a one-night stand with another married man, Hugh. With Hugh she was all set to have a long-term relationship but omitted to ask him the vital question, and he did not volunteer his marital status.

In *Dying for Millions*, Sophie's relationship with Chris still appears fairly unsatisfactory, even though on the one occasion she sleeps with him she says, "as bonks went, it was the most adventurous and satisfying I'd ever had with Chris" (178). Despite this, at the end of the novel, because he believes she will always love and protect her cousin Andy more than she would him, Chris hands her back all the little things she left at his place, and the implication is that the relationship is over.

In *Dying for Power*, Chris is now dating his colleague Diane Stephenson; however, in a drunken rage, she tells Sophie that Chris is "'fucking useless at fucking'" (50). At first Sophie does not seem so regretful that the relationship is over, stating, "There'd never been a future for us" (110). Chris is clearly not happy with Diane, however, and by the end of the book, she is off the scene, and Sophie and Chris are planning a getaway to her cousin Andy's farmhouse retreat. Both with Chris and her other relationships, Sophie does not have Loretta Lawson's insouciance or Penny Wanawake's "love 'em and leave 'em" attitude, so one feels that she resembles Anna Lee more than the 1990s women. According to Cutler, "Sophie likes sexy men, physically desirable.... However much she likes Chris, he simply doesn't turn her on" (personal e-mail February 7, 2000).

If Cutler's depiction of Sophie's rather puritan attitudes to numerous sexual partners remind us of earlier times, so too does the behavior of the police. Detective Chief Inspector Chris Groom and his sidekick Detective Sergeant Ian Dale are the nicest and most thoughtful policemen seen in all of the books mentioned in this work. In *Dying Fall*, after Sophie's first encounter with death, Wajid's, Ian takes her to the local police station by car after first giving her strong mints when she vomits. At the Rose Road station, he gives her coffee with extra sugar and is described: "He might have been a favorite uncle, in his worn sports jacket with archetypal leather patches" (17). Later in the novel not only Ian but also Chris are described as "avuncular" several times. As Sophie becomes more and more involved with different crimes, her relationship blossoms with both men. All of Chris's team refer to Sophie as "the gaffer's woman," and on numerous occasions Ian and his wife offer her shelter, a meal or a bed for the night. Not once does Cutler voice any criticism of the behavior of the police or their inefficiency, and in *Dying to Write* when one of the characters refers to the police as "filth," Sophie thinks "I try to be broad-minded, always, but words like 'filth' upset me. The only policeman I know at all well is not at all filth-like. He is eminently civilized in most respects" (28–29). In the same novel when the murderer, Toad, dies of an epileptic seizure, Chris and Ian feel guilty: "It was better for all if justice could be seen to be done, and neither anticipated a very favorable reaction from those in power when it became generally known that they had allowed an epileptic to drown" (412). Since there were major problems with the police force in Britain in the 1990s, Sophie's views of them seem unrealistic, naive and sugar-coated.

Indeed *Dying for Millions*, Cutler's fourth book in the series, does not show the police in as good a light as the earlier books. Diane Stephenson, who is the acting detective inspector while Chris Groom is taking a course, is portrayed as overly formal and insecure in her own abilities. Sergeant Ian Dale criticizes her saying, "'She's not a bad lass, young Diane Stephenson, but she hasn't Chris's clout with them upstairs. They tell her they can't afford something, she believes them. Chris would spend all night preparing a set of figures to prove they could—and get the other resources he wanted to boot'" (68). At the end of the book when it is indicated that Diane should have made sure that Sophie knew the murderer was not dead as she was previously told, Sophie accuses Diane saying, "'You people have put me at considerable risk, and I'm very far from happy.'" She continues to say that she won't make a formal complaint since she's "angry not vindictive" (199). Not only is Diane shown as inefficient but Chris is also seen as mistrustful when he steals some of Sophie's private papers, suspecting she has destroyed some computer records which implicate her beloved cousin, Andy, who has been stealing medicines and forging records so that he can send the medicines to help the poor in Africa.

All the books take place in the city of Birmingham and thus continue the trend of moving the detective novel out of London and the cozy countryside of the Home Counties. Although the books do not have the stylistic nuances of McDermid's similes or P.D. James's detailed descriptions, the sense of place is very strong with depictions of the traffic jams at Five Ways, the numerous tandoori restaurants, and even the canals, which are described as being not quite as beautiful as those of Venice:

> In Birmingham there might be vistas, but any that we saw ended in sixties flats or the unkempt sides of churches or factories. Mostly factories. The odd brewery, of course. These days efforts were being made to smarten them up, not just round the Music centre, and exploit the austere beauty of the blue brickwork. What was once a nice, cheap mooring in Gas Street Basin, for instance, was now being developed, much to the dismay of the narrow-boat owners. And the early-nineteenth-century bridges, elegant cast-iron affairs, were being lovingly restored and reappointed [*Dying Fall* 222].

Another social issue Cutler's Sophie Rivers series raises is inner-city college teaching. If we compare her descriptions to those of Joan Smith and Amanda Cross, we can see that university teaching, however problematic, is still vastly more privileged than teaching at Sophie's city college which is an old, inefficient building of 15 floors. Much of the time the lifts do not work, so the staff are having to climb hundreds of stairs as they move from one class to another. All the books show Sophie horribly overworked and underpaid, and in *Dying for Power* we see the effects of a stressful life which is causing her to have the symptoms of a stomach ulcer. In addition, the large salaries paid to the principal and head of department are contrasted to Sophie and her colleagues' low raises which cause some of them to take early retirement. Sophie also plans to look for another job at the end of the novel and decides to take a sabbatical. When I asked Cutler about her further education topic, she told me that as far as she knew, no one else was examining it and "at the time [she] was writing, there was an enormous amount of corruption generated by changes to FE management.... [T]he background [of FE] is one of deprivation and under-funding no university teacher could begin to imagine" (personal e-mail).

In addition to her Sophie Rivers series, Cutler has written the first of a new series, *Power on her Own*, with Kate Power as a detective sergeant in Birmingham CID. Having been involved in a horrendous car accident which killed Robin, her lover and partner in the Metropolitan police, Kate decides to make a new start in Birmingham where her great-aunt has moved into an old-people's home and left her the house.

In many ways this first novel does not appear to be saying anything very new or different from Lynda La Plante's *Prime Suspect*. Kate is shown experiencing a great deal of sexual harassment from her colleagues, starting from the first day on the job:

> A hand clamped her mouth, the thumb rough against her nose. She tried for a bite: it pressed harder. She struggled, elbowed—used all the tricks in the book and then some—but he was bigger, heavier. Her chest was parallel to the desk top. Now something was pressing hard against her skirt, against her buttocks. Into the cleft between her buttocks. Thrusting, again and again [5].

Kate is rescued from this first attempted assault and only finds out who caused it much later on. When her boss, DCI Graham Harvey, asks her if she wants to make a formal complaint, she replies, "'If I make a complaint, Sir, I've blown my job here. There's these things wherever you go, aren't there? And I've got to work with—with everyone on the squad. Last thing I need is the reputation for being a grass'" (8). Both the initial attack and Kate's response are reminiscent of Jane Tennison. Interestingly enough, when Kate does turn to Harvey on occasion for his advice, she is immediately presumed by everyone to be having an affair with him. Unlike in *Prime Suspect*, which analyses in depth Jane's difficulties forming relationships, not only with her colleagues but also with her lover and her family, Kate is shown as having a good relationship with her great-aunt and, quite quickly, fairly good ones with her colleagues. Thus, similar to the first Sophie Rivers books which only touch on the fascinating racial issues and do not go into them in depth, the harassment issues in *Power on Her Own*, which could have been a very interesting aspect of the novel, are not really analyzed. Another topic which could have been made more of, is that of being gay on the police force. One of Kate's colleagues, Colin, tells her how hard it is to be gay when "'everyone thinks being gay equals being a pedophile'" (86), but again further analysis of homosexuality in the force is not hazarded.

The plot too is not very innovative in that it is concerned first of all with the rape of a 16-year-old Asian girl, which is portrayed in only a few details, similar to the rape in *Dying to Write*. When the victim claims her assailants were Afro-Caribbean, Maureen, the WPC dealing with the case, says, "'They would have to be sodding Afro-Caribbean—can't interrogate anyone without being accused of racial harassment and damaging community relations. As if raping a sixteen-year-old isn't pretty harmful to community relations'" (153). Later the boys attack another girl, this time an Afro-Caribbean, and we are told that her parents are very supportive, and the girl herself is vowing revenge. In neither case, however, do we learn from the victims themselves how they feel, and this third-person narration gives a sense of distance which prevents the reader from feeling involved.

The plot also concerns the abduction and abuse of young boys, another topic that is hardly innovative. However, there is a striking twist in Cutler's story and a striking contradiction to her earlier treatment in that one of the chief police officers is the main pedophile. Although it is fairly clear who one of the perpetrators of the pedophile ring is, the unmasking of the ringleader comes as a total surprise. Reg Cole, the archetypal nice family copper, is revealed as a monster whom everyone has thought of as "the model officer, full of old-fashioned virtues [but] who comes home from Australia a couple of weeks early and buggers a kid with a toy engine and throws him in the path of a lorry so he can't talk" (276).

It will be interesting to see how Cutler develops this new protagonist and whether or not she uses her detective fiction to encompass greater social realism and criticism. As I have said, to date she appears to be touching on several fascinating topics but does not analyze them in depth, and so for some readers there may be an element of frustration that so much which could be said is not.

Another interesting voice among the latest to appear in detective fiction is that of Denise Mina. Val McDermid recommended her saying, "*Garnethill* has been short-listed for the John Creasey Dagger for the best first novel.... The novel is remarkable for the way it gives voice to those who are usually unheard" (personal e-mail October 13, 1998). The novel concerns Maureen, a woman who has had a nervous breakdown following recovered memories of childhood sexual abuse by her father. Like Joan Smith in *Full Stop*, and Americans such as Linda Barnes' in *Coyote* and Elizabeth Bowers' in *No Forwarding Address*, Mina examines a woman's sense of marginalization when she is forever regarded as unreliable, in this case because of her history of mental illness. Although Maureen receives help from her brother, Liam, and her best friend, Leslie, when her lover, Duncan, is murdered, she finds herself doubted not only by the police, but by her family and even at one point by herself as well.

The novel is unusual for a detective novel since it depicts in graphic detail the full horror of mental illness. Mina, thus, is continuing the trend of the late 1990s authors of combining the detective novel with a detailed analysis of a present-day problem. Maureen has been incarcerated in a psychiatric hospital for several months after being found cowering in a cupboard under the stairs following her father's final vicious sexual assault. In the hospital she meets and remains friends with several women patients some of whom, like her, are suffering depression. After her release, she continues to have out-patient therapy with Angus at the Rainbow Clinic, where she also meets Duncan, a therapist there. Though married, Duncan becomes Maureen's lover and often stays the night at her apartment. When Duncan is murdered at her place, the way the crime is committed, plus the fact that he obviously opened the door to his killer, limits the number of suspects. For the police, the prime suspect is Maureen.

Maureen is suspected and treated in a harsh and unsympathetic way, not only because she has just had it confirmed to her that Duncan is married and she could conceivably have killed him in a fit of anger, but also because Liam is a known drug dealer and her mother an undesirable alcoholic. At one point when Detective Chief Inspector Joe McEwan and Hugh McAskill are interrogating her for the fourth time, McEwan unexpectedly asks her if she is a feminist and then says, "'I thought you liked men'" (142). When Maureen mocks him as clearly not knowing a lot about feminism, his reply is "'I know what they look like and they don't look like you.'" He pointed openly to her large tits and looked away, leaving Maureen—and McAskill—aghast. He knew he'd offended her but he didn't give a shit" (142). Although McEwan is not particularly cruel to her because of the time she has spent in psychiatric care, he clearly feels that since she has lied about receiving treatment at the Rainbow Clinic, she is probably lying about the murder. Mina stresses the woman-as-victim. In McEwan's eyes, Maureen is totally unreliable as a woman and especially as a former mental patient.

As the novel progresses, we learn that Duncan was murdered because he was investigating the rapes of patients at the Northern Psychiatric Hospital that were probably committed by a doctor who tied the women down with rope which over time left horrific rope burn scars on their wrists and ankles. One of these former patients, Yvonne, is described as having suffered a stroke after the rape and now "Her glassy blue eyes were half open, her cheek was resting on the plastic-covered pillow in the slick of warm saliva dribbling horizontally out of her mouth. She was forty at most" (224). Another patient, Siobhain, refuses to talk to the police about what happened, and McEwan asks Maureen with irritation why Siobhain is trying to protect the man. Maureen replies:

> 'She isn't protecting him, she's protecting herself.'
> He thought about it. 'I don't understand.'
> 'Well, there are different reasons why people can't tell.' McEwan
> was watching her, listening intently. 'Siobhain could have been threat-
> ened during it. Some people feel that if they say it out loud it becomes
> real or they'll make someone else dirty if they tell them about it, and
> other people have other reasons. She isn't trying to outsmart you'
> [254].

McEwan then says that he'll interview Siobhain later when she's calmer, which makes Maureen furious at his complete insensitivity, of trying to make Siobhain remember this traumatic event.

Realizing that the police have no idea that the rapes are connected with Duncan's murder, Maureen decides to pursue the investigation on her own with the help of her friend, Leslie. Maureen's relationship with Leslie is typical of the feminist detective in that it is an extremely supportive one. Leslie is her drinking partner, her shoulder to cry on, and, above all, her sounding board: "Leslie was great to talk to. Whatever had happened she unconditionally took her pal's side, happily badmouthed the opposition and then never mentioned it again" (11). Leslie works as a counselor at a battered women's shelter and occasionally voices her personally felt horror at the way many of these women are treated by their husbands. When Maureen is scared of pursuing the rapist, Leslie describes Charlotte, one of these women, in order to show that running away from a terrible situation is not going to miraculously make it go away:

'Her husband had been beating her and she came to us. She had these facial scars—you know, the kind that make you shudder when you first see them. Her nose was flattened and one of her eyes was higher than the other. Ina said it was a cheekbone fracture that hadn't been set. You could see the bone sticking out sometimes, when she was eating. She'd scars all over her cheek, there.' She gestured to her left cheek, drawing a circle on it. 'The really vicious ones cut across cuts so that the doctors can't sew it up. There's nothing to sew it onto, just bits of skin hanging off. They can't patch it up, they just have to let it scar' [248].

Leslie continues her tale saying how Charlotte's husband finally killed her. Later when Leslie and the other women at the shelter say they are sure that her death was caused by the husband, the police say that without witnesses, they can do nothing. The feeling of impotence that Leslie experiences in this situation makes her tell Maureen, "'I'll be there, Mauri, I promise'" (249). She is, right through till the end when Maureen unmasks the rapist and makes sure Siobhain is safe. The closeness between Maureen and Leslie is reminiscent of that experienced by Kate Brannigan and Alexis, and by Loretta Lawson and Bridget, and is another reason why this first novel is powerful.

Mina told me that her next work continues to explore "women and violent direct action." She believes that in the future "women's detective fiction will do what always happens: the ground breakers will be turned against by the new generation who will doubtless produce an anti-feminist backlash" (personal e-mail February 8, 2000). I feel that if Mina continues to focus on arenas in which women are still marginalized, she will add something significant to the genre.

The youngest author in this dissertation is Scarlett Thomas, author of a new series with amateur, Lily Pascale. Another winner of the John Creasey Dagger award for the best first novel, Thomas, at age 28, is able to depict the youth of today with a clear-sightedness which may be impossible for older writers. In addition, the drug culture which is the focus of her first novel, *Dead Clever*, is frighteningly real. Lily moves from London and an unsatisfactory relationship to her home town, Mawlish, in Devon. However, Devon is no longer the bucolic, quiet, crime-free county of the 1950s. Lily is hired to teach English at the university when a teacher leaves following a student's brutal decapitation. When another student from the same class, now Lily's class, is also found dead of a supposed overdose of Ecstasy, Lily decides to investigate. What she discovers is a cult following the leadership of the head of the English department who is promising them nirvana through newly synthesized drugs. As Lily investigates further, she learns how by synthesizing MDMA, the chemical compound of Ecstasy, some university science students have been able to manufacture kilos of the drug.

Although she is so young, unlike the other authors I am examining, Thomas does not appear to be using the detective genre to criticize inequities in society or to raise our consciousness on feminist-related issues. In only one instance does Thomas reflect the 1990s view of the inadequacies of patriarchal establishment justice, and that is at the end of *Dead Clever* when the female murderer Nadia escapes, presumably to continue her work abroad if she cannot get a reference from the university in Devon. In addition, unlike Sophie who has a close relationship with the police, and other protagonists who show how the police are prejudiced, we see almost no interaction between Lily and the police. Indeed, in her second book, *In Your Face*, Lily is able to solve the mystery of the serial deaths of three women entirely without help because of her own sleuthing ability.

This novel is especially interesting because, unlike all the other amateur sleuths, Lily is permanently being asked by friends why she is investigating the killings and commenting herself on her problems and motives as an amateur. At one point she thinks, "'I felt guilty, suddenly, for treating [the murder investigation] all as a game. Maybe I had read too many books. In fiction it was all so much *fun*—the "cozy" village murders were just conundrums to be solved like riddles'" (92). Lily's amateur status also poses some questions as to how and why other people allow her to search their houses and interrogate them. For instance, when she goes to visit the apartment of Rebecca, one of the victims, she asks a neighbor if she will use her master key to let her in the flat. The woman asks her if she is from the police, and when Lily says she isn't, she doesn't ask any more questions, just lets her in and even says nothing when Lily takes away Rebecca's diary, which seems rather improbable.

Like several of the 1990s detectives, Lily is close to her family. She is sexually bold, though not careless. In *Dead Clever* she is very friendly with a colleague, Fenn, but in *In Your Face* when he decides to marry a student of his who claims that the baby she is pregnant with is his, Lily has a short-lived affair with Jon, a friend of one of the victims. At first

Lily thinks that her night with Jon was just a one-night stand, but as soon as she realizes that Fenn has gone through with the marriage, she goes on vacation with Jon for two weeks. She describes her time with him as a departure from her normal behavior as "Jon wasn't relationship material ... [but] pleasure wasn't something to be ashamed of. Jon had helped me realize that" (275). Thus, there is a seriousness about Lily which makes her very different from Penny Wanawake, yet she doesn't appear to be as old-fashioned as Sophie Rivers.

Unlike *Dead Clever* which makes a great number of comments about the modern drug scene, *In Your Face* has little social commentary. The plot involves the death of three young women who were interviewed on stalking for a true-life story in a magazine. When it is revealed that the journalist who wrote the story, Lily's old university friend Jess, fabricated the piece, Lily comments on the immorality of pretending that a true-life story is true when it isn't. She is told that this happens constantly in most women's magazines, and it is only the serious newspapers which are forced to check their facts, mainly to avoid lawsuits. However, Thomas, like Cutler does not centralize some of the issues she raises, and in this book at least, seems to be reverting to the more old-fashioned cozy.

Stylistically this book is unusual since it employs a device similar to McDermid's in *The Mermaids Singing*. Interspersed within the narrative is a dialogue of the murderer with what appears to be a psychologist in which he tells of his background and justifies his behavior. The description of his childhood, in particular, is very interesting with its emphasis on his loneliness, hyperactivity, antisocial behavior and love of violent comics. When we learn at the end of the novel how this dialogue comes about, it makes a most fitting finale. However, although Thomas employs some innovative writing techniques, it is difficult at this stage in her writing to forecast whether she will move the detective genre in really different directions.

Unlike the previous two authors whose amateur and policewoman protagonists are to some extent limited in their fields of operation, Michelle Spring with her private investigator, Laura Principal, reflects many of her 1990s American peers, such as Linda Grant and Dana Stabenow, especially in the way her novels are grounded in contemporary situations to "suggest a continuity between the social order portrayed in the book and the social order in the world in which the book is read creating a dialogic relationship between the two" (Walton & Jones 219). Spring, a former professor of Sociology at Anglia University, told me: "I do like to use the novels to give a voice to people who otherwise might not be heard. Connected to this, I like the challenge of writing against stereotype—for example, making the secretary a person of dignity and intelligence (rather than the nail-filing bimbo she is sometimes made out to be)" (personal e-mail February 5, 2000).

Michelle Spring

With the advent of Laura, it is clear that the days of the rather timid Cordelia Gray and the browbeaten Anna Lee are gone forever. Similar to Kate Brannigan, Laura successfully tackles a series of investigations while enjoying a rewarding relationship with her lover, Sonny. Like Kate, Laura carries a gun, but we never see her use it, only her feet and hands. Set in London, Cambridge and Norfolk, Spring's series is evocative, fast-paced, with highly topical plots.

Every Breath You Take, the first novel in the series, introduces Laura and describes her background. As with all the post 1980s protagonists, we are told a wealth of information about Laura. The daughter of a truck driver, she used to be a history tutor at Eastern University in Cambridge, until she decided to become a private investigator eight years previously. She met Sonny Mendlowitz in a jazz club where they both played on occasions. On hearing of his dilemma solving a case, Laura begged to be allowed to go undercover, posing as a secretary, to help him. When she successfully discovered who was swindling the company, Sonny agreed to give her a job. The new job with its traveling and long hours did not appeal to Laura's husband, and when she discovered him cheating on her, she turned to Sonny as a lover as well as a work partner.

Like Kate, Laura not only has a good relationship with the men in her life but also with the women. She has a close friendship with Stevie, who works for her, and with her best friend, Helen, with whom she co-owns a beautifully converted barn in Norfolk. It is the financial burden of the house which makes them decide to let Monica, a colleague of Helen's at Eastern University, become a tenant and share the expenses.

When Monica is savagely stabbed to death, Laura feels a sense of guilt that she didn't take the dead woman's fears seriously and decides to discover who killed her: "'I had left academic work partly because I wanted to feel that what I did made a concrete difference in people's lives. I sure as hell had failed to make a difference to Monica'" (64). As her search takes her into various departments in the university, she learns that the male provost has been sexually harassing several junior female faculty members. One member tells Laura that when she described one episode first to her head of department and then to the branch secretary of the union, the former told Jennifer that she should be careful not to act provocatively and the latter expressed relief that there was no harm done. On hearing this, Laura exclaims: "'No harm done,' I repeated. 'Well, no, I guess not. Not if they ignore the damage to your reputation. To your sense of integrity.... What about your self-confidence? Your capacity to expect that male co-workers will relate to you as a colleague and not as a sexual object?'" (164). At first it appears that the provost is the killer, but through a series of suspense-filled moments we learn that it is, in fact, a student.

Not only does Spring foreground women's issues in her novels, but she also analyzes the efficacy of the police and justice systems. At one point Laura is asked to act for a convicted criminal, and she agrees to do so because she feels those convicted do not always deserve their fate:

> Only the most ill-informed could take conviction in a British court as an infallible guide to guilt. If you think about it, there may be almost as many innocent people incarcerated in our prisons as there are guilty people roaming the streets outside. And it is the innocent ones who have the most need of the kind of services a private investigator can provide [24].

This direct appeal to the reader clearly shows Spring's concern with this topic. However, Laura rarely thinks the police are ineffective, or worse corrupt, and indeed enjoys an excellent working relationship with Inspector Nicole Pelletier, a former student of hers. Nicole can always be relied upon to help her with background information and takes her suspicions seriously.

Like the American hard-boiled investigators, Laura is very fit and easily able to defend herself. Although she does carry a gun in her car, in *Every Breath You Take* when she is attacked in her office, she defends herself physically. "I flipped over onto my back and pulled my knees up to my chest, kicking out powerfully as he dived at me. The soles of my boots connected joltingly with his breastbone, and though he tried to clutch my leg, I managed to throw him onto his side and launch myself upright" (185). In *Running for Shelter*, Laura does use her gun and is obviously a good shot since she manages to hit her target in the thigh as she feels: "Aiming for the legs is always risky; they are slender targets and they don't stay in one place. But I knew I couldn't bring myself to discharge a bullet at his chest" (256). However, she feels she should never have to use a gun because it is "a surefire admission of failure" (262). In fact, after this episode, she mentions that there will be an inquiry into the shooting, and the police revoke her firearms license, which is very different from the attitudes in the United States.

Not only is Laura very similar to Kate Brannigan but Spring also resembles Val McDermid in that both writers have particularly topical plots. Following her reading of a news article about migrant workers and her meetings with Filipino women working in the West London area, Spring wrote *Running for Shelter* which describes the harrowing life of one such woman and her consequent death. The evident research which went into this novel adds enormously to its interest and power.

Similarly there is a great deal of topical interest in *Standing in the Shadows*, which was nominated for the Arthur Ellis Canadian award, and which examines the idea of a child committing murder and people's general reaction to such a crime. While Laura tells Helen that the whole idea of children as innocent is a 20th century one that would have been unthinkable in the olden days, Helen reminds her of the rise in crimes against children saying "'we're on a point of decision today. Unable to make up our minds whether children are victims or villains'" (116). She says later in the book, when Laura goes with Sonny and his boys to a virtual reality video arcade:

> But my growing hostility to guns doesn't fit with my experience of Laserquest. Racing through the maze, ducking and weaving, I certainly did feel alert, on edge, eager—even aggressive. What I didn't feel was

murderous.... And that probably applies to the rest of the players, too [200].

Thus Laura seems to imply that for most normal people playing violent games does not necessarily lead to violence. However, as we discover in the novel, the child, Daryll, is not really normal as he has been severely affected by his dysfunctional family.

What Spring depicts so well in this novel is the way young people often feel abandoned by their families and by so many of the adults with whom they come in contact. When they try to form bonds and gain support from these older people, they may be rejected and find themselves unable to cope. As we learn in *Standing in the Shadows*, Daryll's "saintly" foster mother is not the loving, kind little old lady everyone presumes, and the unselfish social worker, Kelsey McLeod, is, in fact, the villain of the piece. The "wicked" Darryl, in fact, is just a naughty little boy, not the psychopath as first portrayed.

Spring's willingness to analyze the very latest problems which are overwhelming British society today in tightly woven, exciting plots bodes well for the success and interest of her future books. Unlike Cutler and Thomas, Spring is writing in a similar vein to Joan Smith and Val McDermid, and her books have the power to engage and move the reader as do theirs. When I asked her where she thought the female detective novel was headed, she replied:

> I sense the boundaries that have divided hard-boiled from soft-boiled and male from female dimensions of the genre being well and truly dismantled. By that I mean, that there are increasing numbers of male-centered, action-oriented writers who nevertheless pay careful attention to the full route in terms of gristle and gore, but still retain some of the sensibilities and the themes that we have come to expect of women-soft-boiled authors [personal e-mail February 5, 2000].

Since Spring feels that "crime fiction is a wonderful lens through which to take a critical look at the contemporary world," I feel sure that she will continue to find fascinating topical problems on which to focus her work and be a popular author for years to come.

As has been mentioned earlier in this work, there is a strange lack of ethnic voices in British female detective fiction. To date, there are no female or male minority authors writing detective fiction in Britain; however, *Without Prejudice* by Nicola Williams is worthy of analysis here, even though it is more of a legal thriller. Williams, whose family came to Britain from Guyana, was educated in Georgetown and Croydon. A barrister, she is eminently qualified to take a long, hard look at Britain's justice system and depict today's typical criminals. Her first book, *Without Prejudice*, has as its protagonist a female barrister, Lee Mitchell. If we compare this novel to P.D. James's *A Certain Justice*, we see how pervasive is the racial prejudice encountered by Lee. As she waits for a solicitor's clerk to appear, she is talking to her client, a habitual criminal, though a particularly clean-cut young man. When the clerk arrives, he immediately presumes that the man, Ray Willis, is the barrister, since he is white. An angry Lee rebuffs him, "'You just assumed that Mr. Willis here was my counsel in this cannabis case.... You did, I trust, read enough of the papers to know it was a drugs case?'" (12). Although this altercation appears at the start of the novel, the book focuses on the issue of inequality towards women as much as it does on racism. Several times Lee comments that she has had to struggle, as a woman, to reach the position she is in as a criminal barrister mainly because the law courts are so deeply a male preserve. In addition, her schooling did not prepare her for even the possibility of a career.

Early in the novel, Lee has been asked to speak to the pupils of her old school about how she became successful. Expected by the headmistress and the guidance counselor to praise the formative years she spent at Fordyce Park Secondary Modern, Lee shocks the teachers and amazes the students by telling them what her experiences were really like. "[W]hen I was a pupil here, the only work experience we could have, even the brightest of us, was to be someone's office clerk. You were never, ever encouraged to aim for anything higher" (24). Later we are told that even having gotten an upper second law degree, Lee's lack of connections due to her working-class background also means that she is forever denied entry into the old-boy network, linked as it is to private school and Oxbridge.

Being a woman in the world of the Middle Temple will always be hard, but if one adds being lower class and black, it is excessively difficult to imagine being given anything but the sleaziest of cases. Thus, Lee is thrilled when she is given the chance to defend Clive Omardian, one of two brothers accused, along with their aged father, of fraud. This is a case for which all the top barristers have been vying, and Lee is excited to pit her wits against them in an intriguing battle. Her frustration is enormous, therefore, when she learns that the only reason she was hired is because her client thought she could be bought and would turn a blind eye when he perjured himself on the witness stand.

As well as examining the world of fraud and the moneyed criminal, *Without Prejudice* also deals with the issue of the date rape of a black former school friend of Lee's. The two cases are linked in a very well-developed convoluted plot which keeps our interest. The victim of the date rape, Simone, waits before reporting the event to the police because she is afraid that she will not be taken seriously. When she meets with Giles Townsend, Lee's head of chambers, who is the prosecutor in the case, even he treats her without respect:

> [H]e had That Look—the look she had seen on the faces of more white men than she cared to remember. One of speculation. Appraisal. Sometimes subtle. Sometimes not. But always underpinning the same question: is it true what they say about black women? How could someone who looked like that possibly believe she had been raped? [145].

George Amery, the counsel for the rapist, Steve Payne, is also quite happy to entertain the idea that Simone probably "asked for it" since Steve is a good-looking black man. "Being good-looking didn't hurt either. Funny, that, how good looks worked against a woman in a rape case but in favor of the man. After all, why would a good-looking man need to rape?" (180). As it turns out, Simone was correct to fear the outcome, and, as she tells Lee, the court case is like a second rape (193). When Steve walks free, Simone decides to take justice into her own hands and has a transvestite friend of hers assault him viciously.

Without Prejudice is particularly pertinent to this survey for the light it sheds on the justice system. Amery is shown as being totally without scruples, getting a child molester off on a technicality and later badgering Simone, putting her in a bad light so that her rapist goes free. At one point Lee describes him as "good, very good. He's also completely without conscience. That's a very dangerous combination" (169). As Lee also says, "'justice and the law have very little to do with each other'" (169). Even Lee does not appear to be immune from twisting the law. She leaves evidence in full view of the prosecution which will help them indict Clive Omardian—she knows he is guilty but cannot say so without endangering herself.

Although it is difficult to judge an author simply by her first novel, I feel sure that further novels by Nicola Williams will prove to be as exciting and illuminating as *Without Prejudice*.

Works Cited

Cutler, Judith. *Dying Fall.* Long Preston: Magna Large Print Books, 1998.

____. *Dying for Millions.* London: Piatkus, 1997.

____. *Dying for Power.* London: Piatkus, 1998.

____. *Dying on Principle.* London: Piatkus, 1996.

____. *Dying to Write.* Long Preston: Magna Large Print Books, 1998.

____. Personal e-mail interview February 7, 2000.

____. *Power on Her Own.* London: Hodder & Stoughton, 1998.

Mina, Denise. *Garnethill.* London: Bantam Press, 1998.

____. Personal e-mail interview February 8, 2000.

Spring, Michelle. *Every Breath You Take.* New York: Pocket Books, 1994.

____. *Nights in White Satin.* New York: Ballantine Books, 1999.

____. Personal e-mail interview February 5, 2000.

____. *Running for Shelter.* New York: Pocket Books, 1996.

____. *Standing in the Shadows.* New York: Ballantine Books, 1998.

Thomas, Scarlett. *Dead Clever.* London: Hodder & Stoughton, 1998.

____. *In Your Face.* London: Hodder & Stoughton, 1999.

Williams, Nicola. *Without Prejudice.* New York: St. Martin's Press, 1998.

Conclusion

In his 1972 book *Bloody Murder*, Julian Symons predicts the direction of the detective novel. In a 1985 update of the book, he returns to his predictions and shows how close or far off his crystal-ball prophecies have proven to be. In this conclusion I would like to do something similar, but be even more specific than Symons and examine where I feel the detective novel is traveling. Whereas Symons makes clear distinctions between detective, crime and police procedural novels, I think one of the fundamental differences with the post 1980s novel is a blurring of the demarcations between these subgenres, especially between detective and crime fiction.

One of the new directions in which I see female detective fiction moving is further into the more violent and graphic. As we have seen already in books like Patricia Cornwell's *Postmortem* and Val McDermid's *Wire in the Blood*, detective fiction and horror can go happily hand in hand. However, the big change appearing is the movement away from the female protagonist as diminished victim. As Sandra Tomc describes, "rape/homicide, while surely the crime feared by women, is one that the older school of feminist mystery writers never deals with, very likely because it is guaranteed to highlight the female detective's helplessness over and above any victory she might manage at the end of the story" (53). Tomc continues to remind us how at the end of *Postmortem* when confronted by the serial killer in her bedroom, Scarpetta is too paralyzed to defeat him, and it is her policeman friend Marino who saves her by gunning down the killer. While women may be disadvantaged by killers because of their physical weaknesses, their cunning and deep-seated ability to be as vicious as a man will change the protagonist of the future. In addition, tomorrow's female writers will be able to describe horrific crimes as graphically as necessary as their protagonists deal with violence more easily. Up-and-coming detective writer, Karin Slaughter, told me that violence might be tempered in interesting ways in the future:

> As men lose their "dominance" over women (i.e: women can take out the garbage, build an addition and move up the corporate ladder just as quickly as men) and thus their control, women's mysteries will show a softer, gentler side to take up this gap. I think this will happen as a backlash, because despite what women are doing in the world, a lot of them still think that they need a man to define themselves. This ultimately gives men back the power. Though, I think once women break that new ground of killing and raping and general violence in their writing they won't go back [personal e-mail April 19, 1999].

In the 1990s, one of the main issues for female writers was that of the efficacy of justice and the brutality and corruption rife in police forces. With greater numbers of women both in the courts and the police force, the depiction of justice in crime novels is bound to change. Will women be fairer, less corrupt?—not necessarily. Will they be less brutal in their dealings with criminals?—probably. How will having numerous women in positions of authority in the judicial system affect society? One of their major problems may be juggling home and a career, but even that may change as laws are passed allowing more childcare facilities, more flextime. Clearly, the old-boy network which exists today will cease to have as much power and influence. Women will have to spend less time persuading their colleagues and their juniors to take them seriously, leaving more time for solving crime efficiently. One of the changes may occur in the way crimes against women are detected. What happened in the Yorkshire Ripper murders should not occur with women in charge. As Joan Smith describes in *Misogynies*:

> The police and the press had convinced themselves (and each other, the relationship between detectives and crime reporters being a symbiotic one) that they were dealing with a prostitute killer, a latter-day Jack the Ripper, that *this* was the significant link to look for in establishing which were the man's victims; from this point on, both evidence and suspects would be judged according to the yardstick of how well they measured up to the theory.

Three major errors flowed from the acceptance of this hypothesis. First genuine Sutcliffe victims were excluded from the list of his crimes because they were the wrong 'type' of woman, while a murder in Preston which he did not commit *was* included on grounds of the unfortunate woman's character and habits. Second, the police fell into the trap of expecting the killer to behave like the nineteenth-century Ripper. Third they convinced themselves that they 'knew' the killer in some mysterious and undefined way; that if they were suddenly confronted with him, they would recognize him at once. George Oldfield, Assistant Chief Constable of West Yorkshire and sometime head of the Ripper Squad said in 1980: "If we had twenty or thirty suspects in one room we would know very quickly which one was the Ripper" [123].

The arrogance of these policemen coupled with their refusal to see the victims for what they really were, innocent women who had been attacked by a man who hated women, not prostitutes, was amazing. The policemen did not listen to the accounts of the earliest victims who survived, that the man had a local accent, nor did they believe that Sutcliffe was the man, even though the women said he resembled the photofit picture created after their attacks. It was easier and more comfortable for them to think he was an outsider, a Geordie from Newcastle, totally different from them. The very ordinariness of many criminals who commit horrendous crimes is already seen in detective fiction. With more women in charge in real life and presumably in fiction, we may see more innovative solving of crimes, more risktaking, and less fear that unusual ideas will be rejected by male colleagues, as happens to Shaz Bowman in McDermid's *Wire in the Blood*. As all these changes occur, albeit gradually in society, many of the social inequities leading to injustice and much of the poor police work which we see as the focus of novelists' attention today, should diminish and cease to be of concern.

Most of the protagonists of the books examined in detail in this book are middle class and educated. The exception, of course, is Cody's Eva Wylie. Melville's Charmian Daniels has a working-class background but is also a scholarship recipient and does marry up. Eva, however, is working class, coarse, common and crude. I foresee many more protagonists of clearly working-class origins and attitudes. In the United States there are ethnically diverse private investigators and amateurs but no real "poor white trash" contenders. What makes Barbara Neely's Blanche White appealing is not only that she is black, but that she works as a cleaning woman and is proud of her humble origins. Why does an investigator have to have education and class? In McDermid's non-fiction work *A Suitable Job for a Woman*, she interviews numerous real-life private investigators who entered the field either from the police or after being a secretary or filing clerk. Many of these women did not have higher education and came from the lower-middle or working class.

With more working-class protagonists will come a shift in focus on societal ills. As John Grisham's novel *The Street Lawyer* depicts, the homeless are voiceless, and so too are other members of the underclass. Reginald Hill's novel *Blood Sympathy* states very clearly the harsh aspects of living in a housing development which he calls Hermsprong:

> Here is the original urban black hole into which all social subsidy and welfare work is sucked without trace.... Here everyone has a place and a function. Here there are none so poor they cannot be robbed, none so insignificant they cannot be reviled, none so inoffensive they cannot be hated [163].

However, this focus on the underclass does not appear to have gained much ground yet, and one can only make assumptions about which direction authors will move in.

As we also see in Hill's first book in this new series, *Blood Sympathy*, one of the new areas for detective fiction to examine is the situation of the ethnic minorities in Britain. As I have already mentioned in this work, it is intriguing that there are no female or even male Pakistani or Indian writers of detective fiction so far in Britain, even though these nationalities have been living in the country for over a generation in some cases. Although Judith Cutler mentions racial tensions in her works, and Ruth Rendell's novel *Simisola* paints a compelling picture of the murder of an ethnic immigrant worker, what is most interesting is that an in-depth analysis of a racial murder is depicted not by a British author but by an American, Elizabeth George. In her masterly work, *Deception on His Mind*, George examines the murder of a Pakistani businessman in a small seaside community in Essex. Her protagonist, Sergeant Barbara Havers, working without her usual boss, Lynley, follows her Pakistani neighbors to Balford-le-Nez to try to solve the murder of Haytham Querashi. Her neighbor, Taymullah Azhar, has been called in by his cousin Muhammad Malik to liaise with the local police and make sure that this murder is not swept under the carpet. Barbara discovers that her old friend, Emily Barlow, is in charge of the case and offers her services, claiming to be on holiday and willing to act as an impartial link between the local police and the enraged Pakistani community. The depths and complexities of the tensions between the two communities are extremely well-analyzed, with the racial prejudices felt by so many of the characters giving the book a dimension which is truly innovative. George herself pays tribute to a great many people who helped her write this novel, but I feel that when an Asian writer chooses to write on this type of topic, the result is bound to have an effect on the detective novel which is long overdue.

As we also see in both George's and Hill's works, one of the fears of many minorities is the growing number of white supremacist gangs of youths. While such crimes are mentioned by Judith Cutler, too, they have not yet come to the foreground in literature. Today crimes committed by very young children in gangs or small groups against the elderly and even against younger children have escalated. A female protagonist, especially one who is married and with children, would be the perfect detective to solve a mystery perpetrated by a child. Along with our rejection of the older detective writers' views of crimes being committed by a certain "type," has come our rejection of the idea that children are always innocent. In the United States children under 17 are one of the fastest growing groups of criminals, and the sheer numbers of children between ten and 17 committing violent crimes is horrifying. Figures from the *Statistical Abstract of the US* tell us that, whereas in 1980 there were 77,220 violent crimes perpetrated by ten to 17 year olds, this number had risen to 123,131 in 1995. In 1980 there were 21,203 weapon-law violations, and in 1995 46,506 (U.S. Bureau of the Census 219). In addition, a *Newsweek* article written after the Littleton, Colorado, massacre described, "Just as girls could be the next wave of killers, so could even younger children. 'Increasingly, we're seeing the high-risk population for lethal violence as being the 10–14-year-olds,' says Richard Lieberman, a school psychologist in Los Angeles" (Begley 34).

With the possible depiction of a murderer as a child, so too may come more books with gangs of female criminals. Jennie Melville had her gang of four in *Murder Has a Pretty Face* as long ago as 1981. So why should there not be more female masterminds and more gangs with only women members? Is the idea of female bank robbers still far-fetched? So far my premise has been that detective fiction reflects society; however, does it not also influence society? With gender blurring there is a real possibility of women becoming as willing to commit "masculine" crimes as men, bank robbery, for instance. Moreover, with a woman's attention to detail and ability to plan meticulously, a crime like bank robbery might not end up with a murder, since many women would probably be prepared to back away from committing the robbery if they felt the situation was not ideal and might lead to killing. The rashness of many younger males, which often leads to unplanned deaths, is not seen so much in women, especially older women.

Another huge change in detective fiction has to be linked to the increasing accessibility of computers in many people's lives. Possibly one of our great fears is that of Big Brother. With lives dominated by credit cards and easy computer access to all our private matters, we may lose all control of our personal information. Computer fraud crimes are bound to increase, as are crimes of blackmail and even bizarre crimes like the one which occurred in Sandra Bullock's film *The Net*. Tomorrow's detective fiction may be less concerned with murders and more with the white-collar crimes already written about by Val McDermid and Judith Cutler. The fact that criminals in jail have been known to use computers to continue their criminal activities is another added twist.

Naturally with computers, crimes can cross the world, and many future crimes will start in one country and move to others. So too will our detective become less centered in one town or area and become more of a world traveler. Since this may entail travel on the part of the author, it could be an attractive new direction to go in for everyone. Already many British authors have had certain novels take place in the United States. With the Euro, they may move about Europe more.

Not only will the focus of crime move from murder to many other crimes, so too will the amateur detective continue the trend toward being a specialist in an unusual field. Already we have amateur detectives who are cat lovers, chefs, bridge players, nuns, so on. This may mean that all those readers who also have an interest in these worlds feel immediately connected. The only problem with mixing the detective genre with a distinct area of expertise is that the detection element can become secondary; there might appear a book filled with recipes, for example, as opposed to fascinating detection. Although Julian Symons predicted that the traditional, clue-filled novel would disappear as clues would remain "the affair of the forensic scientist" (235), this does not seem to be the case. There will always be armchair detectives for whom the clues or the puzzle element of detective novels are what make the genre appealing. In addition, at present there are only a few amateur detectives who are also pathologists, but I believe there will be more simply because so much information can be gleaned from scientific analysis. If the popularity of the television show "Silent Witness" is anything to go by, we can predict that there will continue to be a blending of science and detection.

One factor will remain constant, whatever directions detective and crime fiction move in—that is, the books will be entertaining. For those readers who like the horror element, "the mess in a clean place," there will always be novels where "the qualms evoked by detective fiction stamp us, too, however momentarily, with slime" (Trotter 75). Those innovative authors who are truly successful will remember to temper their experiments so that their readers can identify with their protagonists and feel involved in the plot.

This examination of British detective fiction since the 1960s makes it clear, I trust, that there have been huge changes in the genre. Perhaps the most lasting has to do not so much with the new female protagonists but with the readers' responses to the novels. Whereas readers of the genre until about the 1980s were assured of "evil being punished, order restored and endings satisfying" (Glover 68), later readers entered a world which was far more realistic and far less black and white. As the very intricate puzzle formula of the Golden Age disappeared forever, so too did the clear demarcation between detective fiction, the thriller and the crime novel. When this happened, the goals of the authors changed along with crime fiction. Author David Glover also claims today, "crime fiction is conceived as an active force in history, an imaginary solvent of social contradictions rather than a comforting diversion" (68). An ending like McDermid's in *Wire in the Blood* is disturbing precisely because, far from comforting the reader that justice will be served and the serial killer will definitely end up locked behind bars for the rest of his life, there is a strong implication that his money will pervert the already inefficient police force, and he will go free.

How social criticisms in the detective genre will evolve depends, of course, on the way society itself evolves. As Kimberley Dilley reminds us, "Readers interact with the mystery novel; they find pleasure, sources for argument, avenues of discussion, and fantasy" (145). With this in mind, and also remembering how crime fiction is a lucrative market, readers can, by withholding their approbation for one type of novel, influence the types of fiction which will be popular best sellers. However, *What Do I Read Next: A Reader's Guide to Current Genre Fiction* gives us the disturbing news that "Midlist writers—a category which includes most mystery writers—have been badly hurt in recent years by publishers who demand increasing sales numbers each year.... HarperCollins made news when it cut over a hundred titles from its list, including books from such capable mystery writers as ... Val McDermid" (Barron et al. 7). What is clear is that social criticism, in one form or another, will continue to be a part of women's detective fiction of the future. As Symons said so aptly "the modern crime story can ... say something of interest about our time[, and] ... can tell us something about the world we live in, and about the best way of living peacefully in it" (23).

Appendix:
Transcripts of
Personal and
E-Mail Interviews,
and Records of
E-Mail Responses

P.D. James Personal Interview
(July 26, 1998)

MH Cordelia Gray was heralded by critics as the modern woman 'a touch-stone of early seventies feminism' (Nixon 30). What were your aims when you created her?

PD Well, I really wanted to create the type of woman that she turned out to be, that is one who'd had a very lonely and unhappy early life with no real parenting but had the sort of guts and intelligence to make a life for herself, rather fell into this job, but was determined that she would make a success of it. What I did like about her was that she was a woman with a strong moral sense, an ethical sense entering into a world where she's going to encounter people who will have a very different view of life and morals, and how can she do her job well and successfully and retain her integrity. I think she's always very much her own person, and because she's not a policewoman, she doesn't have to act according to rules and regulations, and she can take a line which a policewoman wouldn't be able to take. I think that really was the basic idea. I wanted to set a book in Cambridge, one of Europe's loveliest cities. She seemed to be the right detective. Dalgliesh wouldn't have been able to operate in Cambridge because he's a London policeman, and he wouldn't have jurisdiction out of the metropolitan police area, and the suspects were going to be young, the victim was young, and it really is a very young book in a sense. It was very agreeable to write about a young woman.

MH You have said that she was based in part on your daughter. Can you expand on this?

PD Yes, in some ways she is. Her character is very like Jane—the straightforwardness, the honesty and intelligence.

MH Was there anything inherently difficult in writing about Cordelia?

PD No, the easiest book I ever had to write.

MH We just had it on television and we've also had a newer version.

PD I'm in real trouble with her now—a real problem. Because I thought it unlikely that I'd write another Cordelia Gray, I agreed that the TV company which had made the excellent film *Mrs. Brown* could have the character as a character and continue with it, and this has proved a grave mistake. The second [Cordelia film] is extremely disappointing. Then I read, while I was under the dryer in the hairdresser's of all things, that the actress was pregnant, but the new Cordelia Gray would accommodate the pregnancy. So they hadn't bothered to tell me this, and I asked them, 'what are you proposing?' And they said that they'd say she'd had an affair, and he would go back to America, and she'd courageously have the baby herself. And I said, 'Cordelia Gray would never act like that. She'd never have a child and not let that child know who its father was, and it's a violation of my character.' So this has been a great problem, and I've disassociated myself from it entirely now, and from the whole of the television series.

MH That's interesting because I felt when I saw it that the second Cordelia TV film was just awful. I couldn't believe that you'd had a part in it.

PD No part in it at all. In fact I had said to them, when they discussed the storyline, you must show either the murder or the finding of the body; it's a very important part. In this none of it was credible. We don't even know how that woman died. We're supposed to believe the husband did it without one shred of evidence. It was appalling. So it was a grave mistake to have let them have it, but we all make mistakes in life. I did it on very good evidence because they did the first very well, and Mrs. Brown was a very good film.

MH That was the Mrs. Brown which was the story of Queen Victoria—the same company.

PD Yes.

MH That was a wonderful film.

PD Exactly, so that was my evidence. I was absolutely confident. I met them and I liked them. I think they're in real difficult with the pregnant

Cordelia. So I don't think we'll be seeing any more Cordelias on the screen, or not many, and the ones we shall see will be bad.

MH The whole generational question seems to be a focus in your books. I'm very interested in the way that Kate Miskin has developed from a foil to Adam Dalgliesh in *A Taste for Death* to the comain character in *A Certain Justice.*

PD Yes, I think she is. I'm very interested in Kate because Kate and Cordelia have some things in common. They've both got this very bad background, poor background, both of them are very brave, both of them are quite ambitious. But, of course, throughout Kate is a professional policewoman before she's anything else, so you'd never have Kate acting in the way Cordelia did—covering up a crime.

MH Why did you have Swayne kill the grandmother at the end of *A Taste for Death?* Was it just so that she would be unencumbered by personal ties?

PD No, no! That's just the way the book went. I mean I'd never think, well it would be nice for Kate not to be encumbered with the grandmother. In many ways, having the grandmother there and the personal ties would have made the book more complex. It's just how it worked out. I don't think, when writing that one does it in this analytical way because one is in the process of creation, and that, to an extent, is apart from oneself.

MH The book takes over?

PD Not entirely, because it can't, but to an extent it does. The creative process takes over, and if something seems right for the book, you don't think there's a slight disadvantage if I do that, or some people suggest that I ought to do that because it'd look good on television. Those considerations never operate. That just seemed to be what happened. I suppose I wanted to have an exciting ending to the book [*A Taste for Death*], and I also wanted Kate to realize that she did in one sense love the grandmother, and it was an awful thing that happened.

MH Yes, and she's traumatized by it. And if she feels some relief, most of us can identify with her.

PD Yes, I think so. I wanted all those things which is what made it interesting.

MH There are very few female detectives who are married and especially who have children. Do you think readers prefer their female detectives to be single, or if married, without children?

PD Well, you see I don't write thinking what the readers want. I don't know about that. I think that attitude is totally alien to me as a writer. I would have a detective with a child if I thought it would be interesting to see how she can combine this very difficult job with having a child. But it would rather interfere with the book and that in itself is a subject that has been done so much, so I'm not sure that I feel I want to do it as I think I'd get into the subject of the children and that would throw the detection out. I take the view that I do what I want to do as well as I can and give it all that I've got, and that's what my readers want me to do, because that's what they value in the books. They don't want somebody who's going to say, 'well readers might like that or readers might like the other' because then you would have been untrue to your talent. You just have to do the best you can with the idea that's coming to you. My readers want that.

MH In *A Certain Justice* you have Venetia having the daughter and having problems with Octavia and the whole relationship.

PD And of course the problem of ambition, which is a very common problem now, with professional people both working. I like to deal with social problems in a book, but I think a detective with children would be difficult.

MH Yes, I agree. You yourself balanced a job, family, and your writing at a time when most women stayed at home. Were those days very difficult?

PD Yes, but as my husband was in and out of hospital, I did live with my parents-in-law, so the children had an extremely settled background with their grandparents when they weren't in boarding school. They'd come home for the holidays and we'd all be together. I don't think I could have balanced my life with au pairs or temporary help, not without harm to the children.

MH Did they enjoy having a mother who worked outside the home?

PD No, I think they'd have preferred me not to.

MH Yes, my mother worked at one point and I hated it. Children want that image of you at home baking in the kitchen.

PD Yes, they do. They used to wave goodbye to me from the window when I went off to the station and years afterwards they said, 'we always thought you might not come back.' So, I think one doesn't know what's good for them. But their grandparents were a very stabilizing influence.

MH You have said of Dalgliesh that you 'wanted him to be very professional' and 'because the detective is increasingly becoming a human being, that part of his personality which is evil has to be shown' (qtd. in Cooper-Clark 15–32).

PD I'm sure I never said that.

MH That was a direct quote in an article by Diana Cooper-Clark.

PD I'm amazed at the direct quotes which I've not said.

MH You don't think there's any evil in him?

PD No, I don't think there's any evil in Dalgliesh. I think that you can write that detectives are becoming far more like human beings with human weaknesses. I certainly say time and time again about Dalgliesh that increasingly he's coming to realize the harm that the job he does can do to the innocent as well as the guilty. There are moral implications to this job, and he does cause pain; he has to cause pain to innocent people. But I don't think he's the slightest bit evil. And that quote doesn't sound like me.

MH Dalgliesh himself says in *Death of an Expert Witness*: 'It was possible to do police work honestly; there was, indeed, no other safe way to do it. But it wasn't possible to do it without giving pain' (340). Is this what you mean?

PD That's it exactly. I would also say that he is aware that his job is not always done honestly. He does things honestly himself, but in an organization there are sometimes those who are less honest. We're very lucky with our police, but we know there have been incidents. So he's aware and he has seen that.

MH In *Original Sin*, right at the end when his subordinate lets the murderer go off into the marsh, there's a part of Dalgliesh that's shocked—he feels he shouldn't have done that—but there's another part of him that can understand.

PD Absolutely, absolutely. But nevertheless he would not have done it, and he will not have Daniel [Massingham] in his team any more. That's the difference between the professional policeman and Cordelia. He'll be sympathetic to him; he'll understand it; but he would not do it himself. And I think one has to face that about him. If I make him a professional policeman, he's got to be a professional policeman. I can't sentimentalize by saying he'll be a professional policeman on this or that occasion, but then he'll do this because we don't want our policemen to be like that. That's how he is as a character. He certainly has the capacity for doing wrong, since we all have, but I don't imagine that I would say he has an evil side because evil's a very strong word. I'm not sure I'd use that word about any human being really. There are some who are evil, but it's a strong word to use of Dalgliesh.

MH Maybe she misquoted you.

PD Well, she may have misheard.

MH You made Dalgliesh a poet 'to empathize his sensitivity and to mark him from the ordinary, non-corrupt British detective' (qtd. in Cooper-Clark 29). In the later books he has ceased to write poetry; do you feel he is, therefore, becoming less sensitive, or is there another reason why he has stopped writing?

PD Well, he wrote a very successful book just before *Devices and Desires*, so that's not so very long ago. So we don't know that he's stopped writing poetry. Presumably he's still writing, but he just hasn't published any.

MH One of your greatest strengths as a writer, on which many critics have commented, is your rich, descriptive, almost leisurely style. What do you think are the advantages of the finely crafted detective novel where we are given a wealth of details before the murder ever takes place, versus the fast-paced, action-packed way of writing?

PD Well, I think people write the kind of books they need to write or that they want to write and are capable of writing. These are the kinds of books I like to write, and happily a lot of people want to read them, but I wouldn't make any great claims over my kind of writing because a lot of the other kind is done very well.

MH Do you read detective fiction yourself?

PD Not much.

MH So what sort of authors do you enjoy?

PD I suppose I read a lot of biography and autobiography. As I get older, I like more nonfiction and history. I like women writers in England more than the male writers. I'm not saying they are better necessarily. I like Maggie Drabble and I read Ruth Rendell.

MH You're friends with Ruth Rendell aren't you?

PD Yes. We're very different writers, but we are personal friends. Jane Austen is my favourite author and I read a lot of Trollope.

MH I feel your books are so satisfying. I teach writing, and I can take a passage and say 'look at this description, analyze it, this is exactly how you should write this type of description.'

PD Well, that is very, very flattering. This is of course tremendously important to me. I'm enjoyed by people who do enjoy the classic detective story for their recreational reading, but they do want it very well written. They do want more than an ingenious puzzle. That's the gap that I personally fill.

MH Yes, and I really don't think that you have any competition. I mean I like Ruth Rendell as well, but there's a satisfaction one gets from your books. You can't just dash them off in a two-hour read. This is a 'I've got a whole week of vacation; I'm going to really enjoy this a little bit at a time, like a nice meal.'

PD *(laughs)* Yes, that's how I like to enjoy a book. So that's very flattering and sweet of you to say so. That's certainly what I aim at, and that's why I say I only write to please myself. That's what I'm trying to do. I know that's what my readers want. Because they want what I want.

MH You take quite a long time to write your books.

PD Oh yes! And I do take an awful lot of trouble. I think there is that readership, and I'm the same, who love an exciting story, we all do, but if it's badly written, I cannot read it. I don't want to. It doesn't matter how exciting it is; it's no good. So what I'm trying to do is construct a fascinating and incredible mystery and at the same time write a good novel. And obviously I love my novels to be within this rather rigid format of the classical detective story, and I like the support that the format gives me. I like the sense of order and bringing order out of disorder. Whereas other crime writers want a very different kind of format. I do think we write what we need to write, or what we think we're best at writing.

MH Although you have the format, your books are not formulaic.

PD No, that's the whole thing. They shouldn't be formulaic. All the time I'm just seeing what I can do.

MH Do you feel that Kate, I don't want to put labels on her, but do you see her as a feminist?

PD Yes, I think she is strong. I think it's a difficult label feminist isn't it? Because am I a feminist? It depends on your definition. I am a feminist if by being a feminist you mean someone who very much likes her own sex, admires her own sex, and feels that women are entitled to have equal opportunity, equal right to live their lives in ways that are most satisfying to them. But if by feminist you mean someone who is antimale, then I'm not. Because I feel that it's like all organizations—you can get on the fringe people who really feel half the human race are all potential rapists, and they are not. And I also feel, I've always felt that sexual equality is strongly economic. That middle-class feminists are complaining about all sorts of things in their jobs, and most of the women of the world haven't got equal economic rights; they're overworking for pittances. The greatest freedom for women has come from the right to earn their own money and the right to control their fertility. Those have been the things that have given us our greatest advantages. My mother couldn't have earned a living and people were tied into their marriages. They had no options. But I think that a lot of the things the extreme feminists have fought for have rather backfired on women and have not made women any happier.

MH And we have to be really aware of it.

PD And I think, too, that children have suffered a lot. They really have.

MH And I think more and more are being brought up in single parent families, and then the economics are always bad.

PD Yes, awful.

MH In *A Certain Justice* we first meet Kate, and she's at the shooting range where she is proving to be a better shot than Piers, her colleague. At the end of the novel, however, Dalgliesh does not let her shoot but lets Piers shoot, and he kills Ashe [the murderer.] Kate feels that she would probably have been able to just wound Ashe, and even if she had failed, she wouldn't have done any worse than Piers. When she complains, Dalgliesh says, ' "Come Kate, are you really telling me that you wanted to kill a man?"' (353) Why didn't she get to shoot?

PD It goes on to say that Piers had the better line of fire.

MH Yes, but I'm feeling that she was the better shot, and so yes he had the better line of fire, but he still killed him whereas Kate might not have.

PD I think that at that moment it would have been very difficult to stop him. He [Ashe] was on his way out. He knew he was going to be captured and killed, and he was going to take the girl [Octavia] with him, so it had to be very quick. It would have been very difficult to wound him and at the same time not to hit the girl. So what was important was the one who had the best line of fire. But we don't know and that's the interest of novels. We don't know and that's what one's meant to ask oneself. Was he [Dalgliesh] influenced also by the fact that he thought Kate would be very unhappy if she killed a man.

MH Yes, which is the interesting psychology between the two that to some extent Dalgliesh is always trying to protect her.

PD Well, I think he is to an extent.

MH He's paternalistic.

PD He's a little paternalistic. He's very fond of her.

MH And he admires her.

PD Yes, he admires her tremendously. And of course, he's a terribly difficult boss to work for, and he has her on his team because he has confidence, and he obviously tremendously admires her. But I think what we have here is almost a reproach. 'Are you really saying you'd like to kill a man. And assuming this could hardly be done, without a strong risk of killing him, are you really saying that that is something you would have wanted to do; aren't you rather glad that you didn't have to do it.' But I think that the line 'he had the better line of fire' is key. Dalgliesh would have chosen the one who could do the job best in the end.

MH Okay, good.

PD No doubt about that.

MH So Kate could have got it, maybe in the next book.

PD She'll kill half a dozen people. *(laughs)* He had the better line of fire, and it was a remarkable shot, as somebody later on says, that he did manage not to kill the girl. I like to leave in the books slight ambiguities because I think that's life. I mean in A *Taste for Death* when we have the victim who was in the church and had the stigmata, the book doesn't say he had the stigmata on his hand; it says the priest saw them, and we get the impression that being told this is very unwelcome to Dalgliesh. He doesn't really want to be told this.

MH Yes, I have the quote here when Dalgliesh reacts to the news of the stigmata on Sir Paul Berowne's hands: 'In all his career as a detective Dalgliesh couldn't remember a piece of information from a witness more unwelcome and—there was no other word—more shocking' (52).

PD This is something supernatural and it shocked him [Dalgliesh] that it could have happened. It's a complication of the investigation. And it brings out his own ambiguity about his lack of religious faith. He's a son of a priest, but he obviously isn't himself a believer. We get the interesting difference between him and Kate in the last book [A *Certain Justice*] in the church together where, because of his background, he understands that father Presteign is not going to tell him what this woman said [in the confessional], but Kate, the pragmatic, doesn't understand and says, 'you tell us if we should still be looking for the murderer.' So you get that difference between them, too. One of them not religious but understanding religion and accepting it, and the other not. Also some of the exchanges between Kate and the new detective [Piers]. I like Piers. I think I'm going to carry on with Piers.

MH Well, Piers is very interesting because he's got this whole religious background too, and yet in many ways he's even more pragmatic than Kate.

PD Yes, he is I think. It is very interesting that when she says, 'well, what do you believe in?' it's almost as though she's trying to get some answers to questions, and he says he believes in having as happy a time as possible, not hurting other people, and not whining. And Kate says well that's what she believes. You don't have to go to Oxford for three years to read theology to come to that, but it doesn't answer the other questions—murderers and rapists. So Kate is searching after answers to these questions really.

MH Do you see Kate eventually heading a book of her own?

PD Well, no I don't think so, but sometimes people complain and say Dalgliesh is taking a back seat, and they felt, not in the last one but in *Original Sin*, that he was. But I said he was still in charge of the investigation, and he was there at all the important parts of the investigation, but a lot was seen through the eyes of other people. I'm very interested in Kate and the development of Kate's relations with the detective she works with and in both of their relationships with Dalgliesh. I particularly was in the last one because I was interested in Kate's feeling that somehow for the first time she felt there was a certain male exclusion here. She felt that there was an understanding between Piers and Dalgliesh that somehow she had never got, and it seemed to reveal itself in an attitude to their job, sort of detachment, sort of cynicism, whereas she had this huge commitment. She didn't sense it in them to quite the same extent. There's just a difference. For the first time she's beginning to feel educationally and socially insecure. She's never felt that before. She doesn't like that, of course. It comes out when Dalgliesh says would she like to have been seconded for a university education, and she says, 'would that have made me a better detective?'—immediately on the defensive at the suggestion.

MH She's such a character that one can empathize with. She's all of us who are scrabbling for a really fascinating job. She really loves the element of the job that is really satisfying and she's very ambitious.

PD Oh yes, and it's got her out of this terrible background, and she's tried to make a commitment to it.

MH But she's not quite Piers because she never got to Oxford.

PD Piers is less committed. Piers is entertained by it, likes it, enjoys it but would go off and do something else if it occurred, but she definitely wouldn't. This is her job, and she's extremely good at it.

MH You have said that you spend quite a lot of time planning your novels. Can you describe a typical working day.

PD When I'm writing, I get up early and get started. I write a lot by hand or on the old electric portable typewriter. I don't use the modern technology. Then I dictate it on to tape, and when my secretary comes in, she gets started about 2 P.M., and she will type it back. But when I'm not writing, the day is still as full. There's a formidable weight of post each day that has to be dealt with. I haven't been writing since I finished the last book, yet to have a day to myself is extremely rare. I should have been at the House of Lords yesterday for the debate on homosexuality [the debate on lowering the legal age of consent to 16], but I was at a city banquet because I had to respond to the toast to the guests. I don't go to the House of Lords anywhere near as often as I should. I'm always being asked to open things or give prizes away. Life is getting busier not less busy.

MH *A Certain Justice* is being televised now. What do you think of the production?

PD They always have to cut so much. When they first started televising, you'd have five or six episodes. They're doing it quite well, but they haven't got Venetia's ex-husband; all that has been cut completely. It would have been infinitely better if they'd had five or six episodes and done it in a leisurely way, but it's always money. Drama is becoming incredibly expensive. I think there's also a feeling that nobody wants anything long like *Jewel in the Crown* in 13 episodes and *Brideshead Revisited* in God knows how many.

MH Yes, like *The Forsythe Saga* which we watched religiously every Sunday for years.

PD Yes, those days have gone. Maybe they went on a bit, but my goodness we knew what we were doing on that day of the week. And you had long conversations or discussions between people and nowadays everything is cut, cut, cut. Everyone says a few words and you cut to another picture. It's a totally different way of direction isn't it? Everything shorter, and half the time they do it to the extent that I get very irritated because I find I don't know who the people are. You start something and you'll see two characters dashing up in a car, then you see somebody else in a shop, then you see a couple in bed, and I ask, "who are these people; what is their relationship?"

MH The whole wealth of the description, the whole wealth of the conversations, the depth of the analysis is completely lost

PD Yes, it is lost.

MH That's why we read and that's why we tell our students to read.

PD Oh yes. TV has eliminated conversation except about what was on last night. I mean it has brought people to books, no doubt about it. When they did *Pride and Prejudice*, *Pride and Prejudice* was top of the best-seller list in paperback. Now that is astonishing. So more people read it in a week than had read it since the author wrote it. So it [television] can do that, but I think the way it takes children away from reading, the time occupied watching it, is very bad.

MH What are your plans for the future?

PD Another book I hope, but I'm going to Australia and New Zealand for a tour on August 17 [1998]. I hope this autumn to open my mind to the possibility of an exciting idea, but I don't like to begin until I have an idea that excites me. I think the books depend on my feeling I want to deal with this. I think you can always manufacture a book. I know if somebody said 'you will deliver a good detective story in six months or else,' I could start one tomorrow, but it wouldn't satisfy me. It wouldn't be what I want to do. When I say I don't think about my readers, that's true because I don't write always thinking of them, but I know what they expect and hope for, and I have a huge respect, indeed a huge affection for them, and I couldn't bear to think that I produced something that they thought: 'Oh dear she's slipping. Alas, alas, this is not what we expect from P.D. James.' You have an obligation to your talent.

Gwendoline Butler Personal Interview (July 28, 1998)

MH What is your writing schedule?

GB Persistent and daily! When I started writing, I used to train myself to do 1,000 words a day, and I think I kept that up in those early days pretty consistently. And then when I began being two people, I still did 1,000 words a day on the Coffin books and slightly less on the Melville ones, because when I wrote the first one, it had no buyer or market. Charmian Daniels wasn't in the very first one, *Come Home and Be Killed.* I just work constantly. I did even when I had a child still living at home. But of course I didn't do that when my husband was alive, not so much, although I still was very disciplined and had my own workroom even if it was always in the basement.

MH You have written three different series under two names, the Coffin series, the Daniels and gothic type romances.

GB The book that won a dagger was called *Coffin for Pandora*, and it didn't have Coffin in it. It was set in Oxford, really in the little house we lived in then although I didn't say that, but I think it was, and it was about a mid–19th century heroine who was romantic. I'm always surprised it won a dagger. It was a detective story. Coffin appeared on the last page, or rather his grandfather did, and that got me into a period of the gothics; that got me some large contracts. The publishers wanted gothics, and I wanted the money they were offering, which was quite substantial, so I stopped writing straight detection and veered off for a period which lasted about four years.

MH Do you read detective novels?

GB All the time.

MH Who is your favourite author?

GB Currently I'm rather keen on Reginald Hill. In the past I've liked Elizabeth Daily—still do. I've got all these books. They're the ones I reread.

MH Your writing style has changed considerably in 30 years. What did you find difficult in the past that you don't now or vice versa?

GB No difference at all. If I've changed, it's because one develops and alters, and the books are different.

MH You still use the third person narrator in both the Coffin series and the Daniels. What do you think are the advantages of third person versus first person?

GB I've written one or at least two in the first person, but they haven't been crime books. I don't enjoy writing in the first person because it limits you. You can't range quite so widely.

MH But it has the immediacy, a raciness.

GB It can have.

MH John Coffin is obviously very different from the detectives of the Golden Era in his introspection and admission of faults. In his ability to have a long-term relationship he is also very different from P.D. James's Adam Dalgliesh. What do you see as his greatest qualities?

GB I think his greatest quality seems to be his ability to rise again. Another is that he likes people. He grew from the contacts I made, from the world I saw around me and the people I knew.

MH In several of your books there are implied or stated criticisms of the police. For example, in *A Coffin for Charlie*, Stella is afraid of a stalker and says, ' "She knew enough of her husband's colleagues to know that they might suggest [her fear] was all her imagination. A fantasy blown up in her mind. They would not say so directly to John Coffin, but they had their ways of showing scepticism'"(43). And in *Cracking Open a Coffin*, one influential policeman is a wife batterer and the murderer turns out to be a former policeman. What do you feel are the major faults of Britain's police?

GB Since the Met [metropolitan police of London] is under grave scrutiny for corruption (*laughs*) and several officers have been dumped, quite high-ranking ones, too, the average sins I think of anyone. I like to think that the police officers I put in my books are straightforward, but I don't think there may not be bad apples in any particular barrel. Also I am writing fiction, and you do need a few villains.

MH Do you see a time coming when the British police may all be armed?

GB No, no I don't.

MH How do you research your police facts?

GB From books. Oh, and when I was in New York, I was given a great compendium of police regulations in New York. I do look through that and adapt what's useful to me. And then the police themselves will answer questions. I ring up if I want to, and there are lots of books.

MH What made you create a female protagonist in the first place?

GB We were living in St. Andrews where they trained women police constables, and I saw one red-haired girl being trained in the streets, and I thought I'll have a woman police detective. I didn't realize at the time that it was in any way unique or unusual, and I deliberately made Charmian a professional, so that's when it started. It wasn't a deep motivation.

MH But it was very unusual. Were there any high-ranking policewomen at that time?

GB I think not. There have been and still are a few women assistant chief constables and commanders. They haven't had a lot of luck, and I'm afraid I blame that on their colleagues. The police are very male-oriented.

MH This is the huge difference between Charmian and Jane Tennison in Linda La Plante's *Prime Suspect*. From the word go Charmian is aware of her own power and is quite determined to be successful. She sometimes treads on people's toes but not in a nasty way and everyone respects her. They don't necessarily like her, but no one prevents her from going on up.

GB She was unusual in that, but I was determined she should be a success, and I suppose in a sense I was basing her on what would have happened to me if I'd remained in academic life, when on the whole in my day, even more so now, women do climb the ladder. I was in the generation that was expecting to be successful as a woman in whatever field they ventured.

MH And you were a historian.

GB Yes, I was a historian and probably would have been an academic, although I'm not sure I was totally devoted to the academic life. But I married and left but didn't mind, because I'd already realized that I was free if I wrote. I was independent.

MH Daniels does marry, but you have her husband die of a heart attack, and there are no children. Why did you do this? And do you feel that there is no possibility for a detective in fiction to be married with children?

GB It never entered my head to give her a family. Just didn't come into my mind that she should have one. Since then we've all watched Cagney and Lacey—one of them has a family and a lot of problems. I wouldn't have wanted to do that. It's not what I was writing about. I don't think I'm very family-oriented.

MH Daniels is very human and appealing. As she has grown older, she has clearly grown wiser, but she still agonizes about her decisions and gets into predicaments. Do you feel that the jealousies which arise from having a female boss are still a real problem for policewomen today?

GB Oh yes, I'm sure they are. There just is jealousy amongst any set of professionals as far as I can see. Whether it's publishing, academia or anything. They're all struggling for their place in the sun. It's a very competitive world.

MH Daniels is very successful not only in her job in SRADIC but also in the mysterious job she does for the government in London. Why have you made that job so mysterious, and will we ever be told exactly why that job is important?

GB The thing is I've fallen into the same trap with old Coffin because I couldn't bear them not to be successful; therefore, I had to give them promotion, and then in a mad moment I invented this second city, and I must say I've loved doing that; it satisfies me. There he is, poor chap, he's the head of the place; he can't go out and be a detective, so I have to keep inventing reasons why he should be doing detection. The same with Charmian. I gave her great promotion. Then I thought I must justify her existence, and I said I must have an institution which doesn't really exist, which will enable her to put her hand into whatever she wants to do.

MH I think one of my favorite books is an old one *Murder Has a Pretty Face* because I love the idea of a female gang of bank robbers who will stop at nothing...

GB (*interrupting*) I'm bringing them back in the next book. I haven't signed a contract nor have I written it, but Macmillan say they want it even though I haven't written a word.

MH The book seems to have a major feminist message. You had them showing quite a lot of force and nastiness.

GB Yes, they weren't good people.

MH Is that what your aim was?

GB No! It's just what I thought they were.

MH At the end of the book Baby and Phil have escaped justice and are sitting in Spain planning another bank robbery...

GB (*interrupts*) I couldn't resist Baby. Baby's living in Windsor or nearabouts and is still very friendly with Charmian.

MH Did Baby ever do time?

GB No, she didn't. She's one of the escapees of this world, but she hasn't changed in character. She's not totally honest ever, never will be, but she's coming back. And there's another group formed around her. And the one I killed off, Diana, well she wasn't dead after all, oddly enough. It was all a fake—she's coming back too! (*laughs*)

MH Another aspect of the Daniels series which makes the books unusual is that many of your criminals are women who do not necessarily murder for revenge or out of necessity. Why do you think many women murder? Do their relationships with men cause their problems as Daniels questions in *Windsor Red* ?

GB Well, I think in real life women probably murder less than men—much less—and do it because they've been ill-treated themselves; sometimes they may do it for financial gain of one sort or another, but there must be a few professional women criminals—parts of London harbor them—who are willing to do it for whatever suits them. But I am writing fiction. I have to construct a plot, so I usually have to give my women a good motive really, because even though they are killers, I don't want the reader to feel no sympathy with them.

MH Do you agree with P.D. James when she says that, 'we are all capable of murder in one circumstance' (Cooper-Clark 25).

GB I can't see Phyllis murdering anyone! I'm not sure really. If I think about myself, I find it very difficult to show violence. I don't know about that. I don't think everyone could kill. I really don't.

MH Do you also think that to some extent the victim of a murder is partly responsible for his/her murder?

GB Oh yes. I do certainly believe that one way or another. It's a double act. When the act of killing takes place, they are not two people—they are one.

MH What do you think are the advantages and disadvantages of writing a series?

GB It's nice to create a world that's one I'm very drawn to as you will have noticed in the Coffin books. I always have to create my own world. The city and the world I create are just as important to me as the people I create. I've a very strong sense of the past, what it was, how it grew up. That explains the Coffin things. I'm doing one now when the very first bit is about Samuel Pepys, and you can do that in a series. You can build it up.

MH Do you have many fans who also really enjoy all your secondary characters who grow and change in your books. I'm thinking in particular of Kate when you killed her off in *A Death in the Family*; was that really necessary?

GB No, it wasn't really. Sorry about that. It was quite arbitrary really.

MH You have said that to some extent Coffin and Daniels are extensions of you. In what ways do you relate to Daniels?

GB Yes, they are. Daniels is a successful professional woman, and I admire her for that, and I'm sure lots of things she'd say I would say. Coffin is more like my husband with a mixture of my father. But there's certainly a lot of me in him.

MH Why did you have Daniels marry Humphrey after years of deliberating as to whether or not she would take the plunge?

GB There was no deep significance. I just thought it was about time something like that happened. I think when you get a close relationship, or you're considering it, there are always reservations especially for a woman, and she's obviously a very powerful woman. He's perhaps a less powerful man, not a very strong character, successful. That is because he comes from a world where it was easy for him to be accepted. She isn't that sort of person. She comes from very much a working-class background, as I did myself.

MH Humphrey is a shadowy character. You haven't totally fleshed him out.

GB No, you're absolutely right, and I mean he may die any minute.

MH Oh, may he?

GB Yes! (*laughs*) I wanted her to have a spouse. I didn't want her to seem a lesbian. She didn't seem to have much of a sex life. Detectives don't have a sex life. They are too busy, and isn't it interesting that some of the most successful, like Lord Peter Wimsey, Dorothy Sayers had to be very careful to give him mistresses and then a passionate affair with Harriet, because otherwise he had a chance of getting a different sort of label. Indeed it was hinted that this is what he was, and it is quite a problem. I think what I wanted to show is that men expect women to fit into their lives, and I wanted to create a woman who expected the man to fit into hers. And Humphrey has.

MH What about the relationship between Charmian and Dolly? In *The Woman Who Was Not There*, Dolly is worried about Charmian. The narrator says, 'Charmian had the depressing feeling that her old easy relationship with Dolly was melting away somehow. Her fault or Dolly's?' (147) And then Dolly says, '"Never had you down for one of the ruling class, lady-of-the-manor types ... thought we were mates.' She made a resolve: 'I'll see this case through, then I'll ask for a transfer to another posting, another area'"(147).

GB She's not going to.

MH Oh good!

GB It's a competition. She's not jealous but she is competitive.

MH And she does feel that Charmian has got what she would like.

GB Yes.

MH And she wants to emulate her.

GB Of course she does and why not? She does quite a lot in the book I've just done the proofs for.

MH Oh good, because I really like her. One thing you don't have which has surprised me; you had Ann Hood in one of the very early books, but you really haven't had any ethnic minorities. How come, considering how many ethnic minorities there are in England now?

GB Well, I suppose it hasn't come my way. It certainly hasn't been a deliberate policy. It just hasn't happened. To create a character something's got to attract your creative imagination. You've got to know how they talk, what they wear, how they walk, and that just hasn't happened.

MH There aren't that many minorities in Windsor?

GB No, there aren't and of course not in Scotland.

MH No, of course not, but I was just thinking that with Charmian's job she might be called in to such an ethnic situation.

GB Yes, I think you're absolutely right; it hasn't happened. It's not a deliberate thing. I think if anything I'm nervous as to how I'd handle it. There's an unconscious inhibition slightly because if you're not colored or a so-called minority, you might stumble into all sorts of problems. I think Reginald Hill has in publishing his Joe books—he's invented a black detective. And I do think you're in danger of being patronizing.

MH But you could have a minor character.

GB Yes, you're quite right. I may do so, and if so, I'll give you credit. (*laughs*) Indeed the part of London where I grew up, Blackheath, just close to it is the area where a black boy, a very nice boy obviously, was killed at the bus stop waiting for a bus by a gang of rather horrid white boys. It was a deliberately racial thing. They were the sort of boys you wouldn't want your son to be, flashing their arrogance.

MH The use of ethnic minorities might suit the Coffin books more.

GB Yes, I'll feed it into my psyche. (*laughs*) I think my cast tend to be a bit well-educated and well spoken. Peter Dillon-Parker [Crime magazine editor] said to me, 'They don't even say "ain't" and "isn't" your lot; they always say "is it not."' I thought he's dead right. (*laughs*) But it's the way I write really.

MH It has been said that detective fiction today both reflects societal change and influences it. Do you agree, and which do you feel you are doing more in the Daniels's novels?

GB All fiction reflects social change if it has any quality; it must do, and I know I have done so. But writers are like blotting paper; they soak up impressions and use them.

MH What would be your advice to a budding detective novel writer?

GB Write, just write. That's the important thing to do, plunge in. Beginning a book is always difficult. Sometimes the very first sentence is marvelous, and the whole book grows from there, but sometimes you don't have a first sentence, and then I just write anything. With the word processor you can just go back.

MH Do you start with an idea, you've read something or there's a little titbit?

GB They start in different ways. Sometimes I have a marvelous idea and that's very helpful indeed, but they don't come all that often. Sometimes I know the beginning, and I know the end. It has to be organic for me. It grows towards it. I know some writers have it all mapped out; I couldn't write like that. It would be dead.

MH What are your own plans for the future? Have any of your books been televised?

GB No, radio yes, television no. They often come close to it.

MH Would you like that?

GB I'd love it, and of course it does marvels for the sale of paperbacks. The trouble is there are so many detective series on the air and on TV. They are rather cutting each other's throats. There has been some recent interest in televising Charmian, so we'll see.

Susan Moody E-Mail Response
(January 19, 1999)

Why did I pick a black protagonist? Partly because there wasn't one. But also because, although I dislike the pretentiousness of those crime writers who say they write in the hope of changing society or passing on some 'message', because let's face it, we all write in the hope of entertaining our readers and earning a living while we do it, I do nonetheless think that all good crime novels have a subtext. (This doesn't exclude those written purely for entertainment, of course).

So Penny was always intended to break new ground, to say something political. Black women at the time were almost invisible in fiction, not just in crime fiction. I'd spent nearly 10 years in Tennessee in the 60s, and taken part in the civil rights movement, seen the Ku Klux Klan, even had a cross burned on my lawn and having grown up in liberal Europe, I was absolutely appalled. As I was by the sight of the chain gangs in Georgia, and the fact that the gasstation loos had 3 doors, marked Men, Women and Coloured. I just couldn't come to terms with that.

As you say, she was the first black female protagonist, and although she started out in PENNY BLACK as something of a fantasy figure, she became something more serious in subsequent books. As you will have noted, she has a white boyfriend, a definite political statement, and because of this, the books were banned in South Africa in the pre–Mandela era, something of which I was extremely proud.

I was also proud that my books were displayed on the Women's Rights shelves in a number of the more left-wing council libraries (that is, libraries run by radical councils, such as Brent and Islington). And even more proud when young black women who met me would tell me what a relief, what a breakthrough it was to find a heroine with whom they could identify, a black female who didn't take any s—- from anyone and who was free and her own person.

I can't say I have read many of today's African American female authors, partly because they're difficult to come by over here. In fact, it shames me to realise that I couldn't even name one, except a nice lady called Eleanor someone someone—and that's not much help in getting hold of her books, is it? One of the things that I find interesting to contemplate is the change in publishers' criteria: I wouldn't have a hope in hell of getting the Penny books published today, because I myself am not black. Take that to its logical conclusion, of course, and no middle-class middle-aged English female crime writer will be able to write about anything but middle-class middle-aged English females ...

Hope this is useful,
Susan

Susan Moody E-Mail Interview
(March 25, 1999)

MH In her wealth and privilege Penny does hearken back to the Lord Peter Wimsey type of detective, but she's obviously very different. What are the advantages, in your opinion, of having an upper class protagonist?

SM I would not say that Penny Wanawake harks back to the Lord Peter Wimsey kind of detective! Her upper-classness is entirely incidental, whereas his is crucial. I can't see that today, class of any kind confers advantage or disadvantage on a fictional detective. Class boundaries will always have to be crossed in a contemporary crime novel because none of us live isolated from society. Much more important is the fact that Penny is self-employed, which enables her to take time off to find out whodunnit!

MH Why did you choose to have such an unusual boyfriend for Penny?

SM I usually deny that I have any kind of message for the world. On the other hand, I do realize that the best crime fiction (which doesn't always mean the best selling!) always has a meaningful political sub-text, either as a commentary on the society in which we all operate, or about human relationships, or about the universal emotions which rule our lives. So, given that Penny is a Black woman, the decision to make Barnaby Midas a White South African was a very deliberate one. The fact that he is also a modern day Robin Hood was intended as an extra satirical note. I am exceedingly proud of the fact that in the pre–Mandela days, these books were banned in S Africa.

MH I see Penny's attitude to Barnaby and to the other men with whom she has a sexual relationship as marking a very different type of detective to those who have gone before. She acts like a man, enjoying sexual encounters and having no guilt that she is "cheating on" Barnaby and just saying she has appetites. Do you see her as a typical 1990s woman?

SM When I first began to write the Penny books, it occurred to me that in crime and thriller fiction, the men are allowed sexual freedom, but the women never are. Was this because of the feminine attitude to sex, or to society's view of what women are "permitted" to do? I certainly didn't see her as a typical 1990s woman, much more as an early 1980s woman, aware of her own sexuality and liberated enough to indulge it. The original intention was that, like James Bond, Penny would engage a new sexual relationship in each book. However, AIDS caught up with us, and promiscuity was suddenly not an acceptable message, so I drastically reduced the "sleaze factor"!

MH In her behavior she is very different from your later protagonist, Cassie, who always feels the need to justify why she is "bonking" Paul Walsh, yet clearly likes/loves Charlie Quartermain. I see Cassie as more of a throwback to the gothic heroine, who spends most of the novel saying how unsuitable the man is, but ends up in his arms at the end, much to the satisfaction of the reader. How do you characterize Cassie's relationship with Charlie?

SM I entirely disagree that Cassie is a throw-back to a gothic heroine.

Apart from anything else, the series is not finished, and I really could not be certain that she will end up with Charlie—however unsatisfactory it might be to the reader if she did not. I intended to write 8 Cassie books but so far have only written 6. These eight books were conceived as a means to look light-heartedly at different aspects of current British society, and class is an issue which very much permeates the novels.

MH Would you describe yourself as a feminist?

SM Yes, I'm a feminist, and was one long before the term came into use. Growing up with four brothers, it was a case of embrace feminism or die!

MH Do you agree that the role of the detective novel has changed dramatically because of feminism. And what do you see as the role of today's detective novel?

SM a) I'm not sure to what extent "feminism" is responsible for the change in the role of women in detective fiction, unless you are prepared to attribute to feminism all change in social attitudes to women. Some of this must surely have its roots in the Pill—but feminism alone was not responsible for this. The detective novel has always mirrored the "real" world, and suddenly women were given control over their own bodies. This, in turn, gave them career opportunities which they could not have taken up prior to this. But yes, given that, the feminist movement did then go into the work place and battled for parity—and still has much to do, I'm afraid. That's why there has been such a flood of feisty independent female protagonists in detective fiction—because it was no longer totally unreal to have a women taking on male roles.

b) I'm always uneasy when asked what the "role" of detective fiction is. Does it need to have a role? Surely, whatever political flag we writers are flying, the fundamental role of genre fiction should be to entertain. But see my earlier answer.

MH I realize that I'm not a typical reader and may be reading a lot more into detective fiction than the average reader does; however, what do you think the average reader wants from detective fiction in general and your novels in particular?

SM a) I don't know what an "average reader" of crime fiction is. The genre itself provides such a wide umbrella, embracing everything from historical to thriller to psychological whydunnit, that there can be no such thing as an "average reader." However, I would say that on the whole, readers of crime fiction want:

1. to see justice done, in a way in which it is often *not* seen to be done in the larger and untidier world outside the pages of a book. So the villain should not get away with it.

2. to be involved, which is why character is such a crucial part of good crime fiction—and is one of the fundamental differences between the detective novel and the thriller, where plot is all!

3. to learn something about a world different from their own

4. to be entertained

5. to be moved

b) What does this mythical Average Reader want from my books? I don't know. All or any of the above, I suppose.

MH You have criticized numerous social ills in all your books. Do you think this criticism is now an integral part of detective fiction?

SM No, I don't think social criticism is an integral part of detective fiction. Between us, we could name any number of successful crime writers whose books contain almost none.

MH Is there a danger that an author might become a little too preachy or didactic to the detriment of the plot?

SM Yes, I do think this is a danger. I've heard far too many of my colleagues adopting a preacherly tone on platforms, talking about their intentions of changing the world with their fictions, and I always feel that it is totally hypocritical. What we all want to do is tell a good story—and with any luck, get paid a living wage for it! The detective novel can be a way to comment on social ills as we perceive them, to provide a thought-provoking slant on contemporary society, but it should never pretend that this is its main function.

MH Among the many social ills you critique are classism, agism and sizism. Why do you think these in particular are important to criticize?

SM I would think that all or any social ill is worth criticizing. Classism is so endemic in British society that it's always going to be a worthy target. The abolition of privilege because of birth is fundamental to a healthy society. Ageism: I could go on about this at some length, but will simply say it is important that people should not be stigmatized for their age. In addition, the notion that once you reach a certain age and can be categorized as "elderly," then you no longer have any life worth living is both iniquitous and dangerous, given that we are a rapidly ageing society.

MH For many Americans Cassie's fears about her size seem exaggerated. A size 16 British is a size 14 American which is never considered over large. Since our large sizes go to size 50, Cassie might even be considered thin by some! Why did you not make her really obese? Would a size 24 woman, for example, be considered too large for a protagonist?

SM Sizeism (ghastly word!): I wasn't talking about size as such. I am much more interested in the way women are socialized into perceiving themselves. To be a size 16 is to be overweight but not hugely so. Yet Cassie worries about this constantly. Had I made her much larger, I would have been into a different ball game, where health and mobility would have to become issues. My aim was to critique the way society insists that we are somehow not valuable if we don't look like stick insects. I wanted Cassie, in Book 8 (which I haven't written) to finally accept that she is beautiful, witty, brave and worthy, even if she bulges. Yes, for the reasons in the last para, using as protagonist a size 24 woman would very much have altered the balance of my books.

MH What do you find are the limitations/advantages of writing a series?

SM The LIMITATIONS are that you are to some extent rehashing old ground which a writer can find boring, that it's difficult to be too developmental, that the reader doesn't want your character to change so that you cannot chart full progression. You can make things happen to your character—deaths, loves, good and bad stuff—but the character herself must not change too much because it's the character you produced in the first book which is the one the reader has bonded with. Which means that to an extent, the character is always standing slightly to one side of the action even when she appears to be in the thick of it. That said, there are probably writers out there who have managed to produce a character who has been changed, as real people are, by life's experience, but I can't think of one.

The ADVANTAGES are that you don't have to think of a new scenario, you don't have to produce a new character with a new background, new friends and relatives, new expertises. You've already done your groundwork, all you have to do now is produce a new plot. This can of course get exceedingly boring, as I'm sure Sue Grafton would tell you!

MH Since the US has so many different ethnic and minority authors, I am surprised that there are no female Pakistani/Indian or Jamaican detective novelists in Britain. Why do you think this is?

SM No Chinese or Japanese either! I don't really have an answer to this one. Some of it must be cultural. Some ethnic groups don't assimilate into the host society. Maybe the potential women novelists are still too preoccupied with merely surviving, or, if they've attained some autonomy, too busy clinging on to whatever freedoms they've been allowed to assume. On the other hand, as you say, there are so many ethnic female writers in the US, so why so few in Britain?

MH In my ... [book] I am trying to forecast in which directions the detective novel written by a female will move? Can you make any predictions for me?

SM I would rather not try to forecast! People who do so often end up with egg on their faces. But I would say there is a gap in the market for good strong romantic crime fiction (not the Woman in Peril kind)—Laurie King is already writing something of the sort. I'd say that the really feisty unpleasant female character in the VI Warshawski mode may be temporarily in abeyance. I also believe that the new wave of crime book is much much closer to the literary novel than it ever used to be, and much less puzzle-dependent.

MH When I look at the future of the detective novel, I see a growing move towards more violent works like those of Minette Walters and Val McDermid's latest. Do you see this as one of the trends? Why do you think we enjoy violence in novels?

SM I don't think I agree with you about a trend to more violent works. I can't see much change in emphasis, apart from a very few. Val, yes, but is Minette violent? I haven't read beyond *The Echo*. As for enjoying violence, I don't! I found Val's *The Mermaids Singing* one of the most repulsive books I've ever read, and I also had to put down, never to pick up again, a David Lindsey a few books back because it was so horrible. I don't know that I'm an exception, either.

Judith Cutler E-Mail Interview
(February 7, 2000)

MH What were your intentions in showing Inspector Chris Groom and Detective Sergeant Ian Dale as kindly, gentle types, especially in the first few Sophie Rivers books? I'm thinking in particular of the fact that after Sophie's first encounter with death, that of Wajid's, Ian takes her to the local police station by car after first giving her strong mints when she vomits. At the Rose Road station, he gives her coffee with extra sugar and is described: "He might have been a favourite uncle, in his worn sports jacket with archetypal leather patches" (17). And later in the novel not only Ian but also Chris are described as "avuncular" several times. Not once do you voice any criticism of the behaviour of the police or their inefficiency (as many 1980s and 1990s authors do,) and in *Dying to Write* when one of the characters refers to the police as "filth," Sophie thinks "I try to be broad-minded, always, but words like 'filth' upset me. The only policeman I know at all well is not at all filth-like. He is eminently civilised in most respects" (28–29). In the same novel when the murderer, Toad, dies of an epileptic seizure, Chris and Ian feel guilty: "It was better for all if justice could be seen to be done, and neither anticipated a very favourable reaction from those in power when it became generally known that they had allowed an epileptic to drown"(412). Your views seem to be unusual in light of other female detective writers, such as Joan Smith, and in light of the major problems with the police force in Britain in the 1990s.

JC As the Sophie novels progress, we see more problems with the police. But it's a given that Chris and Ian are as pure as the driven snow. It's important to the tension between Sophie, prepared to cut corners, and Chris, playing by the book. In any case, corruption can be caused by unreasonable pressures, which I also try to deal with in the later books. Of course, there are far more police problems in the Kate series.

MH Also how do you see Sophie's relationship with Chris and men in general?

JC Sophie likes sexy men, physically desirable, like Mike, her new lover. However much she likes Chris, he simply doesn't turn her on. She's also attracted, however, reluctantly, by power—see PRINCIPLE—probably as a result of her working-class background and insecurity caused by events in her late teens (see SCORE).

MH In *Dying to Write* it is clear that Sophie is ambivalent about forming a relationship with Chris, but she is willing to sleep with more unsuitable men. In this book we learn that she has just finished an affair with a married man and has a one night stand with another married man, Hugh. With Hugh she was all set to have a long term relationship but omitted to ask him the vital question, and he does not volunteer his marital status. Yet Sophie doesn't seem to be the "love 'em and leave 'em" type of woman. How would you describe her sexually?

JC Reflect on her relationship with Andy. She's certainly maturing these days (in the novel due out in 2001!!!)

MH I love the sense of place you have in both your series. How important do you think setting is to the detective genre? Also why did you pick Birmingham as your setting? Was it just because it is familiar to you?

JC To be brutally honest, when you have a full-time job, a family, a big house and a big garden to run, you have to cut corners. I couldn't have set a novel in London or Newcastle because I didn't have the background or the time to absorb it. So, faux de mieux [*faute de mieux*], it had to be Birmingham. But I hope I turned a limitation to an advantage. The upside is that noone else writes about it, so I can get local publicity. The downside is that the British media are not keen on Brum, so it's hard to get national reviews.

MH One of the big changes in the detective genre since the 1980s is this use of settings other than London and the cozy village somewhere in the Home Counties. Do you feel your use of Birmingham and Val McDermid's use of Manchester, to name another writer, is effecting the types of crimes your protagonists examine?

JC I think my further education background is the most important. As far as I know, no one else has looked at that. At the time I was writing, there was an enormous amount of corruption generated by changes to FE management.

MH Considering Sophie is an academic, how do you see your novels in relation to Amanda Cross's in the US or Joan Smith's in Britain?

JC Sophie isn't an academic. Further education is a level between school and university, duplicating some school courses and also offering professional exams. It's the Cinderella of the education world (Still)—so the background is one of deprivation and under-funding no university teacher could begin to imagine.

MH You examine cyber crime in *Dying Fall* and *Dying on Principle*; where do you see the future of the detective genre vis a vis technological advances?

JC In the hands of experts, which I'm not!

MH Why did you begin a new series?

JC Money. It motivates most professional writers! I also wanted to explore areas like paedophilia which Sophie couldn't possibly interfere with.

MH How do you see Kate in relation to Lynda La Plante's Jane Tennison?

JC Much more human. It's relationships which drive her. Humans. Sooner or later she'll find a heterosexual relationship which will cause problems with her police life: if you want to get back to someone's bed or have to feed a baby, then you're less likely to put your life on the line. (Think of Mary-Beth Lacey.)

MH What are your aims in this series?

JC To explore pressures, I think. And to develop a new area of expertise. And I have to say all the police officers I've spoken to have been incredibly helpful, even about the bad things in the police service. I know I'm white, middle-aged and middle-class, and thus no threat, but I'm constantly struck by their courtesy, patience, intelligence, sense of justice, etc.

Denise Mina E-Mail Interview
(February 8, 2000)

MH I have included an analysis of Garnethill in my last chapter on "New Voices" and was wondering if you could comment [on] a couple of extracts from my analysis. I particularly like your work since I feel it moves the detective genre in a really innovative direction. This is what I have written: Another interesting figure among the latest voices to appear in detective fiction is that of Denise Mina. Val McDermid recommended her saying, "Garnethill has been short-listed for the John Creasey Dagger for the best first novel.... The novel is remarkable for the way it gives voice to those who are usually unheard." The novel concerns Maureen, a woman who has had a nervous breakdown following recovered memories of childhood sexual abuse by her father. Like Joan Smith's novel, *Full Stop*, and American novels such as Linda Barnes's *Coyote* and Elizabeth Bowers's *No Forwarding Address*, Mina examines a woman's sense of marginalization when she is forever regarded as unreliable, in this case because of her history of mental illness.

At one point when Detective Chief Inspector Joe McEwan and Hugh McAskill are interrogating her for the fourth time, McEwan unexpectedly asks her if she is a feminist and then says, "'I thought you liked men'" (142). When Maureen mocks him that he clearly doesn't know a lot about feminism, his reply is "'I know what they look like and they don't look like you.' He pointed openly to her large tits and looked away, leaving Maureen—and McAskill—aghast. He knew he'd offended her but he didn't give a shit" (142). Although McEwan is not particularly cruel to her because of the time she has spent in psychiatric care, he clearly feels that since she has lied about receiving treatment at the Rainbow Clinic, she is probably lying about the murder. In his eyes, she is totally unreliable as a woman and especially as a former mental patient. Hence Mina, unlike Cutler, follows in the footsteps of several of the authors in this survey in depicting the police as prejudiced against women.

Maureen's relationship with Leslie is typical of the feminist detective and is an extremely supportive one. Leslie is her drinking partner, her shoulder to cry on, and above all her sounding board. She is first described as: "Leslie was great to talk to. Whatever had happened she unconditionally took her pal's side, happily badmouthed the opposition and then never mentioned it again" (11). Leslie works as a counselor at a battered woman's shelter and occasionally voices her personally felt horror at the way many of these women are treated by their husbands. When Maureen is scared of pursuing the rapist, Leslie describes Charlotte, one of these women, in order to make her realize that running away from a terrible situation is not going to miraculously make it go away: "Her husband had been beating her and she came to us. She had these facial scars—you know, the kind that make you shudder when you first see them. Her nose was flattened and one of her eyes was higher than the other. Ina said it was a cheekbone fracture that hadn't been set. You could see the bone sticking out sometimes, when she was eating. She'd scars all over her cheek, there." She gestured to her left cheek, drawing a circle on it. "The really vicious ones cut across cuts so that the doctors can't sew it up. There's nothing to sew it onto, just bits of skin hanging off. They can't patch it up, they just have to let it scar" (248).

Leslie continues her tale saying how Charlotte's husband finally kills her. Later when Leslie and the other women at the shelter say they are sure that her death was caused by the husband, the police say that without witnesses, they can do nothing. The feeling of impotence that Leslie experiences in this situation makes her tell Maureen, " 'I'll be there, Mauri, I promise'" (249). And she is, right through till the end when Maureen unmasks the rapist and makes sure Siobhain is safe. This closeness shared by Maureen and Leslie is reminiscent of that experienced by Kate Brannigan and Alexis, [and] Loretta Lawson and Bridget, and is another reason why this first novel is most powerful.

In my conclusion I would like to comment on where you see your own work moving in the future and where you think female detective fiction is going. Therefore, I would greatly appreciate any help/comments you can make on what I've said about your work. If you feel I'm off track at any point, please tell me, and I'll adjust my comments accordingly.

DM Please forgive my lateness in replying but I have a dead line for my next book on Monday 14th and I'm going mad. I agree with everything you said about my work. My next book is a follow on to Garnethill and is the second in the trilogy which continues to explore women and violent direct action. In the future I think women's detective fiction will do what always happens: the ground breakers will be turned against by the new generation who will doubtless produce an anti feminist backlash. On the shoulders of giants stand monkeys.

Michelle Spring E-Mail Interview (February 5, 2000)

MH Of all the latest writers I'm analyzing, I feel your work best fits in with the earlier 1980s hard-boiled fiction which came out of the States—Grafton and Paretsky in particular, since you have a professional private investigator who is examining topical areas in which women are still marginalized. I have said the following things about your work and would be really grateful if you could comment on them: Michelle Spring's private investigator Laura Principal reflects many of the 1990s American ones, such as Linda Grant and Dana

Stabenow, especially in the way her novels are grounded in contemporary situations to "suggest a continuity between the social order portrayed in the book and the social order in the world in which the book is read creating a dialogic relationship between the two" (Walton & Jones 219). Spring continues in Paretsky's and Grafton's footsteps in developing in her books "the concept of advocacy on behalf of a client, who for one reason or another has little or no conventional legal power to speak for him–or herself" (Walton & Jones 206–207).

Not only does Spring foreground women's issues in her novels, but she also analyses the efficacy of the police and the justice system. [In the analysis of *Every Breath You Take*] At one point Laura is asked to act for a convicted criminal and she agrees to do so because she feels those convicted do not always deserve their fate:

> Only the most ill-informed could take conviction in a British court as an infallible guide to guilt. If you think about it, there may be almost as many innocent people incarcerated in our prisons as there are guilty people roaming the streets outside. And it is the innocent ones who have the most need of the kind of services a private investigator can provide. (24)

This direct appeal to the reader as "you" clearly shows Spring's concern with this topic. However, unlike Loretta Lawson's opinion of the police, Laura rarely thinks they are ineffective or worse, corrupt, and indeed enjoys an excellent working relationship with Inspector Nicole Pelletier, a former student of hers. Nicole can always be relied upon to help her with background information and takes her suspicions seriously.

Laura is very similar to Kate Brannigan, and Spring also resembles Val McDermid in that both writers have particularly topical plots. Following her reading of a news article about migrant workers and meetings with Filipino women working in the West London area, Spring wrote *Running for Shelter* which describes the harrowing life of one such woman and her consequent death. The evident research which went into this novel adds enormously to its interest and power. Similarly there is a great deal of topical interest in *Standing in the Shadows*, which was nominated for the Arthur Ellis Canadian award, and which examines the idea of a child committing murder and people's general reaction to such a crime.

Spring's willingness to analyze the very latest problems which are overwhelming British society today in tightly woven, exciting plots bodes well for the success and interest of her future books. Unlike Cutler and Thomas, Spring is writing in a similar vein to Joan Smith and Val McDermid, and her books have the power to engage and move the reader as do theirs.

MS I have no quarrel whatsoever with your comments on my approach. They capture some of the things that are most important to me, and I am delighted that you place my books in the company of those written by Paretsky and McDermid.

You are quite right, I think, to highlight the focus of my books on contemporary issues. Of course, my primary intention is to write the best novel I can, which should be enthralling and entertaining. But as a writer, my best work comes when I feel passionate about something, and so when issues about which I feel strongly—such as violence by (and to) children, or the unprotected status of domestic workers, or sexual harassment, or student prostitution—are incorporated in a story of mine, they tend to make the writing more powerful.

Yes, I do like to use the novels to give a voice to people who otherwise might not be heard. Connected to this, I like the challenge of writing against stereotype—for example, making the secretary a person of dignity and intelligence (rather than the nail-filing bimbo she is sometimes made out to be). It would be easier to work with caricatures; but there's no fun in writing if you always take the easy way out!

Where do I see the female detective novel going? At my optimistic moments (and this is one of them) I sense the boundaries that have divided hard-boiled from soft-boiled and male from female dimensions of the genre being well and truly dismantled. By that I mean, that there are increasing numbers of male-centred, action-oriented writers who nevertheless pay careful attention to the full nuances of relationships in their work and increasing numbers of women writers who go the full route in terms of gristle and gore, but still retain some of the sensibilities and the themes that we have come to expect of women/soft-boiled authors. The best of the female detective novels are continuing the job of reflecting (and reflecting on) the experiences and the circumstances of women (and men) today. They are not preachy, but nor are they afraid to comment on the society around them. After all, crime fiction is a wonderful lens through which to take a critical look at [the] contemporary world.

You ask, Mary, about comments by critics other than yourself. There's been quite a number for the last two books (Shadows and Nights) including a wonderful review in the Washington Post book World, picking up on my interest in suspense, and Thomas McNulty's long commentary in Mystery News. The enthusiasm of these critics has fairly made my head spin!

Joan Smith E-Mail Response
(February 14, 2001)

Dear Mary,

You know my work astonishingly well, and I'm glad you linked it with Misogynies, which is its non-fiction analogue. I have always felt that fiction should not be overtly didactic; one of the things I wanted to do with Loretta was draw the reader in to the world of a clever, sexy, political and often pissed-off woman, and persuade them to share her view for a while. I think that's more effective (if it works) than lecturing the reader. I'm also pleased you understand that not trusting the traditional forces of law and order is central to the novels—I wrote A Masculine Ending as the miners' strike of 1984–5 was coming to a close, and I felt very alienated from the police at that time. I was trying to express something that was felt by lots of people on the left, including feminists, without actually mentioning the strike in the novel. And of course the unresolved endings in several of the books were deliberate, as well as a tease in terms of traditional expectations of the detective novel. In the UK, crime fiction was for a long time a right-wing and conservative form—eg Agatha Christie's rants against Bolshevism, and the way in which the social fabric is always repaired by the end of her novels—and I wanted to appropriate it as a radical form. It's certainly true, from readers' reactions, that a lot of people identified with Loretta and her politics when they read the books. I think I also wanted to give a contemporary woman a voice in crime, as I am acutely aware of the way we have been excluded from any role other than victims; when I was reporting the Yorkshire Ripper murders, I was often one of about 5 women reporters at press conferences attended by more than 100 men, and had to listen to them exchanging theories, no matter how crazy, with an entirely male police team. Loretta's awareness of crime, and her exposure to it, is partly an attempt to offer an alternative view of its impact and consequences, as well as giving a woman a chance to make sense of it.

I don't know if any of this helps, but I thought you mind find it interesting. The only other point I wanted to add is that I'm still a journalist—very much so. I write a weekly column for the Independent on Sunday, and occasional columns for the Guardian, as well as a mass of reviews and other stuff.

Very best wishes
Joan

Works Cited

Secondary Sources*

Albert, Susan Wittig. "Tough Girls, Hard Cases: Strong Women in Mystery." *Deadly Women*. Eds. Jan Grape, Dean James and Ellen Nehr. New York: Carroll & Graf, 1998. pp. 99–102.

Bailey, Frankie Y. *Out of the Woodpile: Black Characters in Crime and Detective Fiction*. Westport, CT: Greenwood, 1991.

Bakerman, Jane. "Cordelia Gray: Apprentice and Archetype." *Clues: A Journal of Detection* 5 (1984): 101–114.

Barrieua, Nancy. "What's a Feminist To Do?: Feminism in the Female Detective Novel." Popular Culture Association Conference, Augusta, GA, USA. October 1998.

Barron, Neil et al. *What Do I Read Next?: A Reader's Guide to Genre Fiction*. Detroit: Gale Research, 1998.

Bartell, Gerald. "Deadline for Murder." ewArticle=1:next=html/Article.html.

Begley, Sharon. "Why the Young Kill." *Newsweek* 3 May 1999: pp. 32–35.

Butler, Gwendoline. *Cracking Open a Coffin*. New York: St. Martin's, 1992.

Carter, Steven R. "Amanda Cross." *10 Women of Mystery*. Ed. Earl F. Bargainnier. Bowling Green: Bowling Green State University Press, 1981. pp. 270–296.

Cooper-Clark, Diane. *Designs of Darkness: Interviews with Detective Novelists*. Bowling Green: Bowling Green State University Popular Press, 1983.

Cranny-Francis, Anne. *Feminist Fiction*. New York: St. Martin's, 1990.

Cross, Amanda. *Death in a Tenured Position*. New York: Ballantine, 1981.

Davis, Dorothy Salisbury. "The Topical Mystery." *The Fine Art of Murder*. Ed. Ed Gorman et al. New York: Galahad, 1993. pp. 74–76.

For primary sources, see end of each chapter.

Dove, George N. *The Police Procedural*. Bowling Green: Bowling Green University Popular Press, 1982.

Forshaw, Barry. "Definitely No Thrills." *Times* 9 October 1999., p.13.

Frank, Marion. "The Transformation of a genre—The Feminist Mystery Novel." *Feminist Contributions to the Literary Canon*. Ed. Susanne Fendler. Lampeter, Wales: Edwin Mellen, 1997. pp. 81–108.

Fritz, Kathlyn Ann, and Natalie Kaufman Hevener. "An Unsuitable Job for a Woman: Female Protagonists in the Detective Novel." *International Journal of Women's Studies*, 2 #2, March-April 1979: 105–128.

George, Elizabeth. *Deception on His Mind*. New York: Bantam, 1998.

Glover, David. "The stuff that dreams are made of: Masculinity, femininity and the thriller." *Gender, Genre & Narrative Pleasure*. Ed. Derek Longhurst. London: Unwin Hyman, 1989. pp. 67–83.

Grafton, Sue. *A Is for Alibi*. New York: Bantam, 1982.

____. *B Is for Burglar*. New York: Bantam, 1986.

____. *E Is for Evidence*. New York: Bantam, 1988.

Grella, George. "The Hard-Boiled Detective Novel." *Detective Fiction: A Collection of Critical Essays*. Ed. Robin. Winks. Englewood Cliffs, NJ: Prentice Hall, 1980. pp. 103–120.

Grice, Elizabeth. "Clues to the Mysterious Life of P.D. James." *Daily Telegraph* 26 October 1999, p 25.

Hart, Caroline. "Why Cozies?" *The Fine Art of Murder*. Ed. Ed Gorman et al. pp. 71–73.

Heilbrun, Caroline. "Keynote Address: Gender and Detective Fiction." *The Sleuth and the Scholar*. Eds. Barbara A. Rader and Howard G. Zettler. Westport, CT: Greenwood, 1988. pp. 1–7.

Heising, Willetta. *Detecting Women*. Dearborn, MI: Purple Moon Press, 1995.

Hilfer, Tony. *The Crime Novel: A Deviant Genre*. Austin: University of Texas Press, 1990.

Hill, Reginald. *Blood Sympathy*. New York: St. Martin's, 1993.

Huntley, Edelma. "Susan Moody." *Great Women Mystery Writers*. Ed. Kathleen Gregory Klein. Westport, CT: Greenwood, 1994. pp. 236–238.

Irons, Glenwood. Ed. *Feminism in Women's Detective Fiction*. Toronto: University of Toronto Press, 1995.

Kaufman, Natalie Hevener, and Carol McGinnis Kay. *"G" Is for Grafton*. New York: Holt, 1997.

Kaufman, Natalie. "A New Look at African American Domestic Work in Literature: Barbara Neely's Blanche White." *Sage Journal* (1995): 8–27.

Kinsman, Margaret. "Joan Smith." *St James Guide to Crime and Mystery Writers*. Detroit: St. James, 1996. pp. 939–940.

Klein, Kathleen Gregory. Ed. *Great Women Mystery Writers*. Westport: Greenwood Press, 1994.

____. *The Woman Detective*. Urbana: University of Illinois Press, 1988.

La Plante, Lynda. *Prime Suspect*. London: Macmillan, 1991.

Leonardi, Susan. "Murders Academic: Women Professors and the Crimes of Gender." *Feminism in Women's Detective Fiction.* Ed. Glenwood Irons. Toronto: University of Toronto Press, 1995. pp. 112–126.

Light, Alison. *Forever England: Femininity, literature and conservatism between the wars.* London: Routledge, 1991.

Mandel, Ernest. *Delightful Murder: A Social History of the Crime Story,* Minneapolis: University of Minneapolis Press, 1984.

Melling, John Kennedy. *Gwendoline Butler—The Inventor of the Women's Police Procedural.* London: Britton & Walland, 1993.

Munt, Sally R. *Murder by the Book? Feminism and the Crime Novel.* London: Routledge, 1994.

Neely, Barbara. *Blanche Among the Talented Tenth.* New York: St. Martin's, 1994.

Nixon, Nicola. "Gray Areas: P.D. James's Unsuiting of Cordelia." Feminism in Women's Detective Fiction. Ed. Glenwood Irons. Toronto: University of Toronto Press, 1995. pp. 29–45.

Ousby, Ian. *The Crime and Mystery Book.* London: Thames & Hudson, 1997.

Palmer, Pauline. "The Lesbian Feminist Thriller and Detective Novel." *What Lesbians do in Books.* Eds. Elaine Hobby and Chris White. London: The Women's Press, 1991. pp. 9–27.

Paretsky, Sara. *Blood Shot.* New York: Delacorte, 1988.

____. *Dead-Lock.* Garden City, NY: Doubleday, 1984.

____. *Tunnel Vision.* New York: Delacorte, 1994.

Phillips, Kathy. "Family Plots." http://marse.galib.uga.edu:4000/QU... ewArticle=1:next=html/Article.html

Plummer, Bonnie. "Feminism and P.D. James: An Uncomfortable Alliance." Popular Culture Association of the South Conference, Augusta, GA, USA, October 10, 1998.

Porter, Dennis. "Detection and Ethics: The Case of P.D. James." *The Sleuth and the Scholar.* Eds. Barbara A. Rader and Howard G. Zettler. New York: Greenwood, 1988. pp. 11–17.

Pykett, Lynn. "Investigating Women: The Female Sleuth after Feminism." *Watching the Detectives,* Eds. Ian A. Bell and Graham Daldry. New York: St . Martin's, 1990. pp. 48–67.

Rahn, B.J. "Liza Cody." *Great Women Mystery Writers.* Ed. Kathleen Klein. Westport, CT: Greenwood, 1994. pp. 71–75.

Reddy, Maureen T. "The Feminist Counter-Tradition in Crime: Cross, Grafton, Paretsky, and Wilson." *The Cunning Craft Original Essays on Detective Fiction and Contemporary Literary Theory.* Eds. Ronald G. Walker and June M. Frazer. Macomb: Western Illinois University Press, 1990. pp. 174–187.

____. *Sisters in Crime.* New York: Continuum, 1988.

Reynolds, Barbara (ed). *The Letters of Dorothy L. Sayers.* London: Hodder & Stoughton, 1995.

Rye, Marilyn. "P.D. James." *Great Women Mystery Writers.* Ed. Kathleen Klein. Westport, CT: Greenwood Press, 1994. pp. 167–170.

Silet, Charles L.P. *Talking Murder: Interviews with 20 Mystery Writers.* New York: Norton, 1999.

Slaughter, Karin. Personal e-mail interview October 17, 1998.

Spain, Nancy. *Poison for Teacher.* London: Virago, 1994.

Sykes, Jerry. "An Interview with Val McDermid." *The Armchair Detective* 29 (Fall 1996): pp. 312–315.

Symons, Julian. *Bloody Murder.* Harmondsworth: Viking Penguin, 1985.

Tomc, Sandra. "Questing Women: The Feminist Mystery After Feminism." *Feminism in Women's Detective Fiction.* Ed. Glenwood Irons. Toronto: University of Toronto Press, 1995. pp. 46–63.

Trembley, Elizabeth A. "Sara Paretsky." *Great Women Mystery Writers.* Ed. Kathleen Klein. Westport, CT: Greenwood, 1994. pp. 266–269.

Trotter, David. "Theory and Detective Fiction." *Critical Quarterly* vol. 3, no. 2 (1991): 66–77.

Turnbull, Sue. "Val McDermid and the Fine Art of Writing Murder." *Sisters in Crime Newsletter.* 16 (1998), pp. 1+.

U.S. Bureau of the Census *Statistical Abstracts of the U.S. 1998.* Washington DC, 1998.

Walton, Priscilla L., and Manina Jones. *Detective Agency.* Berkeley: University of California Press, 1999.

Whitehead, Gwendolyn. "Gwendoline Butler." *Great Mystery Writers.* Ed. Kathleen Klein. Westport: Greenwood Press, 1994. pp. 46–50.

Wilson, Ann. "The Female Dick and the Crisis of Heterosexuality." *Feminism in Women's Detective Fiction.* Ed. Glenwood Irons. Toronto: University of Toronto Press, 1995. pp. 148–156.

Index